It Must

Be My

Metabolism!

A Doctor's Proven Program for Losing

Weight by Reversing Metabolic Syndrome

REZA YAVARI, M.D.
WITH RECIPES BY JACQUES PÉPIN

McGraw·Hill

New York   Chicago   San Francisco   Lisbon   London   Madrid   Mexico City
Milan   New Delhi   San Juan   Seoul   Singapore   Sydney   Toronto

Library of Congress Cataloging-in-Publication Data

Yavari, Reza, M.D.
    It must be my metabolism! : a doctor's proven program for losing weight by reversing
metabolic syndrome / Reza Yavari.
        p.   cm.
    Includes bibliographical references and index.
    ISBN 0-07-143760-6
    1. Weight loss.   2. Metabolism—Regulation.   I. Title.

RM222.2.Y29   2006
613.2′5—dc22   2005027377

This book is dedicated to my wife, Paula;
my daughter, Rya; and my son, Dorian

1 2 3 4 5 6 7 8 9 0   DOC/DOC   0 9 8 7 6 5

ISBN 0-07-143760-6

McGraw-Hill books are available at special quantity discounts to use as premiums and sales
promotions, or for use in corporate training programs. For more information, please write to the
Director of Special Sales, Professional Publishing, McGraw-Hill, Two Penn Plaza, New York, NY
10121-2298. Or contact your local bookstore.

The information contained in this book is intended to provide helpful and informative material on
the subject addressed. It is not intended to serve as a replacement for professional medical advice.
Any use of the information in this book is at the reader's discretion. The author and publisher
specifically disclaim any and all liability arising directly or indirectly from the use or application of
any information contained in this book. A health-care professional should be consulted regarding
your specific condition.

This book is printed on acid-free paper.

Contents

Part II
Your Plan of Action

Preface

In just fifty years, we have managed to spoil 200 million years of seamless evolution of human metabolism. Never before has the human race faced a global obesity epidemic as we face today. Worldwide, 200 million individuals are estimated to be affected by *metabolic syndrome*, the obesity link to diabetes and heart disease. While the United States and Europe lead in childhood obesity, India, China, and other countries in Southeast Asia are facing the fastest growth rates of obesity, metabolic syndrome, and diabetes in adults.

Naturally, one asks why. Is it our environment, the foods we eat, our stressful lifestyle, or our metabolism? *"It must be my metabolism,"* people say when they are gaining weight or if they cannot lose weight in spite of dieting. If it is indeed our metabolism, can we change it? Why are the majority of American adults overweight or obese while we spend so much time and money on weight-loss products, diets, and fitness centers? In the United States, one out of every three women and one out of every four men will develop diabetes. (And in some populations, lifetime risk of diabetes related to obesity is even as high as 50 percent.) How can we avoid diabetes related to excess body fat?

Currently, 40 million Americans have metabolic syndrome, and the number is expected to rise dramatically over the next twenty years. If not reversed, metabolic syndrome results in diabetes at a rate of about 10 percent per year. That means that in less than two decades, we should expect to have about 40 million new diabetics in the United States alone (doubling the current number). Today, the cost of diabetes alone in the United States is estimated to be at least $100 billion per year. It is estimated that by 2020, the cost of diabetes will exceed our total health care budget—currently at $1.4 trillion a year.

There is a way out! Healthy lifestyle change aimed at prevention and reversal of metabolic syndrome is the only viable solution. Only lifestyle change empowers us to take charge of our health and enables us to avoid expensive medications, procedures, hospital admissions, and other medical costs related to obesity. There are no magic pills or procedures that can stop the global obesity epidemic. There are no foods or diets that make people lose weight! No dietary approach will work in the long term if it does not address other factors, such as stress, body composition, metabolic burn rate, and exercise. More importantly, only healthy lifestyle change results in a better quality of life, a fit body, and a peaceful mind free of disease-related worries and fears.

This book aims to refocus our efforts on the basic premise that by changing our metabolism, we can avoid consequences of excessive weight gain such as metabolic syndrome. As such, this book is not a diet book nor an exercise manual. It is not a medical textbook either, but it is supported by recent advances in medicine and our own clinical experience. It is a *medical coaching* book aimed at metabolic syndrome. There are many academic books on obesity, metabolic syndrome (also called *syndrome X*), and diabetes. For example, an excellent and comprehensive textbook on obesity is the recently published *Handbook of Obesity*, edited by Bray and Bouchard (Marcel Dekker 2004). However, such an academic textbook, as comprehensive as it may be, cannot be used as an "advice book" or a guide for daily implementation of a lifestyle change program. Our book translates scientific knowledge of metabolic syndrome into a consumer-friendly *lifestyle guide*. Using our clinical experience with our patients, this book lays out the process of change and health coaching in simple and practical steps.

To educate our reader (before the process of change is to begin), recent medical and scientific concepts related to metabolic syndrome and metabolism are covered in detail in the first two chapters. Metabolic syndrome is not just a repackaging of obesity and diabetes into a single syndrome. There is indeed a lot of new information about this syndrome that even health care professionals do not know yet. In the remainder of

Part I, every essential aspect of lifestyle change to reverse metabolic syndrome is discussed in detail. Understanding body composition, fat distribution, metabolic burn rate, and the role of stress and exercise is as essential to successful weight loss as dieting. Learning about mindfulness, relaxation techniques, and different types of exercise is as important as learning about food types, calories, and appetite. This book balances the equation between food intake and energy expenditure. More emphasis is put on balancing our metabolism by fat loss than dieting to lose weight. Understanding our metabolism and what controls it is the subject of Chapter 3. Chapter 4 is all about the role of stress in metabolic syndrome and our approach to stress reduction. All you need to know to design an exercise program is covered in Chapter 5. Chapter 6 is our diet. It includes our meal plan and the rationale behind it as well as recipes by celebrity chef Jacques Pépin. Last but not least, Part II of the book is a day-by-day guide for the implementation of lifestyle change. At our center, participants in our lifestyle change programs use a similar guide called "the companion." We have found that those who faithfully use the companion and follow its recommendations daily have more success.

Acknowledgments

I would like to thank all of our patients, whose experiences and life stories have opened my eyes and enriched my life as a physician and a lifestyle coach. Without their daily encounters with me and my staff, this book would be another textbook. Because of their efforts and struggles, this book has become the first "hands-on" guide for metabolic syndrome. For that, I am extremely thankful. I would like to thank my staff, who through their compassionate and expert care have made our center in Connecticut a premium referral source for metabolic syndrome. Thanks to my patients and staff, Beyond Care's lifestyle medicine approach has attracted national attention. In fact, my program will soon be offered nationwide by MDVIP, a leading "concierge" medicine practice focused on preventive care.

I would also like to acknowledge and thank Nicole Wise for her efficient and creative editing of the entire book. Nicole's help in the original rendering of "the companion," now Part II, is also much appreciated. Finally, I am grateful to my friend, the celebrity chef and author Jacques Pépin, for his wonderful recipes and his generous support of my approach to lifestyle change. Last but not least, I would like to express my thanks to my extended family for their encouragement and support of my vision of a different practice of medicine, one that is not based on disease but is built on health promotion.

Is It Your Metabolism?

1 Why You Need to Know About Metabolic Syndrome

There was a time when most people didn't wear seat belts, didn't worry about cigarette smoking, and didn't think twice about drinking and driving. But people think differently about these dangerous practices now. And perhaps someday being overweight will also be perceived as the hazard that it is. Conquering obesity would have more of an impact on our health profile as a people than any other single initiative—and the same thing is true on an individual scale as well. We are just beginning to grasp the consequences of the lifestyle too many of us have been enjoying. It's not a pretty picture, and it's not a healthy one.

Everyone knows that obesity causes health problems, but it is easy to push that awareness aside as we go about our lives—too busy to plan and prepare healthy meals, too tired to exercise, too stressed not to soothe ourselves with chips, cookies, ice cream, or a few cold beers. Many people today accept weight gain as inevitable, partly because it's a harder battle to fight as we age and partly because it usually happens gradually, so we barely take notice. By the time those few extra pounds have turned into "obesity," it has become an overwhelming problem. We now know that just a few pounds of excess fat in the belly can disturb our metabolism to such a degree that the risk of diabetes and heart disease is dramatically increased. This newly discovered link between excess fat, diabetes, and heart disease is at the center of metabolic syndrome—a syndrome that affects over 200 million people worldwide.

But understanding how we gain weight and how we can reverse metabolic syndrome does not have to be so overwhelming. That's what this book is about. As you read it, you will learn surprising facts about why you feel out of control, how your genetic programming affects your drive to eat (including what and when), and what actually happens within your body when you make unhealthy food choices, immediately and over time as the extra pounds accumulate. You will not only understand what this thing called metabolic syndrome is, but also the insidious way it affects your metabolism and all your body systems, leading to diabetes and heart disease. You'll be given the information you need to change your eating habits, based on your genetic predisposition, your age and health status, and your lifestyle preferences. You'll get advice, ideas, and recipes. Most important, you will learn that it's not difficult to change your life and become healthy. It's simple, straightforward, and utterly predictable. And the payoff is immediate. By understanding the difference between a healthy and lean metabolism as opposed to that of a yoyo dieter's, you will be able to lose fat the right way and keep it off forever. By acting as your own health coach, you will begin to take charge and gradually change your health profile and your body. One day at a time, life will get better and better.

Metabolism, Not Diet, Is the Key to Fighting Obesity

Over the last 2 million years of human evolution, our primary metabolic goal in day-to-day energy balance has been to survive by eating while there is food and storing the energy for future use. *Metabolism* is the process by which our body breaks down food to be used as fuel for physical activity and bodily functions or as energy stored for future use. Until recently, our metabolism has been in tune with our energy needs and physical activity. A century ago, an average man would burn about 5,000 calories in a day just going about his daily life. For comparison, that is how much a professional athlete in training burns a day! Most of us don't even spend half as many calories most days. In the last fifty years, a change in our body's metabolism has led us to get fatter, resulting in the global obesity epidemic. In spite of all of our serious efforts to diet, as long as we ignore our metabolism, no diet will give us a healthy, lean, and energetic body. We now know that signals from the gut and from fat cells inform the brain to control appetite, satiety, and the metabolic burn rate. I will discuss these hormonal pathways elsewhere in this book. In addition to hormones, other factors, such as food itself, the autonomic nervous system, and exercise and stress, contribute to the total energy expenditure or burn rate. Our body has a tighter grip on mechanisms that control *energy storage*, such as appetite and satiety reflexes and glycogen and fat deposition, than those regulating our metabolic burn rate. The tendency to gain fat may point to a certain genetic makeup favoring energy storage or a bias toward a sluggish metabolism and low burn rate. Frustrated with their inability to lose weight, when lifelong dieters say "it must be my metabolism," they may just be right!

We do not fully understand how our metabolic burn rate is controlled, but it is clear that a healthy metabolism is essential for a lean and strong body. In the next decade, scientific understanding of these important players will make us more successful in our battle against obesity and metabolic syndrome. Based on recent medical evidence and our own clinical experience, this book describes a program for weight loss that puts more emphasis on improving your metabolism by exercise, stress reduction, and healthful eating than it does on strictly cutting calories. Indeed, the best way to avoid diabetes and heart disease is to enhance your body's metabolism to burn fat. Adult-onset diabetes, which is a key component of metabolic syndrome, is as much about the body's inability to control blood sugar levels as it is about a dysfunctional metabolism favoring excess fat storage. Metabolic syndrome, the main topic of this book, is indeed a disorder of metabolism caused by an imbalance in various hormones, resulting in excess body fat and ultimately leading to diabetes and heart disease.

Close to 20 million Americans today have been diagnosed with diabetes—and there are many more who have the disease but don't yet know it. The American Diabetes Association estimates that within just fifteen years, one out of every four American will have diabetes. Along with diabetes, excess body fat causes a large share of cardiovascular disease, kidney failure, sleep disorders, and, in women, infertility. We now understand that these seemingly separate health problems are actually a constellation of disorders that we call *metabolic syndrome* or *syndrome X*. This "syndrome" is not just obesity repackaged under a new name. Understanding how fat cells cause insulin resistance and ultimately diabetes, while at the same time causing inflammation and cholesterol plaque buildup in the arteries, has led to a unifying concept connecting heart disease to obesity, diabetes, and other hormonal disorders.

Metabolic syndrome is *not* synonymous with your metabolism, obesity, excess body fat, diabetes, or insulin resistance, even though these are all features. This chapter will explain the clinical connection between obesity, diabetes, and the metabolic syndrome and describe its consequences.

To understand metabolic syndrome and how it causes diabetes and cardiovascular disease, you have to first understand that there are different types of diabetes, different types of obesity, and of course different types of people (with the primary differences, of course, being those between men and women). After reviewing our most recent understanding of this syndrome, you will be able to assess whether you have metabolic syndrome. Not all overweight or obese people have metabolic syndrome. In women, for example, the risk of metabolic syndrome increases significantly after menopause, a finding that we now understand to be caused by body fat redistribution resulting from the loss of estrogen.

The following chapters will help you design a preventive approach and a treatment plan to reverse metabolic syndrome using my therapeutic lifestyle change (TLC) plan. But to understand my TLC approach and avoid metabolic syndrome for life, it's best to begin by learning about what metabolic syndrome is and what causes it. Then you can figure out if you have metabolic syndrome and learn what you can do to avoid its complications.

What Is Metabolic Syndrome?

The roots of the metabolic syndrome go back to the 1960s, when the link between diabetes, dyslipidemia (abnormal cholesterol profile marked by low HDL cholesterol and high triglycerides), and cardiovascular disease was brought to the attention of the medical community. Gerald Reaven, M.D., a pioneer scientist and expert in the field of metabolism, is often credited for having recognized the connection between insulin resistance and cardiovascular disease, first introduced in a widely publicized lecture at the American Diabetes Association in 1988. (Dr. Reaven also coined the less commonly used term *syndrome X*.) The constellation of conditions that he included under syndrome X included hypertension, impaired glucose metabolism, dyslipidemia, and insulin resistance.

Because most patients initially described with syndrome X were *not* obese, obesity and, more recently, excess visceral (abdominal) fat were

---

Definition of Metabolic Syndrome

Three or more of the following criteria:

1. *Abdominal obesity:* waist circumference greater than 40 inches (102 centimeters) in men or 35 inches (88 centimeters) in women.
2. *High triglycerides:* greater than 150 milligrams per deciliter (mg/dl)
3. *Low HDL cholesterol:* less than 40 mg/dl in men or 50 mg/dl in women.
4. *High blood pressure:* 130/85 millimeters of mercury (mm Hg) or higher.
5. *High fasting glucose:* 110 mg/dl or higher.

Source: The Third Report of the National Cholesterol Education Program Expert Panel on Detection, Evaluation and Treatment of High Blood Cholesterol in Adults (*Adult Treatment Panel III* or ATPIII). NIH, 01-3670, 2001.

not initially considered as major criteria for this syndrome. With the increasing prevalence of obesity in the world and in particular in the West, the connection between obesity, diabetes, and heart disease has become more apparent. In fact, the term *diabesity* is often used to emphasize the central role of obesity in this syndrome.

This syndrome, which was officially recognized by the World Health Organization in 1998, is estimated to affect close to one-quarter of the U.S. adult population. In men and women over age fifty, the prevalence of metabolic syndrome exceeds 30 percent. It is highest among middle-aged Hispanics. Although the hallmark of the syndrome is now considered to be insulin resistance, the initial cause of elevated insulin levels and its relation to body fat continue to be studied. *Insulin resistance* is a term that refers to a prediabetic state when the pancreas, sensing difficulty in disposing of glucose in muscle and liver, secretes too much insulin. Excess blood insulin in turn causes some of the other findings seen in metabolic syndrome, such as too much male hormone production in women and hypertension in both men and women. Ultimately, this prediabetic condition leads to frank diabetes.

We have learned a lot in recent years about the biology of fat cells. Many used to think that fat was just inert—it was there and it made it harder to get around, but it didn't have a chemical effect on the body. Now we know that fat cells themselves actually secrete a dozen hormones and other proteins that directly cause insulin resistance and inflammation in the blood vessels—two main features of metabolic syndrome—and are closely linked to diabetes and atherosclerosis. What may come as a surprise is that fat cells also appear to stimulate the body to produce more stress hormones. The main stress hormone is produced by the adrenal glands under the control of the hypothalamic-pituitary circuit in the brain. The hypothalamic-pituitary-adrenal (HPA) axis is responsible for the body's primary hormonal response to acute and chronic stress. By revving up the HPA stress axis, fat cells appear to be a critical link between stress hormones (catecholamines and cortisol) and insulin resistance and hypertension. But not all fat cells are the same. Visceral fat cells, the fat inside the abdomen and around the gut and the

14 Feb

Waterford City Council
Central Library
03 JAN 07 04:14pm
Library Receipt

For renewal/enquiries phone 051 849975

Checkout

Patron Name: Caulfield, Ann

New Loan: It must be my metabolism!: a d
30005003817361   Due: 24 JAN 07 *

New Loan: Mercy
30005003831636   Due: 24 JAN 07 *

New Loan: Baby knits for beginners
30005002536392   Due: 24 JAN 07 *

internal organs, play a more critical role in insulin resistance and its metabolic consequences than subcutaneous (under the skin) fat cells.

Metabolic syndrome is a constellation of disorders that links obesity to diabetes and cardiovascular disease. In metabolic syndrome, diabetes develops gradually over several years. During these "prediabetic" years, the body first becomes resistant to insulin, the main regulator of blood sugars. To control sugar levels, the body has to produce much more insulin. So, for a long time, normal or even slightly elevated blood sugar levels are accompanied by higher than normal insulin levels. Eventually, the pancreatic cells that produce insulin "burn out," causing full-blown diabetes with out-of-control blood sugar levels. During the years preceding the onset of full-blown diabetes, another insidious disease process is taking shape. While insulin resistance is a metabolic response to excess fat, the fat cells themselves release hormones and proteins that cause inflammation and plaque buildup in blood vessels. In addition to vascular inflammation, secretions from fat cell make the blood "sticky," or prone to coagulation—a condition called *dysfibrinolysis*.

Stress also has a direct impact. In people with metabolic syndrome, the hypothalamic-pituitary-adrenal stress axis is abnormal. Several investigators have shown that chronic stress and activation of the hormonal and nervous systems regulating the stress response are linked to central obesity and insulin resistance. Though the exact cause of the metabolic syndrome is not yet determined, excess visceral fat, insulin resistance, and chronic stress all appear to contribute to the abnormal hormonal and metabolic profile. Ultimately, the main clinical consequences of the metabolic syndrome are type 2 diabetes and cardiovascular disease, such as heart attack and stroke.

How Doctors See the Syndrome

The clinical definition of metabolic syndrome is simple: visceral obesity (defined by measuring the waist or the waist-to-hip ratio) and the presence of two associated common conditions, such as hypertension and glucose intolerance (that is, prediabetes). As yet, there is no single blood test to diagnose this syndrome. Metabolic syndrome has five commonly seen features: obesity or at least abdominal obesity; high insulin levels, or hyperinsulinemia, reflecting insulin resistance; dyslipidemia, defined as high triglycerides and low HDL cholesterol; elevated fasting blood sugars or frank diabetes; and hypertension. Metabolic syndrome is also commonly associated with sleep disorders, such as obstructive sleep apnea. In young women who are predisposed to *polycystic ovary syndrome* (*PCOS*), fat gain and high insulin levels "bring out" the disease, which I will discuss later.

To diagnose metabolic syndrome, physicians rely on a combination of blood tests and other clinical findings. For example, a fasting blood triglyceride level of 150 mg/dl or higher, together with a low HDL cholesterol of 35 mg/dl, would qualify for dyslipidemia. Impaired fasting glucose, defined as a blood sugar higher than 110 mg/dl but less than or equal to 125 mg/dl, would be another criterion. A third condition, such

Physician-Ordered Blood Tests

Blood tests your doctor would order to determine if you have metabolic syndrome:

1. Fasting blood sugar and insulin levels
2. Fasting complete cholesterol profile
3. Uric acid level (to determine risk of gout)
4. Male hormone levels in men *and* women

Other useful tests include: tests measuring the levels of blood adiponectin, PAI-1 (plasminogen activator inhibitor), cardio CRP (C-reactive protein), and homocysteine; a glucose tolerance test; and a test for pituitary FSH (follicle-stimulating hormone) and LH (luteinizing hormone) in women with irregular menstrual cycles.

as central obesity or hypertension, together with the first two, would then complete the clinical diagnosis of metabolic syndrome.

Worried about metabolic syndrome? Here are some clues:

- Are you gaining abdominal girth? You do not have to be visibly obese to have metabolic syndrome. Excess abdominal fat is enough to cause insulin resistance in spite of lean and strong arms and legs.
- Have you recently being diagnosed with hypertension or so-called "borderline sugars"?
- Do have sleep apnea? If unsure, ask your significant other if you snore or gasp for air in the middle of your deep sleep, or think about whether you are tired when you wake up and even more exhausted in the late afternoon, despite going to bed at a reasonable hour.
- Do you get sleepy after meals and sometimes have symptoms of low blood sugar, or hypoglycemia (shakiness, perspiration, feeling cold, getting a headache and feeling lightheaded after eating lots of sweets or refined starches)?
- Do you have low good (HDL) cholesterol and/or high tri-glycerides with a strong family history of heart disease?

If you have any of these findings, consider asking your doctor for an evaluation for metabolic syndrome. Your doctor can answer your questions and order additional tests. Meanwhile, the information and the risk assessment questionnaire included in the next section will help you figure out your chances of having metabolic syndrome.

Could *You* Have Metabolic Syndrome?

You're probably reading this because you're concerned about your weight and think it may be due to metabolic syndrome. To begin, measure your waist at your belly button. All you need is a measuring tape. Try not to suck in your belly! An abdominal circumference larger than 35 inches for women and larger than 40 inches for men increases your risk. Next measure your hip circumference at the largest point around your hips. Now, divide your waistline by your hip diameter to obtain a more accurate measure of your risk, known as the waist-to-hip ratio, or W/H ratio.

When the W/H ratio is equal to or higher than 0.85 in women and 1.0 in men, the risk of metabolic syndrome is high. In women, a W/H ratio higher than 0.85 defines "apple-shaped" weight gain, and when the ratio is less than 0.85, it indicates "pear-shaped" weight gain. Apple-shaped obese women are more likely to have metabolic syndrome. Men have bigger bellies than women, so their cutoff for W/H ratio indicating metabolic syndrome is 1.0.

A word of caution: These measurements and their significance are statistical parameters used for risk assessment; they are not diagnostic tests. In women, the W/H ratio also depends on body frame and shape. So if a woman's W/H ratio is less than 0.85, the diagnosis of metabolic syndrome is still possible. For men, the W/H ratio is even less reliable. Men with large body builds may have excess abdominal muscle, which causes a large waistline but does not indicate excess belly fat. Finally, these measurements, which are best done first thing in the morning, can vary quite a bit if the measuring tape is not positioned accurately. Perhaps it is easier to have someone else do your measurements. Overall, clinical studies have shown that the W/H ratio is a convenient screening test, which can be monitored as needed in the privacy of your home. If you have obvious central obesity, the test is useful for the diagnosis of metabolic syndrome, but it is even more useful in assessing fat loss as you lose weight.

Weight loss efforts may seem frustrating if the scale is the only measure. Younger men and women who diet and exercise at the same time (as opposed to those who only diet) may not lose much weight initially because they build muscle while they lose fat—and muscle weighs more than fat. If you belong to this category, compare your weight loss on the scale with the inches off your waistline. Waistline shrinks before any other changes in body shape are noticeable—that is, before hips, legs, and arms show any significant change. Abdominal fat loss also means better cardiovascular and metabolic health. So you should take pleasure that not only are you trimming down; you are also reversing your cardiovascular and diabetes risks with every belt notch you pull in. Your body is reporting to you about your better health, just as a physician's blood tests would show an improved metabolic profile, including lower blood insulin and sugar levels.

Your physician can diagnose metabolic syndrome with blood tests. You can also measure your own W/H ratio to assess your risk of metabolic syndrome. What else can you do? If you have access to a body fat measuring device using electrical impedance, especially the handheld device as opposed to the scale, you can measure your upper body fat fairly accurately. In our experience, an upper body fat of 30 percent or higher using these instruments makes the diagnosis of metabolic syndrome likely.

Another measurement you can use to help assess your risk is body mass index (BMI). BMI is usually defined in terms of weight in kilograms and height in meters (the metric system), but you can also calculate your BMI using pounds and inches. To calculate your BMI, take your weight in pounds, divide it by your height in inches to the power of 2 (or divide weight by height once then divide the result again by height), and then multiply the final result by 703. A BMI over 25 may be a concern.

Body Mass Index (BMI) and Obesity

$$BMI = [(\text{Weight in pounds}) / (\text{Height in inches})^2] \times 703$$

BMI	Classification
18.5–24*	Normal
25–29	Overweight
30–34	Obese (class I)
35 or higher	Clinically obese (classes II and III)

*For Asians, the upper limit of normal is 23, and obesity is defined as BMI over 25. Although BMI and fat percentage both increase in obesity, the amount of local fat deposits, which has more clinical significance, cannot be estimated by BMI.

So, weight, W/H ratio, excess upper body fat, and BMI are readily available indicators that you can use to assess your risk and follow your progress. In addition to these measurements, your family history and personal medical history can help you better determine your risks. Answer the questions in the appropriate risk assessments, pages 18 and 19, then see if your score indicates that you are at risk.

Count each "yes" answer as one point and add them up. ("No" answers are zero points.) If your total score is less than 10, you are at low risk of metabolic syndrome. If your score is higher than 20, you are at high risk. And in between (scores 11 to 19), you are at moderate risk. Of course, this survey is not a diagnostic tool; if you have already been evaluated by a physician and confirmed to have the major criteria for metabolic syndrome, you don't need to take this survey—your score doesn't matter. This survey is helpful as a screening tool for overweight and obese people who want to know their medical risks. If your score puts you at moderate or high risk, you should see a physician for a full evaluation. If your score is less than 10, it does not mean that you do not have metabolic syndrome; it just means that you are less likely to have it compared to other men and women.

In women and men with central obesity, the likelihood of metabolic syndrome is quite high. But in obese or overweight women who are pear-shaped and in big men who weigh a lot because of excess muscle, the diagnosis of metabolic syndrome is not so obvious. This questionnaire is most useful for such women and men. For example, in pear-shaped women, medical tests and diagnoses are often negative, even if lifestyle is sedentary and eating habits are unhealthy. Such women would have a score less than 10, even if they are approaching or going through menopause. For them, a low score would reassure them that in spite of their weight, they are at low risk for metabolic syndrome. Heavy muscular men would also get a low score as long as they exercise, eat healthy, and know how to relax. This survey reflects the notion that unhealthy habits contribute to the risk of metabolic syndrome as much as excess body fat does.

If you have metabolic syndrome, do not despair! As serious as it is, metabolic syndrome is a preventable and reversible disorder. I hope you will be able to prevent, reverse, or manage your condition using our clinically validated approach described in this book. On the following pages I will show you how two of my patients, Dan and Jeff, dramatically improved their health profile by adopting our approach for healthy lifestyle change.

Metabolic Syndrome Can Be Reversed or Managed

Dan is a forty-six-year-old engineer, and Jeff is a fifty-three-year-old carpenter. They both have heart disease. Both had angioplasty several years ago and now are followed by cardiologists with regular stress tests. Dan has "prediabetes," or borderline abnormal blood sugars, and Jeff has type 2 diabetes treated with medications. They both followed a lifestyle change plan similar to the one I offer in this book. Their before and after indicators are shown in Table 1.1 to show you how a therapeutic lifestyle change intervention for six months can affect your health.

As you can see, Dan lost a total of 58 pounds, of which 21 pounds were abdominal fat. By the end of the program, his prediabetic blood sugars, his low HDL cholesterol, and his elevated triglycerides and LDL were all normal. He was off all medications and truly proud of his accomplishment. Jeff, who had advanced obesity and frank diabetes, lost 45 pounds, of which 21 pounds were abdominal fat. His diabetes was much better controlled as judged by his HbA1c test (reflecting average blood sugars), which dropped from 8.7 to 5.4 percent without any additional medication. His cholesterol profile improved dramatically with a huge drop in his triglyceride level. Also, both Dan and Jeff were looking good and exercising regularly. For the first time in years, Dan was dating and Jeff had left his depression behind.

TABLE 1.1 Dan and Jeff's "Before and After" Profiles

Parameters	Normal Values	Dan		Jeff	
		Before	After	Before	After
Weight (lbs. lost)		231	173 (258)	281	236 (−45)
BMI (kg/m2)	<26	35	26	44	36
Abdominal fat % (lbs.)	<15–17%	34% (37)	20% (16)	40% (66)	34% (45)
Fasting blood glucose mg/dl	<100	106	83	213	112
HbA1c% (average blood sugar)	<6.0%	5.4 (105)	5.4 (105)	8.7 (210)	5.4 (105)
Insulin uIU/ml	<17	17	10	19	14
Total cholesterol mg/dl	<200	205	161	201	188
HDL cholesterol mg/dl	>40	40	53	31	38
Triglycerides	<150	235	70	474	110
LDL cholesterol mg/dl	<130	115	94	too high to measure	128

Men's Risk Assessment

	Yes	No
Your body measurements		
1. Body mass index (BMI) ≥30	___	___
2. Waist-to-hip ratio ≥1	___	___
3. Body fat ≥25%	___	___
The following conditions in your immediate family		
4. Heart disease or stroke	___	___
5. Diabetes type 2	___	___
6. Central obesity	___	___
Have you been diagnosed with any of the following?		
7. High blood pressure (≥130/85) or under treatment	___	___
8. Borderline or high fasting blood sugars (higher than 100)	___	___
9. Low HDL cholesterol (≤40)	___	___
10. High triglycerides (≥150)	___	___
11. High fasting blood insulin	___	___
12. High blood uric acid or gout	___	___
13. Low blood testosterone	___	___
14. Premature sexual problems, such as impotence	___	___
15. Sleep apnea or poor sleep quality	___	___
16. Premature heart disease or chest pain	___	___
Your lifestyle-related risk factors		
17. You are under high chronic stress	___	___
18. You have a type A personality	___	___
19. Depression, recent emotional setback, or alcohol abuse	___	___
20. You exercise less than 3 hours per week	___	___
21. You do not have a regular relaxation routine	___	___
22. You eat a high-carbohydrate diet	___	___
23. You eat a high-fat diet	___	___
24. You eat large meals	___	___
25. You eat more at night	___	___
TOTAL SCORE	___	___

Women's Risk Assessment

	Yes	No
Your body measurements		
1. Body mass index (BMI) ≥30	____	____
2. Waist-to-hip ratio ≥0.85	____	____
3. Body fat ≥30%	____	____
The following conditions in your immediate family		
4. Heart disease or stroke	____	____
5. Diabetes type 2	____	____
6. Central obesity	____	____
Have you been diagnosed with any of the following?		
7. High blood pressure (≥130/85) or under treatment	____	____
8. Borderline or high fasting blood sugars (higher than 100)	____	____
9. Low HDL cholesterol (≤50)	____	____
10. High triglycerides (≥150)	____	____
11. High fasting blood insulin	____	____
12. High blood uric acid or gout	____	____
13. High blood testosterone or excess body hair	____	____
14. Menopausal symptoms, such as hot flashes	____	____
15. Sleep apnea or poor sleep quality	____	____
16. History of gestational diabetes	____	____
17. History of infrequent menses or polycystic ovaries (PCOS)	____	____
Your lifestyle-related risk factors		
18. You are under high chronic stress	____	____
19. You are a worrier and have chronic anxiety	____	____
20. You exercise less than 3 hours per week	____	____
21. You do not have a regular relaxation routine	____	____
22. You eat a high-carbohydrate diet	____	____
23. You eat a high-fat diet	____	____
24. You get sugar cravings in the afternoon	____	____
25. You eat more at night	____	____
TOTAL SCORE	____	____

2 There's More to Metabolic Syndrome Than Meets the Eye

Many obese or overweight individuals do not have metabolic syndrome. In fact, many obese women with excess fat in their lower body (buttocks, thighs, and lower legs) are "heavy" but often have perfectly healthy blood tests with no sign of diabetes or heart disease. On the other hand, all men and most women who gain excess abdominal fat develop features of metabolic syndrome. Why is it that body shape and where the excess fat is matter so much? Why did it take medical experts so long to connect the dots and discover that disorders as far apart as the polycystic ovary syndrome and premature heart disease and diabetes were all related? The common denominator to all the consequences of metabolic syndrome is excess fat. But not just any fat! Recent discoveries about the biology of fat cells have provided us with important clues as to why excess fat in the belly can cause metabolic syndrome while fat elsewhere in the body does not. To understand metabolic syndrome and its distinctions from obesity, diabetes, and heart disease, we have to understand fat cells, the main culprits in this syndrome. In addition, we have to understand how excess fat "brings out" different complications of metabolic syndrome. Diabetes, heart disease, and hormonal imbalance are all consequences of excess abdominal fat, but they affect people with metabolic syndrome to a different degree. Once we understand fat cell biology better, we also grasp how these apparently unrelated disorders are linked together. In this chapter, you will read about all the common complications of metabolic syndrome, but first let us review recent discoveries in fat biology as they relate to metabolic syndrome.

Fat cells, or *adipocytes*, originate from stem cell reserves in the body. These stem cells, also referred to as mesenchymal cells, undergo a series of genetic changes to differentiate into preadipocytes and ultimately into fully mature adipocytes. Once adipocytes are fully differentiated, they do not multiply but can grow in size, containing more and more fat deposits.

Adipocytes are not just containers of fat; they are actively involved in the body's metabolism. They respond to and secrete hormones and other biologically potent proteins, which "talk" to other organs, such as the brain and liver. As such, adipocytes are now considered an integral part of the endocrine system, regulating important physiological functions, such as appetite, energy conservation, and fat metabolism.

But not all fat cells are the same. Depending on where they are located, they differ in size and activity. For example, fat cells under the skin (subcutaneous fat cells) and intra-abdominal (visceral) fat cells have different functions. Fat cells inside the abdomen and chest are more responsive to stress hormones such as catecholamines (the "fight-or-flight" hormones) and cortisol, but are less responsive to insulin. This is why excess visceral fat causes relatively more insulin resistance. The opposite holds for the stress response: visceral fat cells release more fatty acids and other substances in response to stress hormones. So it is thought that insulin resistance seen in chronic stress is in part due to excess visceral fat, while chronic stress by itself can promote fat accumulation inside the abdomen.

It has been known for a long time that fat cells are hormonally active in that they can convert male hormones, or androgens (most notably testosterone) to estrogens. In postmenopausal women, for example, the contribution of fat cells to the body's hormones is quite significant and can amount to 100 percent of estrogen production, while in young women, 50 percent of testosterone circulating in the blood can originate from fat cells. Here, too, fat cells inside the abdomen slant the hormonal profile in a different direction than fat cells in thighs and buttocks. Fat cells in pear-shaped women convert more hormones to estrogens, and fat cells in the abdomen of apple-shaped women and in men with central obesity convert more hormones to testosterone. Therefore, fat cells regulate not just the body's metabolism and energy level, but even libido, mood, and sexuality.

Fat cells also cause metabolic syndrome by perturbing the body's stress response. It is well known that obesity influences the hypothalamic-pituitary-adrenal (HPA) stress axis, but just recently it was discovered that visceral fat cells can also convert the inactive stress hormone cortisone to the active form cortisol. Could this be the key to the stress-fat puzzle? It is known that visceral fat cells are more responsive to stress signals than fat cells elsewhere in the body. Could it be that visceral fat cells thrive off stress hormones? As if cortisol is required for their livelihood, visceral fat cells rev up the HPA axis to produce more cortisol, and they also convert back cortisone (the inactive form of cortisol) to cortisol for renewed consumption. Mice genetically engineered to overproduce the cortisol in fat cells develop a picture similar to metabolic syndrome, with visceral obesity, insulin resistance, and hypertension. In the opposite scenario, in mice with defective cortisol production in fat cells, no such effect is seen. When these mice are overfed, they do not gain fat in the abdomen; it's almost as if they are protected against metabolic syndrome. It also appears that the HPA stress axis and the autonomic nervous system, the two pillars of our stress response, also interact with fat cells. The combination of all the available data suggests that visceral fat cells play a critical role in the metabolic response to chronic stress and in the onset of insulin resistance, hypertension, and vascular inflammation—all major components of metabolic syndrome.

Fat cells secrete dozens of hormones and other proteins. The most notable ones are *leptin, adiponectin, resistin, plasminogen activator inhibitor 1 (PAI-1),* and *interleukin-6 (IL-6).* Some of these are discussed elsewhere in this book. Here's what we already know about the factors released by visceral fat cells and how they are linked to various features of metabolic syndrome:

- We have found a solid link between appetite, energy storage, and expenditure: *leptin*, secreted by *fat cells*.
- We have discovered at least one key link between central obesity, insulin resistance, and diabetes: *adiponectin*, secreted by *fat cells*.
- We now know that a number of proteins secreted by fat cells cause inflammation in the arteries and platelet aggregation, thus causing heart disease and stroke: *PAI-1, TNF-alpha and IL-6*, also secreted by *fat cells*.

It seems clear that the culprit in metabolic syndrome is the visceral fat cell itself. This was a surprise. No one ever expected that those boring fat cells, which for the longest time were ignored by serious researchers and doctors, would end up as a central command unit shaping the body, influencing the stress response and even our eating behavior. This is why fat has become so fascinating! Recent studies show that even a modest loss of body fat (as little as 5 percent of body weight) reduces risk of metabolic syndrome and its complications. Therefore, fat loss—especially visceral fat loss—has become a top priority for physicians and public health officials.

Metabolic Syndrome, Obesity, and Diabetes

Although we have learned a lot about fat cells, there is still much to be learned about obesity as a clinical syndrome. Are there different types of obesity, and do some carry a higher risk of metabolic syndrome? Is obesity caused by unhealthy lifestyles, or is it genetic? With obesity becoming such a global and expensive health threat, which types of obesity will more likely benefit from a *therapeutic lifestyle change* plan like the one described in this book?

Experts often point out that obesity cannot be genetic, because our genes have not changed in the last three decades, while we have seen a huge explosion in obesity all over the world. This would argue in favor of an environmental, or lifestyle-related, cause for the obesity epidemic. Other scientists argue that many obesity genes have already been dis-covered and many more will be identified in the next decade—ultimately explaining why some people get fat and others do not. The truth will probably be somewhere in between: although environmental factors, such as easy access to high-energy foods and less active lifestyles, are the main reasons behind the global obesity pandemic, genetic mutations and variations in certain genes *predispose* some populations to weight gain more than others. In addition, there are specific genes that, when mutated, cause profound metabolic dysfunction resulting in extreme obe-sity, often at an early age. It is possible that less dramatic mutations of some of these obesity genes may explain the preponderance of obesity in some families.

Metabolic Syndrome, Obesity, and Genes

Some studies suggest that 25 to 80 percent of the variation in body weight may be due to genetic factors. In a study of twelve pairs of identical male twins who were overfed by 1,000 calories a day for 100 days, researchers discovered three times as much variation in weight gain between the dif-ferent families than between the twins themselves, suggesting that inher-itance (genes) was a major force controlling body weight in the twins. In particular, fat distribution and visceral fat gain seemed more likely to be inherited. In a study of childhood obesity among 284 schoolchildren in Iowa, genetic contribution to obesity was estimated to account for approx-imately 75 percent of the variation. Only 23 percent of the variation was shown *not* to be related to genetics. Other studies of families have shown inherited susceptibility, pointing to a higher risk of obesity among cer-tain families, among ethnic groups (such as the Pima Indians), and even among siblings of high-risk individuals. These studies, taken together, suggest a genetic predisposition to obesity. Genetic research also shows that while there is not one "obesity gene," obesity is associated with a number of genes located on many different chromosomes. As a whole, it appears that those of us who may have a genetic makeup favoring weight gain are at higher risk of obesity, but the obesity epidemic is not caused by any specific modification of the human gene pool.

In humans, a handful of single obesity genes have indeed been found to be responsible for "syndromic obesity." In these rare syndromes, obesity is often striking but may not be the most specific feature. Obesity syndromes include Prader-Willi syndrome, Angelman syndrome (also known as the happy puppet syndrome), Bardet-Biedl syndrome, and Alström syndrome. Other specific genetic defects have been identified in humans, and some may be responsible for more of the common cases of genetic obesity. But so far, no such gene has been identified for metabolic syndrome.

Taking together all recent studies and advances in the genetics of obesity, it is almost certain that there is a *genetic predisposition* to metabolic syndrome. But a single "metabolic syndrome gene" may never be found, and different combinations of mutations necessary for metabolic syndrome may affect different families and to various degrees. Even when such mutations are discovered, they may not yield clinical results for large-scale application anytime soon. But identification and investigation of such genes provide invaluable information about risk and prevention of metabolic syndrome. Discovery of these genes and their mechanism of action will also open doors to the development of medications that soon will help control weight, appetite, and metabolic burn rate. However, these medications are not likely to work alone, but rather in conjunction with healthy lifestyle change.

Diabetes, Insulin Resistance, and Excess Fat

Diabetes used to be a disease of the elderly or, in the case of the less common juvenile diabetes, one diagnosed in children and teenagers. Now, the new face of diabetes is that of a middle-aged overweight or obese person who lives a sedentary lifestyle. Because of metabolic syndrome, it is now all too common to diagnose people in their thirties and forties with

diabetes. Diabetes mellitus (from the Greek *diabetes*, for frequent urina-
tion, and *mellitus*, for sugar) is diagnosed when high blood sugars cannot
be controlled and brought down to the normal range without medication.
But this is a very simplistic view of diabetes. Not only are there different
types of diabetes, but the severity of diabetes is quite variable as well,
depending on other medical conditions, age, and lifestyle.

Juvenile, or type 1, diabetes and adult-onset, or type 2, diabetes are
the most common types. The prevalence of type 1 diabetes in the United
States is about 1 million and is not growing much from year to year. Type
1 diabetes is an autoimmune disease in which the body's own immune
system attacks the insulin-producing islet cells in the pancreas. In type
1 diabetes, there is no causal relationship between obesity or sedentary
lifestyle and disease risk. Type 2 diabetes, on the other hand, is a fast-
expanding epidemic affecting at least 16 million people in the United
States alone. It is a slow-progressing and for the most part symptom-free
disease often referred to as the "silent killer." It takes years for it to
become clinically apparent. During this time, the diagnosis of early diabetes or prediabetes can help reverse the disease altogether. At the center of this kind of diabetes, which affects one out of three women and
one out of four men (in Hispanics, African-Americans, and Native Americans, its prevalence is even higher), is the inability of the body to
respond to insulin, referred to as insulin resistance. In this situation, in
contrast to type 1 diabetes, the body makes plenty of insulin—in fact, too
much—but the insulin doesn't work well. The pancreatic cells sense that
blood sugars are high and compensate by secreting additional insulin. So
for a few years, the pancreas is able to maintain fasting blood sugars in
the high normal range, but it eventually fails to keep up. When beta islet
cells fail to produce enough insulin, blood sugars creep even higher and
reach the diabetic ranges. So type 2 diabetes is marked first by an insen-
sitivity to insulin, followed by a reduced insulin secretion. That is why,
initially, lifestyle changes such as dieting and exercise are effective in
treating type 2 diabetes, and later they are not.

Metabolic syndrome is the link between insulin resistance, type 2 diabetes, and cardiovascular disease. There is no increased risk of metabolic

syndrome associated with type 1 diabetes. But people with type 1 diabetes who gain a lot of body fat also become resistant to injectable insulin and require ever-increasing doses. Therefore, when clinicians first meet an obese patient with diabetes who needs insulin treatment, it is important to obtain a detailed history to distinguish the two types of diabetes.

In diabetes (no matter what type), there is an imbalance between glucose in the bloodstream and glucose taken up by target organs, such as muscles and the liver. The process of removing glucose from the bloodstream, called "glucose uptake" or "glucose disposal," is controlled by insulin.

Insulin is an anabolic hormone; it helps the body grow and helps the body store and use energy efficiently. It helps cells in the body take up circulating sugar and fat for immediate use or for storage. Its target organs are the liver, fat cells, and muscle cells. A critical loss of control results early in the muscle cells. Excess fatty acids circulating in the bloodstream cause fat deposits inside muscle cells, damaging their ability to take up and use glucose. Once the transportation and processing of glucose into muscles is impaired, blood sugars remain persistently high. This leaves muscles, which normally utilize glucose quite efficiently, in a bottleneck, with the net result being high circulating blood sugars while muscles are starving for energy; that is the paradox of type 2 diabetes. Even before the onset of diabetes, excess fatty deposits are found in the muscles of people who have metabolic syndrome but who may not yet have diabetes. Similarly, excess deposits are found in otherwise healthy relatives of people with metabolic syndrome. Exercise and a healthy diet flush these fatty deposits out of muscle cells, making them more responsive to insulin. Therefore, insulin resistance in muscle cells is a common, early, and reversible feature of metabolic syndrome.

Other than muscles, the liver is a key site of insulin action after eating, and its role has been carefully studied for decades. Under the influence of insulin, the liver takes up to 25 percent of glucose absorbed from meals to store as glycogen. Indirectly, however, the liver can take up to 40 to 60 percent of ingested carbohydrates. In the fasting state, the liver breaks down and releases glycogen as glucose for use by other organs. In insulin-resistant individuals, the liver does not respond to insulin and continues to release glucose instead of storing it as glycogen. Once again, this results in rising blood sugar. So the inability of muscle and liver cells to hold on to and use glucose efficiently explains how insulin resistance causes high blood sugars or diabetes, in spite of high levels of circulating insulin.

Yet another mechanism involves fat cells. Normally, insulin acts on adipocytes—all fat cells, regardless of where they are located—to stop the release of their triglyceride reserves. Insulin is able to keep triglycerides in fat cells by blocking an enzyme in fat cells called the *hormone-sensitive lipase*, which normally breaks down triglyceride deposits and releases them into the circulation as free fatty acids. When insulin does not do its job, free fatty acids are released nonstop, and their blood level rises. In metabolic syndrome, a clue to this problem is an elevated blood triglyceride level (tested as part of the cholesterol profile). So high triglyceride levels together with high insulin levels are indicative of metabolic syndrome, even in the absence of frank diabetes.

Within 2 to 4 hours after a meal (the postprandial period), 80 percent of the glucose uptake is insulin mediated, with most of that activity occurring in liver and muscle cells. So resistance to insulin action as seen in type 2 diabetes causes more havoc after a meal or a carbohydrate-rich snack. In insulin resistance, fasting blood sugars may remain normal, but postprandial values are always abnormally high and remain higher for hours longer. In fact, even in early stages, abnormal blood sugar and insulin levels after eating can be formally tested by doing an oral glucose tolerance test (OGTT). During this test, the individual is asked to eat a high amount of pure sugar (75grams), and his or her blood sugars are tested every half hour for 2 to 3 hours. Abnormal values are clearly documented and confirm insulin resistance. After a sweet snack, if there is not enough food ingested to respond to the rise in insulin, blood sugar sometimes drops precipitously. This phenomenon is called *reactive hypoglycemia*. (That's why people in a prediabetic stage sometimes get hypoglycemic after a high-carbohydrate meal.) Symptoms of hypoglycemia include perspiration, palpitations or rapid heart rate, and light-headedness. This kind of hypoglycemia often suggests a high risk of diabetes in the near future. Frequently, though, insulin resistance causes high blood sugars *without* hypoglycemia and can go unnoticed for years.

People with diabetes and metabolic syndrome also have trouble clearing fat particles from blood circulation. So the postprandial metabolism of sugar *and* fat are both severely impaired. Each meal causes mayhem in the body. In the hours immediately following a meal, blood sugar shoots up and remains excessively high, while insulin action is being further impaired because of the rising tide of fatty acids in the bloodstream. Excess fat in the blood, either from food or released from fat cells, further worsens glucose uptake by muscle cells. The liver and muscle cells are stressed out, while endothelial cells in the arterial walls are burdened with plaque-building particles. Fat cells, which are supposed to store fatty acids in the form of triglycerides, instead release them into the blood. The period following meals, therefore, is a highly turbulent and stressful time for the body's metabolism. The blood is rich with sugar, fat, and other substances, such as proteins. This is the time when metabolic syndrome does the most harm to the body. Excess sugars and fats circulating for hours in the body cause toxicity to the cells and inflammation in the arteries. Insulin-resistant people often feel drowsy and sluggish after meals, as their metabolism slows down and their blood is thickened. In fact, if their blood is drawn into a test tube during that time, it has a creamy white hue called *lipemic* due to the presence of excess circulating triglycerides.

Just as insulin resistance influences postprandial metabolism most, lifestyle changes, including dietary restriction of sugar and fat, have a quick impact on insulin resistance and metabolic syndrome. For example, an obese person who is overeating and gaining fat is more likely to be insulin resistant than a person of the same weight and body fat percentage who has recently started dieting. It turns out that with appropriate dieting, insulin resistance begins reversing even before any significant weight loss. This appears to be in part due to the relation between dietary carbohydrate and fat intake and insulin resistance. In animal models and in some people, a diet rich in fat causes insulin resistance. On the other hand, a diet rich in carbohydrates that have a high glycemic index, such as refined sugars and starches, often causes high blood insulin levels and weight gain.

Finally, an exercise program may not yet have had an impact on weight loss but may have already reduced insulin resistance by activating previously lazy muscle cells. Exercise, even gentle aerobic activity such as riding a stationary bike, if done within the 2 hours after a meal, enhances glucose uptake by muscles. A gentle walk after a meal, for example, may not help you lose weight but will effectively improve blood sugars and help clear the bloodstream of all the circulating fatty acids and proteins and sugar. Regular exercise will improve insulin resistance in one week even if there is no sign of fat loss yet.

But how does insulin resistance finally lead to full-blown diabetes? In the first few years, insulin resistance, which is caused by excess body fat, accumulation of fatty deposits in muscles, and a sedentary lifestyle, can be reversed completely with diet and exercise. At this stage, diabetes is around the corner but it is still preventable. A change in eating habits

Meals and Insulin Resistance: Some Practical Pointers

Taking into account just the impact of insulin resistance on metabolism during the postprandial hours, people with metabolic syndrome should:

- Have smaller and leaner meals.
- Be active and move around after meals to help muscles take up more blood sugar.
- Avoid big high-fat meals, which aggravate insulin resistance and raise blood sugars even more.
- Be warned that elevated *fasting* blood sugars suggest the onset of frank diabetes caused by insulin *deficiency*, not just insulin resistance.

together with a gentle exercise program leading to a weight loss of as little as 5 percent of body weight is enough to prevent diabetes. As insulin resistance progresses, the pancreatic beta cells, which release insulin when they sense high blood sugars, are no longer able to keep up with the increase in demand for insulin production. When diabetes is fully developed and the pancreas is "burnt out," the disorder may no longer be reversible and medical treatment becomes necessary. Traditionally, the first line of treatment for type 2 diabetes consisted of medications that stimulated the pancreatic islet cells to pump out more insulin. These medications are commonly referred to as sulfonylureas. This does not make as much sense if the body is insulin resistant. A variety of more modern medications are now available, and the first line of therapy consists of medications that act as insulin *sensitizers*. By reducing insulin resistance, these new medications, such as rosiglitazone (Avandia) and pioglitazone (Actos), also reverse other associated complications of metabolic syndrome, such as inflammation in the arteries. These insulin-sensitizing medications also give the pancreatic beta cells a rest and may help prolong their lives, thus avoiding insulin injections. Often, though, the pancreatic islet cells eventually burn out and insulin injections become necessary. If no measures are taken to reduce the body's insulin resistance by fat loss or to cut back dietary intake of sugars, insulin injections become necessary earlier. This is when type 2 diabetes reaches its final phase of insulin dependence as in juvenile (type 1) diabetes. The time separating these stages of insulin resistance, prediabetes, established type 2 diabetes, and the insulin-requiring stage could be years.

It's important to note, however, that even though prediabetes related to insulin resistance may be considered a mild condition ("a touch of diabetes," as some say) and years away from full-blown diabetes, it is already causing subtle but undeniable cardiovascular changes in blood vessels, resulting in hypertension and atherosclerosis, or plaque buildup. Since early intervention prevents both diabetes and cardiovascular disease, every effort must be made to reverse metabolic syndrome. Therapeutic lifestyle change is the only viable way to accomplish this goal.

Metabolic Syndrome and Heart Disease

The American Heart Association considers obesity, regardless of its association with insulin resistance and diabetes, as a major risk factor for coronary heart disease. However, how much of the higher risk is due to metabolic syndrome and its features, such as low HDL cholesterol and hypertension, which are also independent risk factors for heart disease, remains open to discussion. Further, sedentary lifestyle and poor eating habits, which most obese individuals struggle with, also predispose to heart disease, regardless of body weight.

Nonetheless, everyone agrees that central obesity of midlife men and menopausal women is more closely associated with cardiovascular disease than "pear-shaped" obesity, seen mostly in premenopausal women. Once again we see the connection between body fat distribution and disease, in this case linking excess visceral fat and heart disease. We now know that this link is metabolic syndrome itself.

It has been established for decades that diabetes increases the risk of coronary heart disease and the risk of death from it. Several large studies, some with a ten-year follow-up period and involving thousands of subjects, have recently shown beyond any question that even at the early prediabetes stage, the risk of death from coronary heart disease is increased by at least 200 percent. In fact, the risk of death from coronary heart disease increases from 200 to 400 percent beginning with prediabetic blood sugar levels and then rising incrementally with average blood sugars as reflected in the hemoglobin A1c (HbA1c) test. Even in patients with known coronary heart disease, new onset of diabetes increases the risk of heart attack or stroke by about 300 percent.

There is clearly a close relationship between blood sugars and risk of cardiovascular disease. HbA1c, a blood test averaging blood sugars for up to six weeks, is a very useful measure of the degree of diabetes control. HbA1c has to be less than 7 percent (and preferably closer to 6 percent) to significantly reduce the risk of death from coronary heart disease and stroke.

How is it that elevated average blood sugars correlate with increased risk of cardiovascular disease? Elevated blood sugars damage organs with small blood vessels, such as the kidney and the retina layer of the eyes. Several large studies have shown clearly that the lower average blood sugars are, the less chance there is of diabetic retinopathy (retinal damage from inflammation and bleeding) and kidney failure (again caused by inflammation and leakage of the small blood vessels). Based on the data related to small blood vessels and diabetes, it is proposed that high blood sugar, or hyperglycemia, directly damages the arteries and causes stiffness, narrowing, and inflammation of the vessel walls. However, there isn't very strong evidence incriminating high blood sugars as the main culprit in damage to large arteries and increased risk of heart attack and stroke. In fact, several large and extended studies have demonstrated that cardiovascular disease exists early in patients with metabolic syndrome, even before the onset of diabetes and persistently high blood sugars. At these early stages, the markers of inflammation in blood vessels, such as C-reactive protein (CRP), are already elevated, indicating that diffuse inflammation in the arteries is already causing atherosclerosis.

The endothelial cells of arterial walls are intricately involved in many processes related to cardiovascular health. When the arterial wall is filled with toxic fat (oxidized LDL cholesterol plaques), it becomes inflamed, a dangerous surface for the aggregation of platelets and fibrous debris (fibrinogen), leading to the formation of a friable clot called a *thrombosis*. As soon as a thrombosis is formed or a cholesterol plaque is ruptured and breaks off from a blood vessel wall, the body's endogenous clot busters launch a cascade of biochemical steps called *fibrinolysis* to dissolve the clot. Most serious cardiovascular events, such as heart attack or stroke, involve a sudden thrombotic event blocking the flow of blood (and thus oxygen). The balance between factors that dissolve clots and those that form clots by promoting platelet aggregation (to stop bleeding, for example) is essential for a healthy vascular system. One of the factors promoting platelet aggregation is *plasminogen activator inhibitor 1*, or PAI-1, a prothrombotic protein secreted primarily by abdominal fat cells. Excessive production of PAI-1 correlates with increased risk of death from cardiovascular disease, even at early stages of metabolic syndrome and diabetes. The levels of PAI-1 also correlate closely with insulin resistance in men and women of all ages with central obesity, regardless of body weight. PAI-1 levels increase with central fat accumulation and decrease with dieting and weight loss. With the accumulation of visceral fat, PAI-1 follows the abnormal cholesterol profile, with leptin, adiponectin, insulin, and other markers of insulin resistance showing abnormal levels as well. PAI-1 is just one of the many proteins produced by fat cells that make blood "sticky" (thus inflaming arteries). These include cytokines such as TNF-alpha and IL-6, known to activate inflammatory reactions.

Why are fat cells so closely implicated in arterial wall damage and clotting? Could it be that visceral fat is just unhealthy—like cancer cells—or could it be that fat cells have a natural role to play in the balance of clotting versus bleeding? The answer, at least for now, eludes us, but measuring these parameters as markers of arterial inflammation may help us screen those people who are at the highest risk for heart attack and stroke.

In addition to causing arterial wall damage by way of cholesterol plaques, thrombosis, and platelet aggregation, insulin resistance causes hypertension directly. Ever since the pioneering work of Gerald Reaven, M.D., who

Cardiovascular Disease and Metabolic Syndrome: Connecting the Dots

- *Insulin resistance*: hypertension, excess fatty acid release
- *Hyperactive sympathetic nervous system*: hypertension, stiff arteries
- *Plaque-promoting cholesterol profile*: low HDL, high triglycerides and small dense LDL
- *Arterial wall inflammation*: excess inflammatory factors, low adiponectin
- *"Sticky Blood"*: procoagulant factors PAI-1, fibrinogen
- *Small-vessel disease*: excess blood sugar levels

first connected hypertension to insulin resistance, researchers have been trying to understand this connection. The link between hypertension and insulin resistance is complex. Not everyone with hypertension is insulin resistant, and not all patients with insulin resistance or metabolic syndrome have hypertension. Nonetheless, a large number of studies have demonstrated that hypertension and insulin resistance are closely related. Even in first-degree relatives of people with essential hypertension, there is a higher prevalence of insulin resistance. Regardless of age, gender, and body weight, insulin resistance by itself is a risk for hypertension and cardiovascular disease. The link between hypertension and high blood insulin levels involves the sympathetic nervous system, which handles our stress response and the quality of arterial walls. Even in the absence of established atherosclerosis and prior to hardening of the arteries, vascular tone is abnormal in insulin-resistant individuals.

Could it be that there is a link between chronic stress, insulin resistance, and stiffening of the arteries seen in hypertension? The existing data certainly suggest that in patients with metabolic syndrome, cardiovascular risk reduction must include steps to turn down the sympathetic nervous system through relaxation and exercise. It is common knowledge that relaxation and exercise lower blood pressure. In the context of metabolic syndrome, it has recently been shown that healthy lifestyle changes improve the quality of blood vessel walls in major arteries such as the carotids.

To avoid deadly cardiovascular events, early preventive measures have to be put in place years before the onset of clinically obvious symptoms such as chest pain. One early blood protein, adiponectin, a marker of damage to arteries in metabolic syndrome, has attracted a lot of attention recently. Adiponectin, which is very reduced in metabolic syndrome, does not appear to control appetite, fat storage, or even energy expenditure. Nor does it appear to be controlled by meal size or time. But it does appear to be a key link between cardiovascular disease and metabolic syndrome: in the blood vessel wall, adiponectin inhibits attachment of inflammatory cells at the damaged sites and prevents the formation of cholesterol plaques. Adiponectin level is also a reliable marker for the presence of insulin resistance.

Among obese individuals, regardless of body weight and shape, a lower adiponectin level indicates higher risk of metabolic syndrome, diabetes, and cardiovascular complications. As such, adiponectin testing will be a promising tool for medical practitioners treating patients with metabolic syndrome. Based on the available data, it appears that adiponectin is a health-enhancing molecule and may be a promising medication as well.

To prevent cardiovascular disease in people with metabolic syndrome, lowering the bad LDL cholesterol by medication or by diet and taking an aspirin a day may no longer be enough. Insulin resistance and its markers have to be tested individually and treated early. For cardiologists and cardiovascular surgeons, the treatment of insulin resistance has become a major priority.

Menopause, Fat Gain, and Metabolic Syndrome

A woman's body changes during the menopausal transition. In fact, just as with puberty and pregnancy, menopause represents a critical period of profound hormonal and physical transformation of a woman's body. But unlike puberty and pregnancy, the menopausal transformation is often associated with a higher risk of certain diseases, including diabetes, heart disease, and osteoporosis. If puberty is the springtime of a woman's reproductive life, then menopause is the autumn and as such is often perceived negatively. Many of the negative aspects of this natural process, such as weight gain, fat redistribution, and skin and hair changes, are preventable. In particular, fat redistribution, which is responsible for the "midlife girth" of apple-shaped women, is both preventable and reversible.

During the years before and immediately after menopause, there is a natural predominance of male hormone production, which, together with a state of estrogen deficiency, contributes significantly to the fat redistribution seen in midlife women. Overall women have 10 percent more total body fat than men. Most of the subcutaneous fat in young women is in the buttocks and thighs (called *gluteofemoral fat*) rather than in the abdominal area.

Hence the "hourglass" or "pear" (also referred to as *gynoid*) shape of women occurs because of an estrogen-dominant state. In midlife, the hormonal balance changes in favor of testosterone, and women gain more body fat in the abdominal area. Menopausal women have 49 percent more intra-abdominal, or visceral, fat than premenopausal women, resulting in a rounder ("apple") shape. Several studies using sophisticated imaging studies, such as MRI and DXA scans, have confirmed greater amounts of visceral fat in menopausal women. That apple-shaped body correlates with a significant rise in the risk of diabetes and cardiovascular disease.

Overall, the abnormal cholesterol profile, the rise in markers of vascular inflammation, and the higher rate of cardiovascular risks such as stiffening of arteries, hypertension, and insulin resistance are all consistent with a higher prevalence of metabolic syndrome in menopausal women. In fact, menopause is associated with a 60 percent increase in risk of metabolic syndrome. But this can be turned around. Reversal of metabolic syndrome with fat loss reduces most of these health risks.

Metabolic Syndrome and Infertility: Polycystic Ovary Syndrome (PCOS)

PCOS, or *polycystic ovary syndrome,* is the most common endocrine disorder in young women. Worldwide, it affects 6 to 8 percent of all women of reproductive age. PCOS is marked by the presence of an excess amount of male hormones, or androgens, and irregular periods. Women with PCOS have long cycles and rare menstrual periods. They also have excess facial and body hair—sign of excess male hormone referred to as *hyperandrogenism.* These two clinical findings are often enough for the diagnosis of PCOS. Not all women with PCOS are overweight or obese. In fact,

Polycystic Ovary Syndrome and Metabolic Syndrome

- Majority of women with PCOS are insulin resistant.
- Approximately half of women with PCOS are overweight or obese. But obesity is not a required feature of PCOS.
- Insulin resistance due to excess abdominal fat *precedes* hormonal dysfunction such as irregular periods in PCOS.
- Women with PCOS commonly develop diabetes and cardiovascular disease if they continue to have excess abdominal fat.
- Infertility and excess facial and body hair are as much due to excess ovarian male hormones as they are due to insulin resistance.
- Reducing insulin levels or reversing insulin resistance with lifestyle change or medications balances hormones and regulates menstrual cycles.

depending on the population studied, obesity affects close to 50 percent of women with PCOS. But excess abdominal fat, or central obesity, is a very common finding in PCOS. Even lean women with PCOS and teenage girls at risk of PCOS (that is, before clinical findings are obvious) are shown to have excess abdominal fat and features of insulin resistance. Besides reproductive and hormonal findings, central obesity and its metabolic consequences, such as insulin resistance, a proinflammatory state, and ultimately diabetes and cardiovascular disease, are major clinical features of PCOS. Indeed, PCOS is intricately related and is now considered a consequence of insulin resistance and metabolic syndrome.

The hormonal imbalance in PCOS stimulates the ovarian follicles to grow into groups of small cysts (each less than 1 centimeter in size). When these cysts are visualized by ultrasound, they look like a string of pearls. Sometimes cysts can get much bigger and even rupture, causing pelvic pain.

There is certainly a genetic predisposition to PCOS. But gaining excess abdominal fat may be what is required for the characteristic features to become clinically apparent. The exact mechanisms involved in the onset of hormonal imbalance remains somewhat of a controversy.

Women with PCOS who have apple-shaped obesity almost certainly have metabolic syndrome and are therefore at risk of diabetes and cardiovascular disease. Since a higher risk of diabetes and heart disease are often recognized early in these women (who are often in their twenties and early thirties), doctors tend to advise them to join a weight loss program more commonly than in the general population. Even when normal cycles resume and these women are able to conceive, because of underlying predisposition to insulin resistance, they remain at risk of gestational diabetes, type 2 diabetes, and ultimately cardiovascular disease for years to come. Therefore, women with PCOS have to remain lean for life.

3 How Lifestyle Medicine Fights Metabolic Syndrome

The typical visit to the primary care doctor is 8 minutes long once or twice a year. The current medical delivery system is not suitable for coaching and counseling; it is designed to efficiently diagnose and treat diseases. Where disease-based medicine falls short is exactly where *lifestyle medicine* has its strength: prevention of illness with proactive lifestyle change. Lifestyle medicine examines a person's body, mind-set, profession, lifestyle, medical risks, and conditions. This approach sets realistic goals that can be achieved by a specific exercise program together with nutrition and behavior modification.

This book is a lifestyle medicine coaching manual aimed at metabolic syndrome. Here, as in our medical practice, we use a three-pronged approach of diet, exercise, and stress reduction to prevent or reverse metabolic syndrome.

A healthy metabolism is the ultimate solution, but we need to go beyond our medical knowledge of metabolic syndrome. Weight gain, metabolic burn rate, and hormonal swings are linked to our eating behaviors and activity level, but they are also connected to our stress response mechanisms, our career choices, and real life events. This chapter connects the dots between metabolism (and energy balance) and stress, exercise, eating, and the environment.

How Our Body Composition Changes with Time

No matter how we describe body size, our body's composition is a better reflection of our metabolism. Body composition refers to the percentage of muscle and fat mass in different parts of our body. It is more difficult to measure our body's composition than to measure our size. One reason is that our body composition is always changing. In puberty, all girls and boys gain more body fat. But adolescents who go through puberty rapidly end up being short and often chubby, so their body fat remains relatively high for their age. Those who mature slowly become taller and leaner. Later in life, women often blame pregnancy for permanent weight gain. But other factors, such as hormones, metabolic burn rate, and breast-feeding, determine who loses fat after childbirth and who keeps it. Women going through menopause do not gain weight any more than aging men do (roughly a pound a year). But the menopausal weight gain is almost entirely excess abdominal fat, which affects health risks more than weight gain elsewhere in the body.

Our body shape and physical features are somewhat determined by genes. But as we age, hormones that control our metabolism have more influence on our body. Several hormones—namely, growth hormone (GH), insulin-like growth factor 1 (IGF-1), insulin itself, and sex steroids such as estrogens and androgens—control growth rate, body size, and shape.

We also know that the balance between estrogen and testosterone plays a role in the fat distribution and shape of women going through menopause. During perimenopause, ovaries produce less and less estrogen, but they continue to produce male hormones such as testosterone. Therefore, a predominance of male hormone in perimenopausal women contributes to visceral fat deposits. The gluteofemoral fat deposit in the buttock and thighs, which shapes women into pears, is regulated by estrogen, and that is why men normally do not have as much gluteofemoral fat as women. Overall, the combination of inherited characteristics and hormonal changes throughout life determines how our body looks and where in our body we gain fat.

But some biological characteristics are constant in all humans, regardless of gender and age. In general, our body burns fewer calories as we get older. Older adults burn fewer calories in part because they are less active but also because they have relatively less muscle and more fat.

The fat-free mass (mostly muscle) is responsible for up to 70 percent of our resting metabolic rate. Fat, on the other hand, burns only 2 percent of the energy spent at rest. As we age and gain body fat relative to muscle, our burn rate naturally slows down. Therefore, the elderly should eat fewer calories and be more active. Indeed, many studies have shown that longevity correlates with physical activity and eating less.

What tools do we have to measure body composition, and what are the normal reference ranges? The number on the scale does not tell us how much of our weight is due to fat, muscle, water, or bone. Body weight on the scale does not take into account body size or shape. A 6-foot 2-inch man should naturally weigh more than a 5-foot 11-inch man of the same age. So to correct for height, a formula is used to obtain a more reliable measure, referred to as the *body mass index*. But the body mass index, or BMI, by itself does not tell us much about body composition. Recent studies, widely covered in the mass media because of their surprising

Recommended Range of Body Fat Percentage Based on Age and Activity

Age/Activity	Recommended Fat % for Women	Recommended Fat % for Men
Athletic all ages	12–22	5–15
< 34	20–30	10–25
35–55	25–35	10–25
56 or older	25–35	10–30

Source: Adapted from S. Going and R. Davis, "Body Composition," in *ACSM's Resource Manual for Guidelines for Exercise Testing and Prescription*, 4th ed., edited by J. Roitman (Baltimore: Lippincott Williams & Wilkins, 2001). Readjusted based on our clinical experience.

findings suggesting that NFL players are obese and that overweight people have a lower mortality than thin people, have the same basic flaw: it is not weight or even BMI that matters; it is the body fat percentage that best reflects a healthy physiology.

We need to know the body's fat percentage. BMI and body fat percentage both go up in obesity. But depending on body composition, they may not always increase in parallel. Since muscle weighs more than fat, BMI is disproportionately higher than body fat percentage in strong and muscular people like football players. And small, fatty men and women may have a BMI that is a lot lower than their body fat would predict. If you compare your BMI with your body fat percentage range (see below),

Body Mass Index (BMI) and Fat Percentage

Calculate your BMI using the formula on page 13. Estimate your body fat percentage using any of the methods described in this chapter. Compare your results with the ranges given here. If your body fat percentage is higher than the range predicted by your BMI (for example, a man with a BMI of 25 would have a body fat percentage between 22 and 25) you have excess body fat. On the other hand, if your body fat percentage correlates to a BMI range that is less than your calculated BMI, then you are muscular and you weigh more than most people with your height. Comparing your BMI with your body fat percentage helps you gain a better understanding of your body composition.

BMI	Classification	Fat % Men	Fat % Women
18.5–24*	Normal	10–21	20–30
25–29*	Overweight	22–25	31–37
30–5	Obese (class I)	26–31	38–42
35 or higher	Clinically obese (classes II and III)	>31	>42

*For Asians, the upper limit of normal is 23 and obesity is defined as BMI over 25.

How to Measure Body Fat

- Body circumference to estimate visceral fat: waistline; waist-to-hip ratio.
- Skinfold measurement with caliper to estimate overall body fat: subscapular-to-triceps ratio; femoral-to-subscapular ratio. Not an accurate indicator of fat distribution.
- Dual-energy photon x-ray absorptiometry (DXA): direct measurement of body fat in the trunk and limbs. Considered "gold standard" for total body composition assessment.
- Computerized tomography scan (CT) of visceral and subcutaneous abdominal fat area ratio. A precise but costly measurement of visceral fat.
- Magnetic resonance imaging (MRI). A precise but costly measurement of visceral and subcutaneous abdominal fat.

Source: Adapted from A. Garg, M.D., "The Role of Body Fat Distribution in Insulin Resistance," In *Resistance,* edited by G. Reaven and A. Laws (Totowa, NJ: Humana Press, 1999).

you can get an idea of your body composition. For example, if your BMI is in the overweight or obese category but your body fat percentage is less than expected, then you are built solid with more muscle than most people your weight. If, on the other hand, your body fat percentage is higher than your BMI would predict, then you have too much fat and not enough muscle.

Some people confuse intra-abdominal, or visceral, fat with skin fat in the abdominal area. Visceral fat is located inside the abdominal cavity, around the gut, kidneys, and deep abdominal muscles and is attached to the envelope covering internal organs called the *omentum* (the fat attached there is called *omental fat*). Obese men and apple-shaped women have more visceral fat than is estimated by calculating the BMI or by using calipers.

Fat distribution is therefore the most helpful indicator of risk of metabolic syndrome. Accurate measurement of regional body composition—that is, the amount of visceral fat and its percentage of total body fat—is only possible with sophisticated scanners.

Energy, Body Composition, and Lifestyle

If the minute you eat a couple of snacks you feel you gain weight, it may be true! On the other hand, if you hear about someone losing 30 pounds in two months just by cutting out junk food and soda, it may also be true! This is because our body's energy balance depends on our food (caloric) intake as much as on our energy expenditure, or "burn rate." The less we eat and more active we are, the more we lose weight. The more we eat and more sedentary we are, the faster we gain weight.

Of course, things are not that simple. Many factors control our caloric intake, such as hunger, satiety, access to food, type of food, and exercise, as well as psychological determinants. There are also many factors that control our total energy expenditure (that is, how many calories we lose in 24 hours), including ingestion of food, type of diet, exercise, profession, hormonal regulation of our metabolism, body size, body composition, and stress. Our total energy expenditure can be increased or reduced daily, with exercise, for example, but our *basal metabolic rate (BMR)* does not change unless we change our body composition. The main determinant of energy expenditure at rest is the fat-free (muscle) mass. Athletes burn more calories by physical activity than by their BMR. But for most people, BMR contributes the most to the total daily energy expenditure. So any changes, even small, in the BMR have a big impact on our weight in the long run.

To better understand our metabolism—that is, the balance between our food intake and our burn rate—we need to review how our body converts food to energy. As food is ingested, it ultimately breaks down into fat, sugar, and protein—the three main *macronutrients*—and other substances, such as minerals and vitamins—called *micronutrients*. The latter do not contribute much to energy balance. Inside cells, macronutrients are transformed to adenosine triphosphate (ATP) molecules, the body's predominant energy unit. ATP molecules are used by different cells for different tasks, such as contraction of muscle fibers, production of new proteins in freshly generated cells, and synthesis of glycogen in the liver. According to the laws of thermodynamics, the metabolic breakdown of food in our body should yield energy equivalent to the heat generated by the simple combustion of food components measured in calories. *So calories are a measure of energy contained in food, and they are also a measure of energy spent by our body at rest or during exercise.* An adenosine triphosphate (ATP) molecule is not a measurement unit, like a calorie, but is the actual fuel of our metabolism. When we eat food, we generate energy molecules, or ATP. When we exercise, we use these same energy molecules for muscle contraction. The energy balance of our metabolism is *measured* in calories.

If a balance between caloric intake and burn rate ultimately determines weight, then knowing how many calories we burn at rest helps us get an idea of how much food we should eat. So the burn rate, or BMR, is a useful measure for weight loss. BMR is energy spent by our body to stay warm, to keep the heart pumping, to keep the lungs breathing, and for other basic bodily functions. Hormones, such as thyroid hormones, and the sympathetic nervous system control the BMR. If the thyroid gland is underactive, our body slows down and does not burn enough calories at rest. If the nervous system senses a low energy state, say, from dieting, it slows down our resting burn rate to save energy. The rest of the total 24-hour burn rate depends mainly on physical activity.

How is BMR measured? The 24-hour basal energy expenditure may be measured directly through a sophisticated method using heavy isotope water. This method uses a heavy isotope of oxygen in water (the heavy isotope is deuterium and is not radioactive) that is ingested at the start of the test. Incorporation of the heavy isotope allows tracking of carbon dioxide production and its elimination in breath. Carbon dioxide measurement is used to estimate the metabolic equivalent of energy burnt for its production. This is an easy test for subjects under study, but it is too sophisticated for practical purposes. Another way to measure burn rate is to measure body heat generated while resting in a perfectly insolated measurement chamber. This method is also not practical. Recently, breath analyzers detecting oxygen consumption are used to estimate the 24-hour burn rate. This method requires a fasting state for 12 hours and no exercise for at least 6 hours. Although measuring burn rate is especially useful for people who struggle with weight loss, the following formula may be used to estimate basal metabolic rate.

If you are very active and exercise daily, add 500 calories to your calculated resting burn rate to obtain your *total energy expenditure*, or TEE—that is, your 24-hour burn rate. TEE can be much higher than resting burn rate in extremely active individuals, but for most people, TEE is about 500

What Controls Metabolic Rate, or Energy Expenditure?

- *Body size.* Bigger people require and burn more calories both at rest and when active.
- *Body composition.* Lean mass burns 70 percent of energy at rest; more muscles, higher metabolism.
- *Body temperature.* Core temperature raises with exercise, hormones, and genes.
- *Activity level.* Energy used during exercise and oxygen consumption after exercise affect burn rate.
- *Food intake.* Body heat generated after eating foods accounts for up to 10 percent of total calories consumed.
- *Ambient temperature.* Small effect except in very hot or very cold extremes.
- *Hormones.* Thyroid, stress hormones catecholamines and cortisol, estrogens and androgens all affect metabolic rate.
- *Medications.* Stimulants raise the burn rate; mood regulators, such as beta blockers, lower it.
- *Stress.* Chronic stress, regardless of the nature of the stressor, causes visceral fat gain.

calories above the measured basal burn rate. TEE depends first and foremost on exercise and daily physical activities, but it is also impacted by age, gender, race, environment, and, of course, diet. Food itself raises total energy expenditure. During and after eating, our body uses energy to digest food and wastes calories as heat. When we eat a spicy dish or a high-protein meal like chili, we get warm and sometimes we even sweat while eating. That is called the thermic effect of food. Thermic energy or heat generated after eating is the least for fat (5 percent of calories) and the most for proteins (20 to 30 percent). Carbohydrates are in the middle; that is 5 to 10 percent of calories ingested are wasted as heat. So a high-protein meal is less efficient in restoring energy reserves than a high-

---

How to Estimate Your Resting Metabolic Rate (Calories per Day)

	Males	**Females**
Ages 10–17	(8 × BW) + 650	(5.5 × BW) +745
Ages 18–30	(7 × BW) + 650	(6.6 × BW) +500
Ages 31–60	(5.3 × BW) + 880	(4 × BW) +830

These estimates are based on studies done with healthy, nonoverweight individuals and may not apply to everyone. In our experience, these estimates should be considered the minimum burn rate for most people. Most overweight or obese men and women have higher burn rates than predicted by this formula. If you are an overweight or obese woman, you should add 300 calories to the value obtained using the formula given here. Similarly, men should add 500 calories. If you are big but are active and exercise regularly, add another 300 calories to obtain an approximate value of your *total* 24-hour burn rate, or TEE.

Note: BW = body weight in pounds

Source: Adapted from *ACSM's Resource Manual for Guidelines for Exercise Testing and Prescription*, 4th ed., edited by J. Roitman (Baltimore: Lippincott Williams & Wilkins, 2001). Readjusted based on our clinical experience.

carbohydrate meal. In other words, fats and carbohydrates replenish energy reserves (as fat deposits and glycogen) much more effectively than protein and thus cause weight gain more easily.

Energy balance and its mechanisms are not carved in stone. Our body is a living organism, and it responds to challenges in natural ways. When dieting, our body feels the drop in energy taken in, and through a complex physiology regulates our burn rate. This drop in our burn rate happens even before any muscle mass is lost due to dieting, so it cannot be fully accounted for by a change in our body composition.

Cooling down of BMR can add up to approximately one-third of caloric deficit from dieting. This means that if you are losing weight by cutting back 1,000 calories a day, after a while your body fights back and reduces your BMR by 300 calories. In addition, since you now weigh less, you simply burn fewer calories when moving around. Finally, eating less food means wasting less energy in the form of heat. This is another 8 percent drop in energy expenditure.

To *Plateau* or Not

- Weight loss of 2 pounds per week equals an energy deficit of roughly 1,000 calories per day. It requires roughly a 1,400-calorie diet for most overweight or obese people. For smaller frames, a 1,200-calorie diet is needed.
- Often, after two months or approximately 20 pounds less, the dieter's metabolism slows down and weight loss reaches a plateau. So, to continue a weight loss of 2 pounds per week, the dieter has to cut back another 200 calories or burn 200 more by exercising for every 20 pounds lost.
- It is very difficult to sustain a low-calorie diet of less than 1,000 calories. Therefore, when most people stop losing weight, they give up and relapse. The only way to break through a plateau is to increase the burn rate with exercise and if needed by building more muscle.

The combination of these parameters (diet, reduced burn rate, and weight loss) results in a drop of total energy expenditure, or TEE, by roughly 10 calories per pound lost. So when you add it all up, if after ten weeks you've lost 20 pounds by eating 1,200 calories a day, now you have to limit your diet to 1,000 calories a day to lose more weight. Cutting back more calories is not easy. The best way to continue to lose weight is to increase both physical activity and resting burn rate by building more fresh muscle fibers.

Food, Activity, and Weight Gain

Children burn calories even when they are asleep because they are growing. They also burn more energy than adults throughout the day because they are generally more active. So most children and adolescents do not have to worry about weight gain unless they have unhealthy eating habits. Adults, on the other hand, do not grow, and our resting burn rate, or basal metabolic rate (BMR), actually goes down as we age. So in adults, the total daily energy expenditure depends more on activity level.

Foods we eat and our physical activity and rest level balance our metabolism every few hours. The body does not calculate and recall the energy deficit from five days ago to credit against today's excessive caloric intake. If we overeat when our body doesn't need the extra energy, we store that energy as fat. This aspect of weight gain is not difficult to understand.

Using hormonal signals, our fat cells talk to our brain. If we starve ourselves or even skip meals, the appetite centers in our brain get flooded with "*eat eat*" signals from fat cells and we crave more food. People who have an erratic "good day—bad day" eating behavior eat too much one day, starve themselves the next day, only to eat twice as much food the following day. This kind of eating pattern causes weight gain.

The same is true for exercise. When we exercise, we burn calories during our workout. We also continue to burn calories for about 6 hours afterward because of increased body temperature and oxygen consumption. But if we do not exercise the next day, our body does not "remember" the previous day's exercise and will hold on to extra calories. So people who exercise hard one day only to recover during the next two or three days do not lose weight.

We are beginning to understand the mechanisms that control appetite, digestion, and energy storage, but those regulating energy expenditure appear to be more elusive. Although more research is needed, the avail-

What We Know About Metabolic Rate

- Lean adolescent girls and lean young women burn fewer calories than lean males of the same age: about 400 calories less at rest and 600 to 700 calories less when active. So, overall, females burn fewer calories than males even when they are active. Men can lose weight exercising, but women have to diet as well as exercise.

- Overweight women burn 200 to 400 calories more at rest and when active than lean women of the same age. So it is generally a misconception that obese women have lower burn rates. But it may be true that some overweight women and men have slower metabolism than predicted simply by their weight. People with sluggish metabolism (due to hormones, excess fat, medications, or genetics) gain weight quickly when they overeat. That should be a reminder to them to exercise more.

- Overweight men burn more calories at rest and even more when active than overweight women and lean men of the same age. So, obese men have the highest burn rates of all. Even gentle activity such as walking helps big guys lose weight. In our experience, men who weigh over 300 pounds often have a resting metabolic rate above 4,000 calories. If they eat 1,500 calories a day and stay active, they can lose 4 pounds a week.

- Overweight women burn far fewer calories than overweight men, even when they exercise. That explains why men can lose weight so much faster than women. Men burn more calories because they have more muscle but also because they exercise harder. (That is why we do not enroll husbands and wives in our weight loss programs at the same time. Men lose weight faster, and that frustrates their wives, who may be struggling to lose just a few pounds.)

- Bodybuilders often eat a high-energy meal within an hour after an exercise session. They do not lose fat this way, but they get bigger with increased lean mass. Exercise is anabolic: it releases growth hormone, which builds muscles, but it also stimulates appetite so that our body replenishes its energy stores. Overweight people should eat a small meal half an hour before they exercise. That way, they get a better workout and are less hungry afterward. Eating before exercise also blunts the release of growth hormone and prevents the muscles from getting bigger.

- To keep the metabolic rate up, it is better to exercise more often even if workouts are shorter. Excessive exercise often requires a rest period of several days afterward. During these rest days, our body continues to store fat, and the end result is weight gain. Exercising 4 hours split up during the entire week gives much better results than exercising 4 hours on the weekend. In addition to weight gain, "weekend warriors" are at higher risk of injury and stress.

- Finally, exercise is sometimes used as a dietary indiscretion, justifying overeating. In addition to satisfying hunger after a training session, it is not uncommon to eat more and say, "Well, I'll just have to exercise harder tomorrow." An exercise session usually burns 300 calories, equivalent to a small meal.

able data suggest that our body's metabolic memory is about 6 hours. Our appetite centers are stimulated and we get hungry again about 6 hours after a meal. The satiety signals telling our brain that we are full also last about the same time. In principle, if we eat every few hours, we should not experience hunger. Exercise also revs up our metabolism for about 6 hours. Therefore, I recommend to my patients that they eat frequently to keep the appetite centers shut and exercise twice a day to keep the burn rate up. But there is still a lot to be learned about variations in energy disposal, and there are many factors that affect our metabolism. Hormones (such as thyroid hormone, estrogen, and testosterone), medications, body composition, fitness status, stress level, and environmental factors (such as climate) all influence our energy expenditure. Too much focus is put on dieting and not enough on metabolic rate or burn rate.

Recent studies have proved that lean individuals burn more calories doing exercise than overweight individuals. If overweight people burn more calories at rest and during activity, how is it that lean individuals burn relatively more calories with exercise? It is actually simple to understand. Lean people spend more time exercising, and because they are in better shape, they can exercise harder. But we can also conclude that overweight individuals, if they are healthy and in reasonable shape, can burn more calories with a less intense exercise program. For example, heavily built and muscular men and women have the muscles they need to burn lots of energy; they just have to use their muscles more often. Submaximal whole-body exercise such as interval training, walking, or swimming should yield great results for muscular obese people.

On the other hand, overweight people who do not have lots of muscle, either because they have always been couch potatoes or because they have lost significant lean mass due to injury or old age, may not get much out of an aerobic exercise session such as walking. They need to build muscle doing resistance training and then use these freshly made muscle fibers to burn more calories. Because these "fatty" and relatively weak individuals are often sedentary, they typically dislike aerobics but may enjoy slow resistance training and core strength training such as Pilates or yoga. In addition to a low-calorie diet, a carefully designed and personalized exercise program is more critical for these individuals than for the more muscular obese men and women. Muscular and large-framed obese people do not need as much help losing weight as fatty and small-framed obese people.

How Therapeutic Lifestyle Change (TLC) Works

Clinical evidence showing the effectiveness of lifestyle change in diabetes prevention and reversal is continuing to arrive from researchers all around the globe. Diet and exercise are becoming the first-line therapy for adult-onset diabetes and, of course, for metabolic syndrome. Ever since the discovery of the pancreatic origin of diabetes over a century ago, dietary intervention has been a major component of diabetes management. Even before the availability of insulin as a medication, it was known that patients suffering from diabetes would have better control of their blood sugar on a low-carbohydrate diet. But recently, the role of dietary fat and excess body fat in insulin resistance and type 2 diabetes has attracted more attention. Fat loss as a tool for diabetes management is now considered as important a dietary goal as lowering blood sugar has been for the last fifty years. Fat loss is best achieved through a combination of diet and exercise. In fact, physical activity and fat loss have been shown to lower average blood sugars (as tested by HbA1c levels) as effectively as most antidiabetes medications.

It has been known for a long time that type 2 diabetes is more common in sedentary people and that exercise improves diabetes management. In the last decade, numerous studies have shown that moderate exercise ameliorates blood sugars and improves insulin sensitivity. Animal studies using rats have identified this beneficial effect to be due to an increase in insulin receptors in muscle cells as well as a more efficient glucose transport into the cells. Exercise also removes fat deposits from muscle cells, further reducing insulin resistance. But whether type 2 diabetes is preventable or not was not clearly established a decade ago. More than ten years ago, a five-year Swedish study of 181 sedentary men with borderline diabetes (impaired glucose tolerance) showed that men who exercised at home and followed a low-calorie diet had one-third the chance to progress to frank diabetes compared to men who did not make any lifestyle changes. Around the same time, two large studies of 87,253 nurses followed for eight years and another following 21,271 physicians for five years showed a significant reduction in diabetes risk among women and men who exercised at least once per week. Although these studies were powerful enough to show a beneficial *relation* between exercise and diabetes prevention, they were not designed to prove that type 2 diabetes is indeed preventable by lifestyle change. To *prove* that lifestyle change actually prevents diabetes, high-risk subjects have to be divided randomly into one group undergoing lifestyle change and another group followed as control. The two groups would then be followed for a few years before any conclusion could be reached.

In 1997, one such study from China showed clearly that therapeutic lifestyle change, or TLC, consisting of diet modification and/or moderate exercise reduced the risk of diabetes in subjects with metabolic syndrome (with impaired glucose tolerance) by about 46 percent over a six-year period. And in 2001, a Finnish study showed that a TLC intervention consisting of regular exercise, dieting, and counseling prevented onset of diabetes in high-risk individuals by 58 percent over a three-year period. Next, a sixteen-year follow-up of the Nurses' Health Study, published in 2001, showed that 62 percent of new cases of diabetes were due to weight gain, and overall, 91 percent of cases were attributable to lifestyle factors. Nurses who developed diabetes during the study had a higher risk of cardiovascular disease *before* diagnosis of diabetes, and their risk increased to almost four times *after* they developed diabetes.

The same year, the first large-scale and well-controlled study in the United States, called the *Diabetes Prevention Program*, or DPP, was terminated early because of its remarkable results. This study, which was subsequently published in the *New England Journal of Medicine* in 2002, was conducted on 3,234 adult participants in 27 medical centers nationwide and represented all ethnic groups and all age groups. The early results showed conclusively that participants who were in the TLC arm of the study, exercising 150 minutes per week and eating a low-fat diet, reduced their risk of diabetes by 58 percent. Those participants who took a medication lowering insulin resistance (metformin) also reduced their risk of diabetes, but to a lesser degree (by 31 percent.) A modest 5 to 7 percent weight loss correlated with risk reduction in the TLC group.

The DPP trial established in a conclusive way that type 2 diabetes is preventable and that lifestyle changes reducing insulin resistance by (even modest) weight loss are highly effective preventive tools. DPP also showed that the conversion rate from metabolic syndrome, a prediabetic state, to diabetes is about 10 percent per year. That means that if 100 people with metabolic syndrome are followed for ten years, they all develop diabetes and heart disease. But if they change their lifestyle as in this study, approximately half of them will avoid diabetes and reduce their risk of heart disease by roughly 400 percent.

Not only does TLC prevent diabetes, but it also reverses some of the related cardiovascular complications of diabetes, such as thickening and stiffening of arteries (called vascular tone and compliance). It has also been shown to improve fertility and conception rate in women with polycystic ovary syndrome (PCOS), a condition associated with metabolic syndrome. All these studies suggest that the protective effect of TLC is related to visceral fat loss, regression of insulin resistance, and reduction of early vascular inflammation. Medications such as metformin and the thiazolidene family of drugs (TZD drugs, for short, such as rosiglitazone or pioglitazone) are very effective in treating insulin resistance. Use of these medications results in similar benefits as TLC interventions, but without significant fat loss.

Therefore, reversal of insulin resistance, whether with medication or TLC, is key to diabetes prevention in the context of metabolic syndrome. However, all studies to date show that compared to medications, lifestyle change is much more effective in reducing insulin resistance and reversing metabolic syndrome. Overall, the DPP trial and other studies discussed above have shown that TLC reduces the risk of diabetes, PCOS, and heart disease by at least 50 percent (almost twice as effective as medications). *TLC is the way to go!*

Our own experience in Connecticut confirms that TLC is an effective and practical method for diabetes prevention and diabetes reversal in early stages of metabolic syndrome. Preventive medicine has traditionally been a practice limited to research institutions with government funding. Our experience shows that it works in real life, too. Depending on their initial body weight, women and men who enroll in our TLC programs lose 20 to 60 pounds in six months. As soon as meal planning and counseling begin, even before weight loss, blood sugars and insulin levels drop to normal levels. Most of the initial weight lost is fat; visceral fat and facial fat deposits disappear first. On average, HbA1c (a measure of average blood sugars given in percentage points) drops by 1 percentage point in the first three months—better than most antidiabetes drugs. Previously discussed cardiovascular risk markers, such as PAI-1 and CRP, also drop significantly as fat loss continues. After the first eight to ten weeks of meal planning, our enrollees begin exercising. The exercise program is customized according to body composition (measured by DXA scan), body shape, fitness level, and medical history. Those individuals who are very deconditioned or who have advanced cardiorespiratory disease begin with gentle yoga and breathing sessions before they are able to exercise under supervision. Throughout the program, people work with a clinical psychologist for cognitive therapy and stress management training. Relaxation sessions are encouraged and are available. Finally, basic cooking classes and educational seminars are offered to those who are interested. Of course, a medical doctor and a dietitian follow each participant. At regular intervals and at the end of the program, everyone gets a medical evaluation consisting of an interview, anthropomorphic measurements such as waist-to-hip ratio, a physical exam, and blood tests. Once people reach their goals, they are encouraged to enter a maintenance program.

The most remarkable and rewarding aspect of such a TLC program is the true empowerment of individuals who finally learn the skills they need to change their lives, their minds, and their bodies forever. TLC is not a quick fix but has a rewarding return on investment for all parties involved: individuals and their loved ones, clinicians, and society at large.

How TLC Can Work for You

TLC is a process. It is the process of regaining your health. To work for you, the flow of the different parts have to be adjusted for you. These parts include setting goals, activating motivators, overcoming obstacles, reinforcing change, creating a structured schedule, recognizing results, and implementing rewards systems. It all begins with contemplation, which marks the end of denial. Contemplation overlaps with and leads to commitment.

Contemplation and commitment cannot be separated from goal setting. To remain committed, it is important to identify specific goals and targets early on. Goals could include weight loss or fat loss or redistribution or could be limited to a component of TLC, such as exercise training or healthy cooking. For example, an exercise-related goal could be to learn to exercise while avoiding a medical complication such as low blood sugar or chronic back pain. A limited goal related to eating could be to find solutions that work for you while you travel. Goals cannot be set without full and open communication with your clinician, your family and friends, and even with yourself. For example, if your goal is to lose abdominal fat but instead you focus on your looks, you may not change your lifestyle effectively. If you have an eating disorder or suffer from a

Dana Gains at Least Fifteen Years of Life

Dana is only twenty-seven years old. She has early signs of diabetes caused by excess body fat and metabolic syndrome. She was 150 pounds when she entered college. In her first year, she had a traumatic emotional experience and dropped out. In that year, she gaining about 100 pounds. After a year of counseling, she was able to finish college and now has a great job. She has overcome a lot of challenges but has remained obese.

Dana finally decided it was time to change her lifestyle and enrolled in our program. The initial testing showed that diabetes was around the corner: when she was challenged with sugar intake (called a *glucose tolerance test*), she would reach high blood sugars in the diabetic range. Interestingly, her blood insulin level rose to over four times the normal peak levels, causing her blood sugar to drop precipitously. She turned all flushed and felt light-headed. The glucose challenge not only diagnosed her with early stages of diabetes but also explained her symptoms, which, she was told by a coworker, resembled hot flashes.

Table 3.1 summarizes how her profile improved after just six months of weight loss in our program.

Table 3.1: Dana's TLC Experience

Parameters	Normal Values	Before	After	Comments
Weight (lb)		297	232	65 lb loss
BMI (kg/m²)	< 26	44	34	
Abdominal fat				
% (≅ lb)	< 10	45% (69)	35% (45)	24 lb abdominal fat loss
Fasting blood				
glucose (mg/dl)		< 100	105	82
Cholesterol,				
total (mg/dl)	< 200	174	136	
HDL cholesterol				
(mg/dl)	> 40	32	31	See below.
Triglycerides	< 150	173	106	
LDL cholesterol				
(mg/dl)	< 130	107	89	
Insulin (μIU/ml)	< 17	17	7	

Dana has done extremely well. She has lost 65 pounds so far. Her symptoms have disappeared. Her good (HDL) cholesterol and PAI-1 levels did not improve because she did not like aerobic exercise and she continued to smoke. She finally quit smoking after she met with a caring cardiologist. She now looks beautiful, is very confident, and is putting the finishing touches on to a successful lifestyle change.

post-traumatic stress disorder, no matter how hard you try to diet, you may not succeed without counseling. In such a case, you have to communicate your concerns with your counselor. Sometimes your goal is related to your weight but is not weight loss per se. For example, you may wish to renew your romantic ties with your spouse and believe that a better body image and perhaps feeling sexy would help. But what if your relationship with your spouse does not improve, even after you lose weight? Is your goal a loving relationship or weight loss? An honest and open communication (with yourself and with your clinician) is critical if your program is going to be effective.

Once you set your goals, then you have to develop a strategy with specific targets. Targets are different from goals in that they are highly specific, vary with time, and may not be as complex as goals. For example, consider diabetes prevention as a goal set by an overweight woman. She set this goal because she has a family history of diabetes, had gestational diabetes, and has gained 25 pounds in the last five years. It is clear that she is on her way to type 2 diabetes. In fact, a doctor has already told her that her blood sugar is borderline. She knows that her goal is *to prevent diabetes* but she does not know what to target. She knows she has to lose body fat, but how is she going to do that?

After a long interview, we find that she began gaining weight five years ago when she met her husband, a police officer who often works late night shifts. During the day, she is busy and does not eat much, but at night, because she is tired and lonely, she nibbles on crunchy and sweet snacks. Already, two targets are identified: *loneliness at night* and *boredom-related eating*. When she spends time with her husband on his off days, her activities are centered around food: she goes out to restaurants and casinos. So the third target is *leisure time overeating*. These are well-defined targets, which have to be aimed at from the start.

Next we have to identify motivators. Why does she want to lose weight? Is it really because she wants to prevent diabetes, or is it because she does not like the way she looks, or is it because she wants to be attractive to her husband? These are all related, and their common denominator is weight loss. But which motivator is key? It is critical to identify the top motivator that would really get her going. She will have to tap into the main motivator over and over again. It is also important to build a reward system around her personal motivators. We will review specific examples of reward systems elsewhere. But for now, let us just point out the difference between obstacles and challenges, which can neutralize her motivation.

Like sudden roadblocks, lifestyle change *obstacles* are to be expected, looked out for, and avoided. A common example of an obstacle is the family dinner when one parent (usually mom) decides to diet. If she has to avoid certain foods to lose weight, and dinner includes those food items (for example, a pasta dish made for the children), then dinner becomes an obstacle for her. Obstacles are more visible and more readily identifiable than *challenges*.

Challenges are thrown at us, and at first it appears that we have no control over them. For example, a dieter's mother gets ill, and he has to go live with her and ultimately move her back home. That throws a monkey wrench into his weight loss plans. Another example of a challenge is a personal injury, such as a knee or back injury, requiring an extended recovery period. The more committed we are to TLC, the stronger these challenges become. But they are not unique to TLC—they are part of life. Very few projects progress in a straight line. There is always give and take, readjustments, a fresh start.

During TLC, problem-solving and coping skills are learned, practiced, and mastered early in the process so that they can be applied to all obstacles and challenges, big and small. Ultimately, the process of TLC boils down to an individualized range of skill sets that, once learned, will be used over and over again in different contexts and situations.

Rough Start: Change Can Be Hard

Even when everyone agrees that it is time to begin a long-contemplated process of change, things may not get off to a smooth start. After all, this is a process that involves "rewiring" our brain, changing our mind-set, setting new priorities, and leaving behind old beliefs and emotions. Sometimes we begin with healing old wounds from various life traumas and losses. But why should someone who has gone through so much preparation and contemplation be so resistant to change? There are many answers to this question. Resistance comes in different colors and shades, but they all share common elements. I distinguish *resistance* from *inertia*, which (in my definition) refers to difficulties and complications that slow down the process of change. Resistance to change is more psychological in nature; inertia is more practical and includes real difficulties, priorities, and decisions that people often face. Before beginning a therapeutic lifestyle change program, priorities and obligations have to be reset to make room for new commitments, such as exercise and meal planning. This takes time and slows down the process (that is why I call it *inertia*) but does not have to disrupt it.

I have found that the common sources of resistance to change originate in negative thoughts, such as resentment, anger, and pessimism. But resistance is not always negative in nature. Self-aggrandizing beliefs tied to a driven personality or high moral standards, overconfidence, or a combative sense of leadership and rebellion are other sources of resistance.

Resentment and anger are powerful undercurrents that, if not detected early, can lead to an abrupt end of coaching early in the process. A resentful person typically responds with quick, canned answers or statements, often arguing to prove a point. Resentful people think they fail because once again they are handed a program not right for them. It is a waste of time and makes them upset.

Frustration, setbacks, sorrow, and other negative emotions are sometimes felt and expressed as *anger*. In my coaching experience, anger is different from resentment. Like a driver overtaken by road rage, the angry dieter gets totally out of control. Things go well at first. But at the first roadblock, years of bottled up anger erupt. The emotional charge of dieting is blown out of proportion by years of accumulated bitterness, anger, self-destructive behavior, and negativity. For these people, weight gain is a personal setback, a public admission of failure, and is very hard to accept. They would rather mind their own business and eat carelessly; instead they have to focus on their weight loss efforts.

The *pessimist* is both resentful and angry, but is unaware. The pessimist is not a victim and after years of struggle no longer has a grudge and is not interested in proving anyone wrong. A humbling track record of failure after failure has taken its toll. The pessimist does not see the weight she or he has already lost, but sees the weight yet to be lost. The weight of failure overpowers the joy of success.

In the world of obesity, the resentful, the angry, and the pessimistic all end up cycling, losing 30 pounds and gaining 40, year after year. They fail for different reasons, but they all need cognitive therapy and counseling.

Resistance does not always originate from a negative source. For example, pride can be a source of resistance. In my experience, self-aggrandizing beliefs, especially in an egocentric person, are a big source of resistance to coaching. An *egocentric* person sees the world through a personalized prism, which distorts everybody else's opinions. At the same time, the person's ego, accomplishments, wealth, and pedigree form a center of gravity that attracts and holds tight deeply rooted values and feelings. In the world of such personalities, overeating and obesity do not point to failure but are an indication of overindulgence.

Sometimes a person's value system is a source of resistance. Moral and principled people often have a well-structured worldview set around conservative values. Their worldview is well defined with boundaries between right and wrong clearly marked.

They would commit to a lifestyle change program if it somehow fit into their worldview. A spiritual realization or at least a philosophical recognition has to initiate the process of change. If meal planning fits in a spiritual context, it will work for them.

One of my patients, Jane, is a telling example of this kind of personality. She is a vegetarian with borderline diabetes. She was gaining weight and decided to see our nutritionist, who suggested that Jane eat more protein, less carbohydrate, and less high-glycemic and processed foods while getting regular exercise.

Jane began with small steps. But it was not easy because she was a strict vegetarian. She thought that gym goers were vain, generally decadent, and too "hyper." She would rather go to a yoga class or take a hike in the woods. Jane limited her possibilities by choice. To lose weight and reverse her metabolic syndrome, she would have to change her eating habits and exercise in ways that did not make sense to her.

The third category of individuals with a high level of positive resistance includes the *highly accomplished* and decorated "CEOs," "bosses," and other successful professionals, such as lawyers, doctors, and professors. They are leaders, not used to being coached. These "type A" people need a rational approach armed with emotional and healing skills. Once they see results, they will continue full force and stick with the program.

Getting Ready for Change

What if you are not ready for change? What if your life does not offer you enough stability to begin a TLC program now? Should you give up altogether and eat carelessly or fall pray to depression and panic attacks? No. Even in the least favorable situations, there is always a ray of hope. Just the fact that you have reached this point, where you are considering change, puts you ahead of someone who may still be in denial or battling personal demons. What can you do?

The approach here should be that of a mindful watching and waiting for the right time. Do not be hard on yourself, and do not try to take revenge with overeating. When it comes to healthy change, it is never about yes or no, black or white. It is about degrees and steps of change. Here are some baby steps that may help in a big way:

- *Befriend your weaknesses.* Get to know your rebellious side or your feared demons. Recognize your cravings and talk to them (as if they were people!); make deals with them, even contracts with them. Sometimes you can talk them away; other times you may settle for less. Mindfulness is a subtle but important step.
- *Focus on one small change at a time.* If you have a habit of eating two glazed doughnuts on your way to work, do not stop altogether. Eat one till you have an alternative. If you go straight to the refrigerator when you get home, eat a healthy snack (like a protein bar or some nuts) at work or in the car before you arrive home. Once you get home, try not to go straight to the kitchen; instead go for a walk.
- *Plan change for the near future.* Visualize yourself committed to a TLC program, and envision the success in your waistline and in how you will feel. If you have been lean and fit in the past, imagine regaining control of your body. Do not get stressed over future challenges or past mistakes. Instead, see yourself as reaching your goals, and you *will* get there.
- *Do not postpone medical care.* If you already have diabetes and perhaps heart disease, set incremental goals in a medical

context. Say to yourself that you want at least your HbA1c to drop below 7 percent or your cholesterol profile to turn around in the next three months. Plan to book all your medical visits, such as that stress test and sleep study that you have put off for so long. Your doctors' counseling combined with more education will motivate you even more.

- *Exercise: just do it!* If you have not been exercising for quite a while, you may begin by walking for 15 minutes a day. Do not even try to break a sweat. Just do it and you will set yourself on the right track. If you do not like to walk or jog, begin by lifting small weights or just do stretches. If you can afford a fitness trainer, begin gentle exercises under your trainer's supervision and explain to him or her why you want to take it slow. The type of training matters less than a long-term, safe, and enjoyable exercise program.
- *Education first, then action.* You may not be ready to start a meal plan, but you can still benefit from educating yourself about food, portions, choices, and calories. Simply paying attention to labels or learning how to estimate the caloric content of foods may help you lose a few pounds.
- *Learn to relax.* People at risk of metabolic syndrome are often anxious; they move quickly, eat fast, and are restless. Being anxious, nervous, or rushed is not going to get you to your goals any faster.

These are just a few small steps that will empower you—in due time—to take charge and reset your priorities. Armed with a centered and motivated mind and a body craving for well-being, embark on the process of change for a better life.

4 Stress and Fat: How Stress Shapes You

A person who develops metabolic syndrome because of excess abdominal fat is not just overweight. That individual also suffers from a hormonal imbalance that throws off the body's metabolism, affecting mood, energy, concentration, and the stress response. Chronic stress changes body shape by causing excess fat deposits inside the abdomen. Excess abdominal fat in and by itself affects the stress hormone axis, resulting in unhealthy behavioral patterns such as stress eating and psychological disorders like depression and anxiety.

Chronic stress causes excess abdominal fat *directly* by affecting the stress hormone axis. Chronic stress causes fat buildup *indirectly* by causing stress eating. In either case, fat deposits accumulate deep in the abdomen, and the body as a whole becomes obese. This excess body fat is not just dead weight. The fat cells in the abdomen secrete hormones that cause insulin resistance and prediabetes. They also cause inflammation in blood vessels, make the blood platelets "sticky" (or hypercoagulable), and overall promote narrowing and hardening of the arteries, leading to hypertension as well as heart disease. These are all features of metabolic syndrome, as discussed in Chapter 2.

People with excess abdominal fat also tend to be anxious and nervous. Do stress and anxiety build fat first, or does excess fat rev up the stress hormone axis? Most likely, both the overactive hypothalamic-pituitary-

adrenal axis (HPA) and the anxious psyche craving comfort foods contribute to fat buildup. In metabolic syndrome, the HPA axis releases the
stress hormone cortisol in response to carbohydrate intake. This burst of
cortisol is accompanied by a quick rise in blood sugar level. Perhaps
because this "sugar fit" is followed by a drop in blood sugar, or hypoglycemia, it in turn results in a release of catecholamines—the "fight-or-
flight" hormones epinephrine and norepinephrine. These ups and downs
in blood sugar and stress hormone levels contribute to more anxiety and
nervous eating.

Overall, the hormonal, behavioral, and psychological profile of "big
apples," those with excess abdominal fat, paints a picture of stress-
induced obesity. Interestingly, "big apples," as opposed "big pears" (people who are mostly bottom heavy), have high basal metabolic burn rates.
As if the body were an oven, chronic stress has fired it up and the spirit
is boiling over.

Does Stress Cause Metabolic Syndrome?

The "fight-or-flight" response, or the "adrenaline rush," is just one part of
the stress response axis. In prolonged, or chronic, stress, cortisol becomes
the main stress hormone. All stress responses are triggered in the brain—
more specifically, in the hypothalamic-pituitary axis and in the autonomic nervous system. Activation of the autonomic nervous system
results in firing of neuronal signals at sympathetic nerve endings. These
nerve endings store a number of neurotransmitters, including the catecholamines (epinephrine and norepinephrine), which at the target
organs cause the symptoms of the "adrenaline rush," such as a rapid heart
rate, a sudden rise in blood pressure, dilation of the pupils, heightened
alertness, and increased oxygenation. This quick response to a stressor
is often a reaction to a sudden event, such as a speedy car coming at you
or the shock of hearing bad news. Catecholamines are also stored in the
adrenal glands (located on top of each kidney). When our body needs to

respond to a more prolonged stressor, such as a chess competition, an exam, or a long argument, the autonomic nervous system releases cate-cholamines from the adrenal gland directly into the blood circulation. This release of hormones not only affects organs typically regulated by catecholamines, such as the heart and blood vessels, but also impacts metabolism and energy balance—for example, releasing fatty acids from fat cells for energy use. Interestingly, at this early stage, the mind has no time to focus on eating, and appetite is indeed suppressed. As if the body is adapting to a life-threatening challenge, it is calling on all reserves, cog-nitive, hemodynamic, and metabolic. But if the battle goes on too long, the warrior body burns out. The adrenal glands and the sympathetic nerve endings get depleted of catecholamine reserves, and the body fails to respond to stressful stimuli. Some argue that depletion of the adren-als and sympathetic nervous system results in chronic fatigue and depression.

Cortisol release is tightly controlled by the pituitary stress-regulating hormone ACTH (adrenocorticotropic hormone). A slight rise in ACTH results in a major peak of cortisol 20 to 30 minutes later—not as fast as the catecholamine release. Unlike catecholamines, which exert their effect primarily through the nervous system, cortisol plays a direct role in regulating metabolism and energy expenditure. For example, in indi-viduals overproducing cortisol as a result of disease or who take med-ications similar to cortisol, fat accumulates in and around the abdomen. These individuals also become insulin resistant and develop diabetes and hypertension, as in metabolic syndrome. Therefore, cortisol excess has been considered a cause of some of the features of metabolic syndrome in predisposed individuals, but the link between chronic stress and the syndrome itself has been a relatively recent discovery.

Under the influence of the HPA axis, our body releases cortisol in a "pulsatile" manner, with frequent peaks and troughs. In addition, the rel-ative amplitude of these peaks are usually higher in the morning than in late afternoon and evening—a common hormonal swing called the *diur-nal pattern*. During a stable and normal period of life, everyone has a sim-ilar diurnal pattern of cortisol release. Our body releases more cortisol in early morning, perhaps to ready our metabolism for activity. In late afternoon, adrenal glands release less cortisol, perhaps to prepare for rest and sleep. This diurnal pattern fades in psychological disorders such as depression and in some chronic illnesses. In addition to the diurnal variation, frequency of releases and peak amplitudes are both important indices of overall health of the HPA axis.

Because cortisol levels vary from minute to minute and because people have different degrees of response to minor stresses (such as needle pain in a blood draw), investigation of the HPA axis in stress and obesity has not been easy. We know that in all types of obesity, morning blood cortisol levels are low and the diurnal pattern is lost. This is due to a higher turnover of cortisol. When tested with stimulation and suppression tests, the pituitary-adrenal axis controlling cortisol release is generally intact in obesity. But when centrally obese men and women with excess abdominal fat are studied separately from other obese individuals with excess subcutaneous fat (for example, in the thighs), a different pattern emerges. In men and women with central obesity, the amplitudes and the frequency of cortisol release are different. The response to the stimulation test is brisker, and the response to the suppression test is more blunt. Therefore, centrally obese individuals with excess visceral fat appear to have a hypersensitive HPA axis regardless of diurnal pattern and blood levels of cortisol. Using noninvasive salivary measurement of cortisol levels in ambulatory men, Per Bjorntorp, a Swedish pioneer in the field of stress axis and metabolic syndrome, has shown that men who have central obesity tend to have exaggerated responses to day-to-day stressful events when compared to nonobese men. This finding further confirms a hypersensitive HPA axis in metabolic syndrome. Finally, this investigator and others have shown that "apple-shaped," centrally obese women and men have higher and faster cortisol responses to food and in particular sugar.

Taken together, these findings indicate that early in chronic stress, the HPA axis becomes hyperactive, releasing a lot of cortisol. As chronic stress continues, the system appears to burn out. Response to stress stimuli becomes somewhat blunted, as if the axis is fatigued. At this stage, those individuals who have accumulated excess fat around the abdomen (the apple-shaped obese) appear to distinguish themselves from nonobese and "pear-shaped" obese people. Not only do the "apples" have a hyperactive HPA axis stuck in overdrive; it also appears that they metabolize ("use up") cortisol more effectively. As discussed previously, it has recently been shown that visceral fat cells have a much greater "appetite" for cortisol and its metabolites. So people with central obesity produce more cortisol in response to stress and food intake, but they also use it more rapidly. The end consequence of this hyperactive cortisol state is a numbing effect of the stress response. It almost appears that chronic anxiety and stress in these "apples" has resulted in a passive metabolic state, where the body has become used to a "stirred up" metabolism. When further stressed, "apples" resort to stress-related eating of carbohydrates to stimulate the HPA axis. Since overeating aggravates obesity, this vicious circle leads to more abdominal fat accumulation, insulin resistance, and diabetes. Therefore, some investigators now propose that metabolic syndrome is actually caused by chronic stress in predisposed individuals.

What Is Stress Eating?

There are different types of stress eating. Do you recognize yourself in any of these?

- *Afternoon nibbling and grazing.* We all have "bad times," the times when we kind of lose it. For many chronically stressed women, whether they work in an office or at home, the vulnerable time starts around 3 P.M. Could it be because the blood cortisol level starts dropping around that time? Or is it because it is 2 to 3 hours after lunch, and sugar levels are dropping? Regardless, overweight women who are apple-shaped often have more problems with cravings and hunger in late afternoon. Many people

Did a Lawsuit Reshape His Body?

David, a fifty-two-year-old CFO, was always in charge. He was at the top of his game when a class action lawsuit was brought against his company, specifically naming him as the person responsible for millions of dollars of damage. The shock of getting sued hurt him more than anything ever had. He started working out more, going to the gym every night after work. Exhausted, he would then go to his girlfriend's house for the night, where she would give him plenty of good food to eat. On his early nights, they would go out to a restaurant, where he would eat, drink, and vent. Then one day he had a heart attack. The doctors did not believe it at first. After all, he worked out every night. He was lean in the arms and the legs from exercising. But his abdominal fat percentage was over 37 percent. His cholesterol profile showed a low HDL (good) cholesterol and a high triglyceride level, and his blood was "sticky" as measured by a PAI-1 level. His blood was also inflamed, as shown by a sensitive CRP marker. His fasting blood sugar was borderline, and his blood insulin level was very high. All of this is consistent with metabolic syndrome. When David was questioned further, it became apparent that the stress of the lawsuit had made him gain body fat. Yes, he was exercising, but the excess calories and overwhelming stress had taken their toll. David ultimately lost the lawsuit but changed his ways and regained his health.

are also tired and more stressed as the day is ending and are often hungry because they did not have a real lunch. So they are set up for late-afternoon stress eating. Perhaps to get a boost, many people, in particular apple-shaped women, start nibbling on carbohydrates like chips, pretzels, and other snacks at this time. In my experience, this type of stress eating can go on for a few hours till dinner is served. The final damage can add up to 1,000 extra calories.

- *Evening binging.* As opposed to afternoon grazing, evening binging is more characteristically a male behavior. It is not exactly the same kind of eating as stress-driven mindless eating. It is more a form of relaxation. The foods consumed are real foods, not chips, sweets, or other quick fixes. Evening bingers eat large portions, second servings, and continue to eat and drink until bedtime. It is as though these men and women who work very hard all day let go of their guard and get a release by overeating late at night.
- *Emotional eating.* Emotional eating is a whole different type of eating. It is not driven by stress, nor is it used as a relaxation

Chris, the Ultimate Stress Eater

Chris was referred to me for an endocrine evaluation for Cushing's syndrome, a potentially serious condition marked by excess cortisol production. She did not know she was also going to a "fat doctor." In fact, she cried about the fact that she was referred to an obesity center. Visibly apple-shaped and overweight, she was an administrative assistant for a group of about twenty brokers. She admitted to raiding the vending machine every time someone made a comment about how "not smart" she was. On average, she ate a granola bar or a pack of M&M's every hour beginning around 11 A.M. Sometimes, she would leave the office "just to get air," in reality going to sit in her car to eat sweets. Her worst time of day was from 3 P.M. until dinner. Once she got home and ate dinner, her nerves would settle down and she would stop eating. Her trigger, she figured out during our first interview, was the comments her coworkers made about her competence. Because she dropped out of college after six months, she always blamed herself for her lack of education and felt inferior. We calculated that she probably consumed about 1,000 calories per day in just junk food alone. We discussed whether she should go back to college. She is now a part-time student at a local community college, and that has boosted her self-confidence and cut down on her stress eating.

method. Emotional eating can happen at any time, day or night. It can happen when people are happy, excited, or depressed. It is truly an emotional relationship to food—a relationship that spins out of control. It can get exacerbated because of a wedding, a birth, a departure, a separation, or a death. It is truly like taking comfort in foods that have deep roots in someone's life.

Recognize Your Stressors

There are five common categories of stressors. There are, of course, others that may be specific to your current situation. In my experience, however, common stressors fall in the following categories: (1) work related, (2) money related, (3) body related, (4) mind related, and (5) relationship related.

Eating for Company

This respectable, friendly professor named John admits to me—voluntarily—that his biggest problem is late at night when a "family friend" pays him regular nightly visits. He has called him Freddy. John is struggling with early stages of diabetes as a result of metabolic syndrome. He has a caring wife who prepares all of his meals. He watches what he eats throughout the day. But after he gets home and sees the kids to bed, he wants to relax. As if a switch is turned on, he gets the daily paper and sits and eats while reading. It is *his* time. Estimated confessed caloric consumption after everyone is in bed: minimum 500 calories. Others' *real* buddies who want to extend happy hour to a meal at the newest restaurant and then at the bar serve the same purpose. They are enablers for the person who wants to eat and relax with food.

Joan's Emotional Eating

Joan has always been a caretaker. She is the oldest of three, and she remembers taking care of her younger brother and her two sisters when her parents were out socializing. The situation was even more complicated because her two sisters were adopted, and Joan felt that her parents always favored them. Ever since high school, Joan has been bringing home "problem" boyfriends—*people in need*—guys who had drug problems or came from dysfunctional families. Later, it was men who often had financial or emotional difficulties. In each case, she gained weight during the relationship. Sometimes, she would eat when things weren't going well. Other times, she ate because she was excited or she wanted to please her new partner by taking him to a fun restaurant. In all cases, she was eating because of others. In the movies, though, she would let it all go and cry.

With every relationship, Joan gains weight. She then has to lose the weight to attract a new man. If she could get a hold of herself and befriend her inner "other," she would—just maybe—meet the right person who for once would make her happy.

1. Work-Related Stressors

Work-related stressors are often specific to the job: deadlines, pressures, hours, bosses, coworkers, and job insecurity are all examples of these stressors. The more driven an individual is, the stronger he or she feels job-related stressors. In people who are not as attached to their job, work-related stressors do not have as much power. On the other hand if the livelihood of the individual depends on the job, or even a particular project or a deadline, then the stress of "making or breaking it" is intense. Academic scientists who depend on competitive grants for their salaries and those of their technicians know how stressful a grant deadline can be. Sales staff who have to meet a certain target by a particular date know what work-related pressure is all about. And bosses can be stressors to their employees and can also be stressed by their employees' performance or complaints.

Many self-employed men and women don't expect a paycheck every two weeks. They have to plan and strategize to make money and to make it last till the next time. No matter how big a business, self-employed business owners are always under financial stress.

Work-related stress is a major concern for employers as well. Stress reduces productivity, causes illness, and, if it lasts long enough, will force the employee to quit. Every year, stress-related symptoms and illnesses cost employers billions of dollars in direct costs and even more in indirect costs such as absenteeism and loss of productivity. Recognizing this, many large and medium-sized companies have put in place on-site stress management programs. These range from yoga classes, massages, and relaxation rooms to seminars and workshops on stress reduction. Writers and speakers with expertise in stress management are frequently invited to lecture at large companies. For the most part, these speakers use performance psychology, inspirational empowerment, and relaxation techniques to help employess reduce stress and increase productivity.

But not many have focused on stress-related *eating* at work and immediately after work. How many people do you know keep candy on their desk or in drawers and closets at work? How many people do you see hanging around the vending machines in the afternoon? Stress-related eating at work has no limits. It can begin on the way to work, immediately upon arrival, or at "break time." It can be ongoing every half hour or it can be related to certain office activities, such as report time or staff meetings. It is often worse in the afternoon, when people are getting tired and the blood level of the stress hormone cortisol begins to dip. Interestingly, work-related stress is often felt as "anxiety" and not fatigue or "burnout." A quick sugar fix is just enough to finish the workday but not enough to stop the stress response, so the cravings and eating continue after work, in the car and at home.

Finally, in certain work environments, stress and stress-related eating are actually part of the day-to-day ritual. The "doughnut rounds," the "pizza lunches," the "microwave reports" are examples of eating rituals centered around stress. These rituals are very familiar to hospital staffs. Night nurses, in particular, struggle with the workload and stay awake by eating all night. In addition, their nocturnal hormonal and sleep patterns are disrupted, making it unsurprising that so many night nurses gain weight. Another environment triggering stress eating is that of an emergency response task force. When on duty, most emergency personnel grab something to eat in a rush and then they eat again to relax. At that time, whether it is happy hour or dining out or dinner at home, the portions are too large and the choices are often unhealthy and high-energy meals such as fast foods.

Night eating is also commonly—but not always—related to daytime stress. In my experience, there are two types of stress eating related to the day's workload. These both affect hardworking, ambitious, driven, and successful workers who, after a day of hard work, get home exhausted, feeling drained and "brain dead." One pattern is to start eating the minute they get home, heading straight for the refrigerator from the garage. The second pattern is to eat a big dinner. Then second and third servings are continued on the couch as they watch TV until bedtime. This is a type of binging for relaxation. It may be food, alcohol, soda, candy, popcorn, or any other food that, when consumed, will eventually calm the mind and prepare this modern day slave for sleep.

2. Money-Related Stressors

Surprisingly, money-related stressors grow both out of economic hardship or poverty and in the most affluent portfolios. Money-related stress does not know social or economic class. Poverty is simply stressful. It is extremely painful to have to choose between clothes for your kids or medications for yourself. It is hard not to know how you will manage to pay the next month's bills. It is difficult to admit to failure and file for bankruptcy. Everyone would agree that these are difficult financial situations where stress levels would be extremely high. But even in these extreme cases, some people handle stress better than others. More commonly, financial stressors are less dramatic and relatively solvable. It is the bills, the credit cards, the mortgage, the kids' school tuition, the

renovation, the business costs such as payroll and other financial constraints. Aside from poverty, money-related stress depends first on the
person's value system and expectations. People of high net worth also
have finance-related stressors. Managing money can be inherently stressful. First, it is a lot of work, and there are all kinds of legal and technical
challenges involved. Money is fun to spend but not such a delight to preserve. Because our professions and accomplishments are usually valued
in terms of the universal currency that I call the "glory exchange," money
becomes a stressor even when there is too much of it. It is the value and
the emotional charge hidden in finance that cause stress. People who
learn not be attached to money are not stressed by lack or excess of it.

3. Body-Related Stressors

Body-related stressors are wide and varied. They can be physical in
nature, such as a disease. A woman diagnosed with breast cancer has
every reason to be stressed. When a man is awaiting cardiac surgery, he
is under tremendous stress, whether he appears calm or not. Another
common category of bodily stressors includes injury, suffering, and pain.
We take for granted our healthy body until we get hurt. When we are sud-
denly handicapped, limited by pain or a disease as common as arthritis
or back spasm, we are reminded of our physical vulnerability.

We also experience stress related to our *perception* of our body. Women
going through menopause have many complex reactions. It is a natural
event that happens in all different shades and colors. Some feel little,
while others suffer from serious hot flashes, night sweats, and depression for months or even years. More bothersome are the changes in the
body's shape (fat gain in the belly), skin, and hair. These changes signal
only one thing: aging. Though not ill, the menopausal body is perceived
as "disordered" by many women because there is a negative feeling associated with the "change." The constant reminder of this transition forces
many women to take steps toward improving their health. "Menopause
represents years of change but also years of opportunity," I always say
to my patients. Women have to think about the state of their health
because their changing bodies remind them of midlife health risks. Car-

diovascular disease, breast cancer, diabetes, osteoporosis, and weight gain are all more common in postmenopausal women. Being naturally more proactive, women are more likely to get checkups and ask for medical tests. (Men, for the most part, avoid doctors and do not go through the "change," so they do not get a chance to assess their health till they actually get diseases like heart disease or prostate cancer, hence the saying, "Medical care for men is catastrophic care"). Menopause is a good example of a natural hormonal change acting as a stressor on the body and the mind *directly*, by causing insomnia, for example, and *indirectly* by transforming the body image.

Body image, with all the emotions and perceptions related to it, is a strongly felt stressor for most women struggling with weight gain. In our society, body image has become a strong motivator for weight loss for both men and women, but it has also become a huge stressor. Our body image and perception of our body parts belong deeply to our soul and our life mythology. In one woman's eyes, a 34-inch waistline may seem disgusting, while in the eyes of another, it is just perfect. An individual may be stressed by an aspect of his or her body part because it evokes a very personal and hard-to-describe feeling related to a parent, a spouse, or a lover. Commonly, people make references to an elderly parent or another relative: "My legs drive me crazy because they are starting to look like my grandma's before she died."

Our body image is also emotionally tied to our life values: a certain idealized image implies success, happiness, peace, and love. How much of that is achievable, realistic, and honest does not matter too much. Body image, even when well articulated and described in sizes and measurement, is a personal and a cultural construct, which has to be acknowledged in a neutral and nonjudgmental way. Psychologists are quite familiar with the connection between a history of sexual or physical trauma and the body image. This is particularly true for young women who, after a sexual trauma, develop a complex relationship with their bodies. For them, weight gain and a new body image ironically become a response, an answer to the problem. Obesity in this case may define a comfort zone in which they will not have to face being in a sexual relationship again. Weight loss in these cases is often accompanied by tremendous anxiety and sometimes triggers the onset of obsessive behavior. Such individuals need extensive psychiatric support if they want to lose weight and heal from their past trauma.

Individuals (women or men) who have had attractive bodies as adults, even in the remote past, remember feeling good about their bodies. As if engraved in stone, their curves, muscles, and the "fit feeling" they had remain registered in their brains. This reference point may be used as a motivator for weight loss. As long as memories of those years of "looking good and feeling fit" are not associated with any trauma or sad events, reenacting them is useful for weight loss. I tell my patients to bring the pictures out, frame them, and put them up where they are seen often. Take the trophies and the jerseys out of storage boxes and leave them around the house or even in the office. Like souvenirs of a memorable trip, these symbols of a healthy past motivate people to regain their lost confidence, strength, and fit feelings.

No one can fight age-related changes in the body. The point is not to regain that perfect young body. That is unrealistic and probably harmful. The goal here is to regain the confidence, the inner strength, and the sense of beauty and attraction of the past in a new body. A sixty-five-year-old body will never look as perfect as a twenty-five-year-old body, but the person inside can feel even greater strength, stamina, and confidence. *Body pride is ageless.*

4. Mind-Related Stressors

Compare our lives now, in the first part of the twenty-first century, with our lives just fifty years ago. Through our laptops, we have access to more information than previous generations could process in an entire lifetime. Using the Internet, we can order literally anything we want—foods, pets, houses, and even mates—without leaving our bed. In addition, we are living longer. As we get older, we get more pleasure (and more pain) from matters of the mind as opposed to physical pleasures (or challenges). At age fifty-five, we may not play as hard, but we certainly find other ways to remain a player. As life goes on, the emphasis moves from

Playground Stress and the Power of Body Image

Tammy is beautiful. She is the mother of two boys, is a successful business owner, lives in a nice town, and even has horses on her own property. But Tammy is all stressed about her weight gain. Two pregnancies and the stress of juggling work and family have resulted in a 65-pound weight gain. That is a lot for a woman who is 5 foot 4 inches and does not have a big frame. Tammy's biggest failure in her life is with her all the time and everywhere she goes: her body. Her negative body image goes to bed with her, takes a shower with her, goes to work, and even follows her shopping every now and then. But nowhere is she more stressed about how she looks than on the playground where she takes her boys after school. She sees other moms in jeans, their shirts tucked in, looking all fit and relaxed. Instead, she is wearing a loose oversized shirt on top of a loose skirt that comes down to her ankles. She is not comfortable chasing the boys in that outfit.

Tammy would do anything to lose weight—just to be able to shop in a regular store, wear jeans and tight shirts, and show off her toned arms. She would love to be *body proud* once again. But her body image is so stressful to her that she cannot commit to any weight loss program. She is afraid of doing all the work and still not being able to look the way she once looked.

physical achievements to mental strides. The eighteen-year-old football player, proud of his 50-yard dashes, will be proud of his 50-foot sailboat when he is fifty-eight. The *physique* will make room for the *psyche.* Our biological nature dictates that our body changes, grows, and, yes, gains weight slowly. But our mind is different: it can make quantum leaps. Our mind operates very differently than just a few decades ago. Small children can play computer and video games that their college graduate parents cannot. The question is: Is our brain ready for these quick and fundamental transformations? Are we exposed to more mind-related stressors now than ever before?

Mind-related stressors can be clinical in nature, such as with psychological disorders. A panic attack is a clinical entity, often well described by the patient and firmly diagnosed by the clinician. A panic attack can cause significant stress when it occurs. But even when in remission, the person afflicted with panic attacks is often under stress. (Panic attacks are rarely cured, but they can be controlled.) Other common clinical disorders that are mind-related stressors include mood and anxiety disorders, obsessive-compulsive behavior, and endogenous depression. These conditions cause stress and pain when the patient is in relapse; but they also act as stressors when the patient is in remission, because they always appear to be "just around the corner."

However, in my experience these clinical disorders are not the most common or the most potent mind stressors. I believe that the most common mind-related stressors belong to a category that, for lack of a better name, I call "the stuff of life." Bereavement, regret, empty-nest syndrome, loneliness, guilt, broken hearts, and emotional setbacks are the most common and also the strongest stressors. These stressors tend to trigger a more direct behavioral response than, say, work-related stressors. These stressors may be hard to detect, and their stress response is also personal and hard to pinpoint. For example, an individual facing a stressful deadline or a difficult work assignment is more likely to talk about it and seek a solution than one under chronic and relentless stress because of loneliness or fear of being left alone. Mind-related stressors are indeed difficult to identify.

Identifying and neutralizing mind-related stressors is a process of elimination. Mind-related stressors take their roots deep in the personality of the individual. As such, they are hard to identify and analyze. Looking for and ruling out all other stressors will eventually help identify the source of mental stress. This process often requires the help of a counselor, a friend, or even a self-help book.

5. Relationship-Related Stressors

In our center, relationship-related stressors are by far the most common of all types of stressors. Difficult relationships with significant others, parents, children, neighbors, clients, and even pets make up the bulk of stressors in most people's lives. Rivalry, guilt, control, jealousy, and conflicts are among the forces that turn a relationship into a stressor. Relationships do not even have to go bad to cause weight gain. Many men and women take care of their elderly parents by cooking for them and taking them out to dinner. While the elderly parent probably does not

The Tale of Two Obese Sisters and Their Father

Life is not a straight line, not even for two very close sisters like Cynthia (Cindy) and Margaret (Magi). Fifteen years ago, when they were teenagers, their father left the family and moved to the city. The two girls, of course, suffered. They felt abandoned. But life went on, and through their bonding and support, they did fine. Both finished college, married, and had children, but both became obese—Magi 60 pounds and Cindy 75 pounds overweight. Five years ago, Cindy lost her high-paying job as a result of downsizing. She was really stuck, because her husband had recently left her and she had to provide for the kids and pay the bills. Reluctantly, she asked her father for help. At first apprehensive, she was surprised how helpful her dad was. For the next three years, she got to rediscover her father, and they resolved most of their issues related to the separation. Coached by her dad, Cindy started her own business and made it a success. Two years ago, her father died of lung cancer. He kept the diagnosis to himself till the last few weeks of his life. In the last few weeks, Magi and Cindy both went to the city every day to see their dad (alternating with each other). After their dad's passing, Cindy, having reached closure, moved on. She is now active, happy, and losing weight. Magi, on the other hand, regrets that she never got to know her dad and resolve old hurtful feelings. After her father's death, she experienced a major depression and put on another 40 pounds. After a recent heart attack, she was diagnosed with coronary heart disease and is now in a cardiac rehab program. She says it is the *regret* of not reaching out to her dad that *"broke* her heart."

really eat that much, the whole ritual may cause the caring daughter or son to gain weight. This is an example of a relationship that over time becomes a stressor, not because the people involved fight or hurt each other, but because it results in a negative consequence for one participant or the other.

In our experience, most relationship-related stressors have to be resolved (or at least recognized and acknowledged) before a true therapeutic lifestyle change can take root. I recall an obese husband and wife who argued all the time—and everywhere. An argument over the color of the curtains in their new home, for example, would become a huge fight, eventually settled by going out to a restaurant to binge. These two ended up getting a divorce before they could lose weight. Abusive husbands and sons have to be kicked out before wives and moms can lose weight. Self-imposed and rigid "control traps" have to be dissolved for a successful outcome. Examples go on and on. People who are in a difficult relationship that is causing them to engage in stress eating have to seek counseling before they can lose weight and keep it off.

Your Body as a Stress Compass

It was a bright and sunny Sunday morning, and Jim was sitting in his sunroom. He had just showered and finally sat down with a cup of coffee in his hand to read the Sunday paper. Bam, the chest pain started. This was not unfamiliar to him. In fact, it was the same sensation that led him to call 911 just a few months back. He knew that his extensive cardiac evaluation, from stress test all the way to angiogram, showed no abnormality. His coronaries were as clean as a twenty-year-old's. Since then, he had followed the advice of his cardiologist and had seen a psychologist for counseling. He had also continued to exercise and even added yoga to his program. He was also trying meditation and massage therapy as forms of relaxation. So he could not understand why, in spite of all these doctor visits, tests, and exercise and relaxation sessions, he was still getting chest pain—especially on a picture-perfect Sunday morning, when he was all relaxed and at peace. But was he really at peace? Or was his mind still plagued by stressors that he had not identified yet? Peace of mind is very subtle and personal. Jet pilots, astronauts, race car drivers, surgeons, and others who perform precision work have to have "peace of mind." A turbulent and distracted mind cannot concentrate. But this kind of peace of mind is certainly not relaxing. In fact, it is exhausting. There is a difference between mindfulness, a peaceful mind, and passive relaxation (those of us who do yoga know how the mind can be both relaxed and focused).

Going back to Jim, he was baffled by the recurrence of his symptoms. He wanted to call 911 just to make sure that he was not having a heart attack. Then he decided to do a mental exercise. If the pain persisted, he would then call 911. After all, that is what his doctors told him to do. He put the newspaper down. Then he took a gentle deep breath in and exhaled the breath slowly, relaxing from his head down to his larynx, rib cage, belly, and lower back. He took another gentle deep breath in and repeated the same slow exhalation. The third time, while exhaling, he visualized a drop of rain falling into a pond. He saw the ripples, circles gently expanding out.

As each circle would move out away from the center, it would leave no trace—just a pure and perfect circle of imagination. There comes the next breath and the next drop of rain followed by the next circle. Soon, the pain was gone. He was triumphant and happy. He could control his body's symptoms. He had not identified the cause of stress. The stressor was real but had not surfaced out of the depths of his mind yet. That was okay, at least for now. He was happy that he could befriend his stress symptom and learn to live with it rather than fight it or run away from it. He was no longer afraid. Now he was actually interested in finding what the stressor really was. That would take time and a lot of counseling. But at least now he knew that the stressor would no longer be able to paralyze him.

Active and Passive Relaxation

Relaxation includes but goes beyond pampering. Pampering—that is, pleasurable body works, like a massage, or beautification procedures, such as facial, manicure, and pedicure, are most definitely luxuries— even though for some people they may be considered a professional necessity. Relaxation also goes beyond passive rest states, such as taking a nap, watching a good movie, listening to music, or just stretching. The purpose of active relaxation is to relax the body or the mind using tech- niques that are proven to give the desired effect. Just as humans come in all shapes and colors, active relaxation, too, comes in various forms. *Noncompetitive activity*, such as jogging, hiking, canoeing, or gardening, are good examples of outdoor active relaxation. Indoors, yoga, breathing meditation sessions, arts and crafts, and other activities that engage the mind just to relax it are also considered active relaxation. While we do these sorts of activities, we are not asleep. We are not exhausted either. We just want to ease into the day, night, or weekend—or get ready for bedtime—or release tension—or prepare for Monday morning—or get psychologically ready for a competition, interview, or speech.

Active relaxation has to be planned. It requires a certain degree of structure, a plan, and an organized life. Active relaxation also requires mindfulness. If you are not in touch with your feelings, your body, and your place in life at the moment, you may need passive relaxation before you can practice mindfulness! Choosing an activity for relaxation implies that at the least you enjoy doing something. People who are depressed, distracted, and burned out usually do not enjoy much of anything.

When I interview and counsel my patients regarding stress manage- ment, I always ask them what their favorite activities are, even if they are not currently engaged in any such activities (owing to a lack of time or money, a physical handicap, or some other reason). Gardening, shop- ping, reading, and dancing are common favorite activities. But so are more strenuous activities, such as running, kayaking, hiking, and moun- tain biking. These choices give me a clue as to what my patient's pref- erences are. Some patients are surprised by this question and may not have a favorite activity (most men are quick to think sex!). Other patients have a clear and specific set of preferred activities that they enjoy and relax with. Unfortunately, many people relax with food. They bake or cook and eat it to relax. They walk to town to get ice cream or a doughnut. Food-related activities are not considered active relaxation; they are more like indulgences. Active relaxation requires some degree of commitment and engagement. In any case, the purpose of active relaxation is to relax the mind and the body. After 30 minutes of aerobic exercise, the brain secretes endorphins, which relax the mind, release tension, and reduce pain in the body. Yoga centers the mind, and with the right breathing pattern, it also relaxes the mind and releases tension in the body. Yoga instructors often say to "breathe into" the tensions in the muscles when twisting, bending, or stretching. Obviously, one does not "blow air" into the muscles that are hurting. It is a metaphor used to describe relaxation and tension release by breathing and focusing attention on the muscle or the knots in order to "melt them away."

Trainers who work with top athletes are quite familiar with active versus passive relaxation. Overtraining results in injury and "burnout." A successful training program is one that is structured and that has put in place a customized series of active and passive relaxation techniques. These relaxation sessions are scheduled around programmed sessions of hard workouts.

Without rest and recovery, the athlete will not have energy and will not be able to repair damaged muscles, ligaments, and joints. Without active relaxation, the athlete will lose focus, "burn out," get lazy, or sometimes become self-destructive. Active relaxation trains the mind to increase positive energy and performance as opposed to tensing up and getting "mean."

Active and passive relaxations are useful for everyone and not just for athletes. The same approach can be used for the driven type A *corporate athletes*, high-achieving students while preparing exams or reports, and in general for people who are committed to a goal (for more on this topic, read *Stress for Success* by James Loehr, Random House, 1997). In our case, the main goal is healthy lifestyle change. Just like the athlete who needs various stress management skills for different occasions and different phases of training, a health seeker who really wants to move forward and change his or her life also needs these stress management techniques. In addition, as described in the next section, these sessions may be used as "anchors" to put in place a schedule or program that will take on a life of its own.

Time Management, Healthy Anchors, and Rewards

Stress management implies learning skills that proactively neutralize stress before it gets out of control. Too much time is spent dealing with symptoms and consequences of stress. It is so much easier and cost-effective to set up a system that detects stress and allows it to dissipate. Like ancient alchemy, this life system turns stress, with all its destructive power, into a creative and productive energy. Like turning acid into the elixir of happiness, the "stress-proof lifestyle" reshapes both mind and body. A wise mind and strong body, a successful career and a happy personal life are the rewards of healthy change. But how does one do this? Are there algorithms, protocols, or recipes to follow? Is it magic or is it wisdom?

The real answer is that we do not know. What works for me may not work for you. A lifestyle change protocol prescribed for a given individual at a given time in his or her life won't work for everyone else. It probably won't work even for the same person at a later time in his or her life. Nonetheless, there are guidelines that apply to all lifestyle change programs.

Just as our body is constructed of many parts working together, an antistress lifestyle has to have several different components working in harmony. Once they are in place and working together, the process of change will take shape and (as if on autopilot) will work by itself. These components are *time management, planning, healthy anchors,* and *rewards*.

Time management is an essential component of any process. If days start and finish without any sense of priority or order, then there is no possibility of planning. There is no chance to be proactive if we are not in charge of the process. There is no time for strategizing. The only goals achievable are survival and damage control. On the other hand, if priorities are clearly defined, there is a sense of control and management. Time management is an essential part of lifestyle change. In particular, when it comes to eating and exercise, being in charge of the day's agenda is critical.

Admittedly, in real life there are always surprises. For example, you may hit bad traffic on your way to the gym and have to cut back your workout time. Your meal plan may not turn out exactly as you expected. But overall, as long as there is some degree of predictability and a more or less stable pattern of work, eating, sleep, exercise, and travel, then there is room for better planning and time management. Planning a healthy lifestyle change also requires healthy activities: stress reduction, exercise, relaxation, mindfulness, and hobbies and leisure activities. These have to be planned in such a way that they do not take a toll on your livelihood and personal goals. One cannot dictate early-morning healthy activity sessions to someone who has to be at work at 6 A.M. It is unrealistic and unhelpful to insist

Ten Pillars of Change

1. Change is an organic part of life.
2. Change requires commitment and perseverance.
3. Change cannot be forced; it has to take its own roots.
4. Change is not random; it needs planning and strategizing.
5. Change for the better needs order and stability.
6. Change implies identifying and setting priorities.
7. Change without reward is unnatural and forced.
8. Change has to evolve.
9. Change leads to self-realization.
10. Change is healthy; stagnation causes illness.

on a 45-minute exercise session at 4 A.M. But it is not unreasonable to do a 15-minute breathing, stretching, and yoga or meditation before heading out. Moreover, the exercise session can happen later in the day. At noon, instead of de-stressing and relaxing with a big lunch, it may be more beneficial to take a break for a walk, a gym session, a massage, or even a power nap. If going home at 3 P.M. means rushing to pick up the kids from school, taking them to afterschool athletic activities, cooking dinner, and doing house chores, it is unrealistic to plan to go to the gym on the way home. De-stressing activities, such as exercise, relaxation sessions, massage, and other body-works, are best used on a fixed schedule to transform the self-imposed structure into an organic flow. A massage booked last minute is a sign of an unorganized and stressed schedule. But if, for example, you truly enjoy a Saturday morning yoga class, you will stick to it and will want it so badly that you do not overindulge the night before. More than that, even your exercise routine Friday morning has to take into account the Saturday yoga. If you push yourself Friday morning, lifting heavy weights or running faster than usual, your body will be sore and you will not be able to do the Saturday morning yoga as well as you would like to. The yoga class also influences how the rest of your Saturday is spent. Typically, after yoga, you feel relaxed and stretched. Saturday afternoon is best spent taking it easy rather than going to work or doing more strenuous physical work. This way, 1 hour of yoga impacts two days of your life. If you stick with the yoga class on Saturday morning, it will influence two days of your weekly schedule in a way that works for *you*. It is a reward for you to look forward to. It wraps up the week and starts the weekend. It releases stress because the week is left behind and the body is rejuvenated.

With two or three more of this type of structured and rewarding activity built into your schedule, your whole week's planning will be set. When these healthy sessions become an integral part of our lives, I call them "healthy anchors" because they hold the healthy lifestyle in place. They reinforce change and bring rewards in an effortless and organic fashion. There is no need to figure out every Monday morning what the week will look like, since it is to a large degree predefined around these anchors. After a while, these healthy anchors begin to reinforce not just change but also rewards. The yoga class is no longer difficult. All that sweating is paying off: you breathe better, you are more centered, and you have a toned and flexible body to prove it. The midweek massage is paying off, too: your body does not have as many aches and pains. The massage is a good excuse to get away and relax, and as a result, you have become less tense. The Monday-Wednesday-Friday morning workout sessions have paid off also: you look great while your performance at work has improved dramatically. You are succeeding in life thanks to *healthy anchors* and a personal *reward system*. This pattern of healthy anchors and rewards will allow you to ground and sustain your newly changed lifestyle.

Mind, Body, and Environment

If the stressed body is compared to an overheated oven, could cooling off be used as a metaphor for reversing metabolic syndrome? People with metabolic syndrome often have high blood pressure, high insulin and sugar levels, high stress hormones, and a high burn rate. All indicators point to a body with an energy balance stuck in "overdrive." People with metabolic syndrome also have a predisposition to anxiety, nervousness, and irritability. How, then, does one "turn down" this revved physiology and relax the anxious mind?

Mindfulness does not always mean meditation. Exercise can be a type of mindfulness. For people with excess abdominal fat, aerobic exercise, breathing (raising the body's oxygen levels), and even sweating (cooling the body and burning calories), when performed with the mantra "easy does it," are effective ways to burn calories, lose body fat, and feel empowered and centered. After 30 minutes of a fat-burning aerobic program, endorphins are released to relax the mind. At the same time, release of growth hormone helps gear the body to burn more fat and build new muscle fibers. Meanwhile, lungs are oxygenating the blood, and toxins are blowing away and washing out in sweat. The sweat and the breathing help cool the body down. Gentle aerobic sessions go a long way for people with metabolic syndrome. On the other end of the spectrum, pear-shaped and older women often have less muscle and more subcutaneous fat. They do better with slow resistance training. Resistance training helps build muscles and raises their burn rate. From a psychological and behavioral angle, "pears" tend to be sluggish and depressed. By doing resistance training, they gain vigor and inner strength. So, exercise can indeed become part of the mind-body equation. When carefully designed and thoughtfully performed, exercise becomes the ultimate mindfulness practice: mind and body in motion for the benefit of both.

A healing environment plays an important role in reducing stress. Healing is different from diagnosis and treatment, which belong to the doctor's office. Healing is a forward-looking process that helps people put their stress, their loss, their suffering behind and opens up the doors of hope and optimism. Healing environments are not limited to health care institutions. Gardens, parks, natural landscapes, museums and cultural centers, spas, resorts, homes, and even bedrooms can become healing environments. I always encourage my stressed patients to change their home environments so that they are relaxing, healing, and rewarding.

Your home should be a sanctuary, a place for rest, reflection, love, and rejuvenation. *Your home has to be part of your therapeutic lifestyle change.* Make it uncluttered, neat with a Zen-quality charm. Music, lighting, decorations, and furniture all have to become part of your healthy change. It does not mean that you have to redecorate your house to lose fat! However, just as you would throw away all the junk foods and high-calorie items in the kitchen at the start of a diet, you would also reassess your home for change. If the exercise equipment is not being used, could it be that you have placed it in an unappealing room? If you tend to eat and watch TV in your bed, should you really keep the TV in your bedroom? If you put a bird feeder in front of your favorite window, would it help you relax and keep you centered? These are examples of healing touches that can help transform a home into a de-stressing and welcoming sanctuary.

5 Designing a Personal Exercise Program

"I'm a short, fat guy who runs every day. . . . I have run tens of thousands of miles over the past forty years, and in the time I've gained 30 pounds," said Dr. Steven Blair in a *New York Times* article that appeared April, 21, 2005. Dr. Blair, a 5-foot 5-inch stocky man weighing 195 pounds, is not just any doctor; he is the chief executive officer of the Cooper Institute, a renowned wellness and exercise center in Dallas, Texas. But Dr. Blair is not alone. We all know someone who works really hard at the gym but still looks overweight. Or perhaps you are someone who works out regularly but do not have the toned and lean body you want. As a physician, I often hear my patients talk about how hard they exercise and how little they have to show for it. They tell me that no one, including their doctors, have been able to explain why their regular exercise is not yielding results. This chapter will teach you how to design a personalized exercise program, how to change it to better fit your goals as your body changes, and how to avoid the common mistakes that people make when they begin exercising.

Since the 1970s, first the American College of Sports Medicine, then the American Heart Association, followed by many other associations and government agencies have regularly published guidelines for exercise. The latest report on exercise by the Institute of Medicine recommends that all Americans walk or jog 4 to 7 miles or 1 hour per day, seven days per week. All recent recommendations take into account the benefits of exercise for general health *and*, for the first time, weight control in a population that is steadily gaining weight. But it is clear that no one can or should engage in the same exact exercise routine on a daily basis. Aside from environmental imperatives like bad weather, increased risk of injury from repetitive routines, "burnout," and boredom, all diminish the practical value of such recommendations. In addition, as our body adjusts to our exercise routine, we get less and less for our efforts. A personalized, effective, and safe program should include variety, periodic change in types of exercise, complementary modalities, mindfulness, and stress reduction. Other issues, such as medical, psychosocial, and time management concerns have to be addressed as well.

When the experts at the Institute of Medicine published their latest exercise recommendations, they defended their cookie-cutter guideline based on the presumption that most Americans do not know what other exercises to do or perhaps do not have access to other types of activity. This consideration may be valid, but it does not go far enough. It is equivalent to saying that since most Americans do not cook every day, they should eat the same type of food every day. The correct approach has to take into account the genetic makeup, life history, medical risks, and goals of the individual.

Before you design your personalized program, you have to know the basics of exercise and the key parameters of an effective exercise program.

Guideline for a Personal Exercise Program

1. In the last fifty years, scientific research in sports medicine and exercise physiology has provided plenty of sophisticated and practical guidelines for trainers and athletes. Even though most guidelines were developed based on studies of young men, with careful consideration, they may safely be applied to nonathletic men and women of all ages, including those who are overweight and out of shape.

2. Qualified trainers must provide such guidelines and training. Even young individuals with no medical condition are better off learning the basics of an exercise program, such as resistance or endurance training, from a qualified trainer than from a friend, a book, or a video.

3. Understand that a program that worked for you when you were in your twenties may not be advisable for you in midlife. Also, a program, that worked for a friend of yours or even a family member may not give you the same results.

4. Don't lose focus of your goals. You may have long-term goals, such as fat loss or fitting into a certain dress size. You may also have short-term goals, such as increasing your cardiorespiratory capacity. And you may even have weekly and daily goals. Don't lose sight of your goals, and if you get discouraged or lose motivation, remind yourself of your goals. An individual without a fitness goal becomes a "gym rat"—that is, a person who just hangs out at the gym wasting time!

5. Be kind to your body. Don't use exercise as a means to stress your body or to "punish" yourself for acts or feelings that frustrate you, such as overeating. Use exercise as a positive tool to de-stress and to feel good about yourself. Don't push yourself beyond reason, and don't get into a competition with yourself.

6. If you have a medical condition talk to your doctor about exercise. Your doctor may not be an expert in exercise physiology, but he or she may alert you to certain risks and conditions that you should discuss with your trainer. For example, you may have forgotten that you once suffered from abdominal hernias, or you may overlook some nerve damage in your feet.

7. Finally, your body changes, and so do your goals. It is important to reassess your program periodically. If fat loss is your primary goal, then every few months you need to reconsider the frequency and intensity of your routines, the specifics of your program (for example, isotonic versus isometric, aerobic versus resistance training), and the nature of your rest intervals. Once you have reached your weight loss goals, you have to reassess your program for maintenance or toning purposes. No single program is effective forever. In fact, for an exercise program to be both

practical and effective, it has to be broken into several phases. The sequence of phases is referred to as *periodization*. Each period, or phase, usually lasts two to ten weeks and has a certain level of *intensity* of training. The frequency and intensity level vary, depending on the fitness condition, age, and goals of the trainee.

Most exercise physiologists recommend working out no more than 45 to 60 minutes per session. So to address all the targets, such as strength, flexibility, and fat loss, a 1-hour session per week is not enough. Therefore, it is often recommended to split routines into alternating days or at least three days per week. If you are not previously trained or if it has been years since you last exercised, stay with a simple program for the first few months. Later you will learn to alternate, and you will modify your program as you go. For example, one day you may do more resistance training for the upper body, the next day resistance training focused on the lower body. One day you may spend more time stretching during warm-up and cooldown, the next day more aerobic exercise. If a body part is sore, do not abuse it the next day; let it rest and focus on other body parts. If one day your stress level is high, do the routine that relaxes you. If you feel sluggish, do the routine that energizes you. If you feel frustrated, do the routine that helps you release tension. Your exercise program will become an organic part of your life; it will not be what the trainer prescribed a year or so ago. You will be in charge of your own program and thus your mind and body. However, to get to that point, you have to be patient. After all, this excess weight gain did not accumulate overnight, and it will not melt away either.

The Right Exercise Program for You

Nowadays, we categorize exercise programs according to the science of exercise physiology and the latest fitness trends. For metabolic syndrome, all major categories, including cardio, fat burning, resistance, and core strength training, are useful. All exercise sessions lasting at least 30 minutes raise the metabolic rate during the workout and for up to 6 hours afterward. Therefore, such exercise programs are all *fat burning* in that they increase caloric expenditure, causing fat loss. But some routines burn body fat more effectively than others. If your main goal is to lose fat, each of your exercise sessions should include an extended period of moderate-intensity aerobic workout.

Fat-burning aerobic sessions are defined as submaximal aerobic workouts lasting 30 minutes or longer. Submaximal means that your heart rate is maintained on average at 60 percent (55 to 70 percent) of your theoretical maximal heart rate (maximal heart rate is equal to 220 minus your age, plus or minus 10 percent). During aerobic exercise, muscle fibers use both stored glycogen and fat deposits. People with metabolic syndrome and/or diabetes have excess fat deposits in their muscles. By increasing fat oxidation, aerobic exercise mobilizes and depletes fat content of muscle cells, making them more energy efficient. Therefore, aerobic exercise must be a major component of any program designed for metabolic syndrome. Aerobic sessions do not have to be long (and boring); they can be broken up into two or even three shorter intervals mixed with resistance training. To keep heart rate above 100 beats per minute all the time, no prolonged rest period is allowed in between aerobic intervals. This kind of session, consisting of shorter intervals, is usually referred to as *interval training*. Interval training can emphasize different body parts on different days. The key is to keep your heart rate and thus your oxygen consumption in the aerobic range at all times.

In *cardio training*, heart rate is generally higher and is maintained close to 80 percent of the maximal heart rate. The duration of exercise is again at least 30 minutes without interruption. Cardio training is usually beyond the ability of most obese patients and may not be safe for them. There is also significant risk of musculoskeletal injury associated with cardio training in obese individuals. In addition, most obese people are de-conditioned and may not reach the cardio threshold without significant cardiorespiratory strain. As a result, in the beginning of a lifestyle change program, we do not recommend cardio training for people with metabolic syndrome. In fact, we do not even expect them to be able to participate in a fat-burning program for more than a few minutes. For de-conditioned people whose cardiorespiratory capacity is compromised, resistance training can be a useful alternative.

Resistance training can achieve significant calorie burning when either resistance is high or the number of repetitions is increased to reach the anaerobic threshold (muscle fatigue). Resistance training is good for people with metabolic syndrome. It reduces insulin resistance and improves glucose control. We recommend a low-resistance, high-repetition routine to be integrated into a submaximal aerobic exercise session.

Core strength training is also effective for people with metabolic syndrome. People with metabolic syndrome are centrally obese, carrying more weight in the lower front of their body and putting their lower spine at increased risk of muscle spasm and injury. For better back health, it is important to strengthen core muscles. Using exercises with the Physioball or the balance board or simply borrowing some poses from yoga, muscles deep in the abdomen and in the lower back and buttock areas are strengthened. Since people with metabolic syndrome do not usually engage in such exercises, by doing so, they actually build core muscles and enhance their basal burn rate while correcting their posture in the lower back and hips.

Metabolic syndrome is an insulin-resistant state. Based on our previous discussions of insulin resistance, we know that the time after meals is when the body's metabolism is most disturbed and harmful. Therefore, in the context of metabolic syndrome, a good time to exercise is *after* meals. Since it is difficult to exercise with a full stomach, we suggest you walk, bike, or get on an elliptical cross-trainer type of machine for 15 to 30 minutes *after* meals. Postprandial exercise should be low-intensity exercise similar to a stroll in the park or the shopping mall. Finally, exercise when performed at low to moderate intensity has a relaxing effect—a de-stressing benefit of exercise not to be forgotten. During the day, exercise at lunchtime (for example, a walk or a 30-minute gym session) is a perfectly suitable stress management technique for the rest of the workday. At night, a gentle workout after dinner may prepare the body for sleep better than a sleeping pill or a glass of wine.

In summary, exercise for metabolic syndrome has many benefits, ranging from fat loss and cardiovascular toning to diabetes control and stress management. Your exercise does not have to be limited to a rigid set of routines. There are many enjoyable and effective forms of exercise that can be combined to add variation, get better results, and avoid injury and boredom.

For safety reasons, if you have not been exercising regularly, you need to get in shape and reach your fitness goals slowly and methodically, through the four phases, or periods, I describe below. A trainer should help you assess your fitness level at the end of each phase before moving to the next.

Phase 1

Preparation: *Four to Eight Weekly or Biweekly Sessions.* The purpose of the preparation stage is to focus on the basics of body awareness, breathing exercises, and fitness education in order to build confidence and prepare your body in a gentle and natural way. Your body is not going to go through a dramatic transformation overnight. Appreciate the slow pace of change.

Phase 2

Cardiorespiratory Fitness: *Ten Weekly or Biweekly Sessions.* This phase improves lung capacity, cardiovascular tone, and the neuromuscular response to exercise. Lower body aerobic exercises using the treadmill or stationary bike are preferred in the beginning. Upper body aerobics should be done at low resistance in order not to increase systemic blood pressure and place additional strain on the heart. Use of free weights and resistance training should be limited to isotonic repetitions. Isotonic exercises do not require excessive force or straining, instead utilizing multiple repetitions to burn calories. For example, if you are doing biceps curls or bench presses using dumbbells, begin at low weights, such as 2 to 5 pounds each, and repeat 20 to 25 times. If after this number of repetitions you do not get fatigued, you know that you have to either repeat the cycle or increase the weight slightly. The goal here is not to get stronger (that will come later) but to increase your cardiorespiratory capacity. So whatever combination you choose, your heart rate and breath frequency should remain high for the entire duration of active exercise. Your trainer will tell you what level of aerobic exertion you should be at. As a rule, you do not want to exceed 60 percent of your maximum heart rate at this time. For most midlife people, this corresponds to a heart rate of 120 beats per minute. The breath work should be such that you are slightly aware of breathing when you talk and exercise. If you are able to engage in a conversation without any difficulty, you are not working hard enough. But if you cannot catch your breath, slow down. As always, discuss your concerns and medical risks with your trainer and, if necessary, with your doctor, since your case may be different.

Phase 3

Full Exercise Program: *Twelve to Sixteen Weeks of Full Workouts Three Times a Week.* This phase takes shape under the supervision of a trainer but does not require meeting with him or her every time. One session with the trainer per week may be enough. The other two sessions are done alone. Of course, if you need more specific and closer monitoring, then more frequent guided sessions may be helpful. The key difference between this phase and the previous preparatory phase is in the variety of choices, the order of exercises, and, most importantly, a transition from aerobic to resistance training. By this time, you should be able to engage in aerobic exercise routines comfortably and safely. As the body is getting in shape, it will burn fewer calories performing submaximal aerobic exercise. Several options may be adopted, and for most people we recommend only one of them. The first option is to increase the *intensity* of the session. If the cardio session included walking 30 minutes on the treadmill, we will replace it with 30 minutes of jogging. Although this is a viable option, it is not always possible for very big people and may not be safe. The second option is to increase the *duration* of the session to 45 or 60 minutes of walking on the treadmill, for example. This newly prolonged session could be split into two sessions: 30 minutes in the morning, 30 minutes in the afternoon. This option is not recommended often because it is not practical and may cause boredom. The third option, which we prefer, is to add a variety of other routines that complement aerobic exercise and further increase caloric expenditure. These complementary routines include resistance training with tubing or free weights, use of the medicine ball, Physioball training, calisthenics, core strength training, and balance exercises. They may also include yoga for strength and for stretching.

Phase 4

"The Sky's the Limit" Program: *Six Months to Forever*! This phase of the program is designed for the rest of your life! For that reason, it is flexible and somewhat complex. This phase corresponds, therefore, to the maintenance phase of a dietary program. But it differs from a maintenance program per se because it still contains goals that go beyond fat loss. For example, one goal may be to reshape or sculpt your body to gain more definition. The fat in the belly is gone, but there is still subcutaneous fat to get rid of in the arms or buttocks. Or in other cases, fat loss or even the toning may not be the goal anymore. It may be power, endurance, or external goals like being able to kayak or mountain climb.

How to Design Your Program

Intensity, duration, order, periodization, and record keeping are the basics of all exercise programs. Other parameters for a successful program include the number of sets, rest intervals, cycles, and rotations. Here I will explain these parameters and how they are used to design a program.

From a metabolic point of view, the *intensity* of an exercise is measured by maximum oxygen consumption, which in turn correlates with calories burnt per minute or per session. In practice, the intensity of an exercise is measured in *METs (metabolic equivalents)*: 1 MET is the energy expended during 1 minute of rest. A 5-MET exercise intensity means burning calories at 5 times the rest rate per minute. To convert METs to calories, we need to know the weight of the person exercising. For example, a 70-kilogram (154-pound) person exercising at a 5-MET intensity burns $1.2 \times 5 = 6$ calories per minute. Energy expenditure also depends on age, but MET charts usually do not correct for age or weight. Table 5.1 shows relative and absolute intensity of exercise based on age.

Most exercise and weight loss experts recommend spending at least 1,000 to 1,500 calories per week on physical activity. This caloric loss may be achieved by burning roughly 200 calories per session per day or burning 300 to 500 calories every other day. After a few months of exercising, you will gain a personal and intuitive impression of how much exercise is enough, taking into account the intensity and duration of each session. For safety reasons, short and very intense sessions are not usually recommended. Also, keep in mind that intensity values (METs) seen in various charts are based on values measured for lean and young men. Older and heavier people exert more effort for the same exercise intensity. Therefore, older obese men and women could work at lower intensities and still burn as many calories as shown on METs charts. Don't be too hard on yourself. As long as you engage in moderate-intensity exercise frequently, you *will* get results.

The *duration* of your exercise session is also important. If possible, each session should be between 30 and 60 minutes, no matter what combination of routines you choose to do. Up to the first 10 or 15 minutes, muscles are using up glycogen stores; after that, the fat stores get used. That is one reason aerobic exercise for fat loss or resistance training for strength has to be longer than 15 minutes.

In resistance training, intensity is often measured by comparing strong resistance resulting in a maximal repetition of one contraction to the least resistance allowing 25 repetitions or more. At the start of a weight loss program, a repetition of 25 (for example, working with small weights) resembles aerobic- or endurance-type exercise. This kind of low-resistance high-repetition exercise is quite adequate for fat loss as long as two or more sets are incorporated into the routine with no rest in between. However, at later stages, if strength and power are the new goals, resistance intensity should be such that it allows no more than 10

Table 5.1: Intensity of Exercise for Different Age Groups

Relative Intensity	Absolute Intensity* (METs)			Examples of Activities
% of Maximal Heart Rate	Young (20–39)	Middle Years (40–64)	Seniors (65–79)	for the Middle Years
Very light < 30	< 3.0	< 2.5	< 2.0	Washing dishes
Light 30–49	3.0–4.7	2.5–4.4	2.0–3.5	Stationary bike
Moderate 50–69	4.7–4.8	4.5–5.9	3.6–4.7	Brisk walk
Hard 70–89	7.2–8.2	6.0–8.4	4.8–6.7	Running 5 mph
Very hard ≥90	≥10.2	≥8.5	≥6.8	Swimming fast
Maximal 100	12.0	10.0	8.0	Cross-country skiing fast

*To calculate calories burnt, divide your weight (in pounds) by 154 and multiply the result by 1.2 × the METs value × the number of minutes. For example, if you weigh 200 lbs and walk briskly for 30 minutes, you burn (200/154) × 1.2 × 5 × 30, or approximately 240 calories.

repetitions before muscle fatigue. So if you can do 25 repetitions easily with a 5-pound dumbbell, increase the weight gradually to get a "burn," or muscle soreness, by the sixth or eighth round. This also holds true for tubing, machines, and even resistance training using the Physioball.

The *order* of exercise is based on your fitness level, the target intensity, the available equipment, and your choice of muscle groups. The less fit individuals get best results using large muscle groups in a whole-body mode or in a leg-arm or arm-leg rotating pattern. For example, performing squats with dumbbells in both hands burns more calories and may be easier for most big people than using leg presses followed by biceps curls. When performing bench presses, using a Physioball for support activates the whole body, as opposed to when presses are done on a bench and the arm muscles are isolated. Using isolated small muscle groups for toning or strength is more useful for advanced individuals who can reach exhaustion (lactate threshold) without compromising safety. The order of exercise may also be determined by the frequency and intensity of the program. If exercise is intense and performed every other day, then you can begin with upper body one day and lower body the following day. Vary the order of exercise, since beginning the session with the same order favors specific body parts and may cause early fatigue and injury.

Repetitive dynamic routines that use large muscle groups with or without resistance are called isotonic exercise. During isotonic exercises, muscles contract and elongate, but resistance is minimal to moderate. The benefits of isotonic exercise, such as steps, crunches, Physioball, or other types of whole-body exercise such as swimming or gymnastics, are mostly fat burning. Isotonic exercise also enhances muscle endurance and cardiorespiratory capacity. If the goal is to increase lean muscle mass in addition to losing body fat, the number of repetitions and the resistance level are gradually increased and isometric exercises are introduced. Isometric exercise refers to resistance training, which emphasizes strength and power as opposed to duration and endurance. Extreme isometric or static resistance refers to a muscle contraction that is unable to move the body, like pushing or pulling a very heavy weight. A less extreme intensity is when a weight can be lifted or moved once. A proper level of isometric resistance is such that a low number of repetitions (for example, 10) is achievable before onset of muscle fatigue. For fat loss, we often recommend longer aerobic sessions broken up into intervals. In between aerobic routines, we introduce resistance training using free weights, tubing, Physioball, and machines. Typically, *rest periods* between routines are reduced to 1 minute or as long as needed to reach a level of comfort (such as a level of 5 on scale of 10, 10 being exhaustion).

When designing routines, keep the above parameters in mind. Just as food variety is the key to healthy eating, it is best to avoid the same exercise routines day after day. Try new combinations and different orders, but always consider safety first and do a quick risk assessment: Am I hurting or fighting a cold today? Did I get a good night's sleep? Am I dehydrated? Did I take my medications? Most importantly, do not push yourself beyond reason. Body shaping and toning take time and patience. Keeping logs and records with comments is a useful habit that will not only help you answer puzzling questions (such as, Why does my right piriformis muscle—near the tailbone—hurt on days that I go to the gym?) but also help you reach your goals more efficiently. I routinely review my patients' activity logs to help them improve their program. An activity log also points out risks of injury and other potential setbacks. It also helps to change the program periodically to burn more calories, making a long-term weight loss program more effective.

Designing an exercise program begins with properly and completely assessing risks, reviewing body composition, and taking into account other lifestyle and body-related specifics. For example, let's design a program for John. John is a fifty-year-old businessman with metabolic syndrome. He is out of shape but has strong limb muscles. He has a history of back injury and is at risk of overeating at night. At the end of our assessment, interval training in the morning and strength yoga in the evening are recommended for his initial program. For someone else, a different program may be designed, but the process would be the same.

Therefore, for this man with metabolic syndrome who is out of shape, who suffers from back pain, and who binges out of boredom and perhaps depression, we design a program that addresses his body composition

John's Exercise Program

Medical Risks

Metabolic syndrome

Goals

Fat loss; activate muscles

**Body Shape and
Composition**

Strong limbs and excess
abdominal fat

Recommended Program

Aerobic fat-burning routines or
interval training; core strength;
isotonic repetitions

Condition

Deconditioned

Beginning Sessions

Short sessions of cardiorespiratory
toning with breath work and
frequent, short isotonic routines;
include yoga in the beginning

History of Injuries

Back pain

Precautionary Steps

Yoga to emphasize core strength
and develop back muscles,
correcting the posture; Physioball
training; frequent massages

Stress Level

Grade 2 on a scale of 5 (low)

Performance Psychology

Low level of stress and sluggish
metabolism: needs an invigorating
and disciplined program

**Time and Other
Practical Issues**

Is bored and engages in
night binging

Solutions

Encourage interval training in the
morning and yoga at nighttime

and fitness targets but also safety, his mind-set, and his lifestyle. His program will also take into account his prior history of injury and other medical risks. The final program will be revisited periodically and readjusted to reach new fitness goals.

Out of Shape? Here's a Program for You!

What is a deconditioned and overweight individual to do? In our experience, the first step in a long-term exercise program for overweight individuals is a *change of attitude*. The new approach involves reeducating the mind to think of exercise differently and rewiring the body to become mindful.

We often recommend slow routines together with breathing and a lot of stretching in the beginning. After a few weeks, nonimpact aerobic exercise is added. Finally, more traditional conditioning, cardio, and resistance exercise routines begin. So, here a program would begin with mindfulness, breathing, and relaxation exercises. Nonimpact and slow exercise routines emphasizing yoga and stretching as well as low-level aerobics would be next. Fat-burning routines using the elliptical machines, treadmill, and stationary bike are then combined with isotonic exercises with free weights, tubing, and other tools such as the "medicine balls." Finally, based on other data, such as body shape and composition as well the individual's goals, the final phase of training includes high-resistance training, calisthenics, and core strength and balance exercises.

Activity Log and Planning: A Few Examples

See pages 106 through 108 for a few sample activity logs.

AC: 27-year-old female

5'5", 140 lb, body fat 20% but formerly obese with history of eating disorder

Time of Day	M	T	W	T	F	S	S
Morning							
Noon			gym		gym		gym
Afternoon	run 4 miles			run 4 miles		run 4 miles	
Evening							

This is a very active program. The only problem is that AC is gaining weight. Her program appears somewhat limited in choices, and she may be doing too much resistance training at the gym. Since AC has an ideal body fat, if she wants to trim down (she thinks she is too stocky), she will have to replace the gym sessions with Pilates and yoga. This will stretch and relax her muscles instead of bulking them. She should also watch her diet.

DJ: 53-year-old male

5'10", 220 lb, body fat 35%, busy insurance broker

Time of Day	M	T	W	T	F	S	S
Morning	jog 3 miles		jog 3 miles		jog 3 miles		
Noon							swim
Afternoon		garden		garden		garden	
Evening							

DJ needs to lose body fat. Jogging three days a week is effective. Jogging three days a week is effective. Gardening on off days is also a good idea, as is occasional swimming. The problem with this program is that it only works for the summer months and good-weather days. If DJ wants to lose weight year-round, he needs to sign up at a local gym. He is also not helping his back problems (except when he swims). He should stretch more and try to do nonimpact aerobics (such as the elliptical cross-trainer).

DK: 44-year-old male

6'1", 240 lb, body fat 26%, business owner diagnosed with diabetes last year

Time of Day	M	T	W	T	F	S	S
Morning	power lift	power lift	machines	power lift	power lift	machines	
Noon							
Afternoon							
Evening							

DK has excess abdominal fat, the main cause of his type 2 diabetes. The program he follows keeps him "buffed up" but is not enough for him to lose body fat. His body is used to the power lifting. In fact, he cannot build any more muscle (based on his body DXA scan). He needs to incorporate aerobic exercise and cut back on his food intake. He also needs to stretch and gain some core strength. He would look and feel better if he walked two or three afternoons per week and signed up for a relaxing yoga class.

Breathing Exercises

One of the most serious complications of obesity is cardiorespiratory failure. This condition, also referred to as heart failure or respiratory failure, results from mechanical and metabolic consequences of excess weight. Imagine trying to breathe through a narrow pipe; how you would have to exert yourself to inhale and exhale, both of which are now harder and take longer. Now imagine doing the same, but with a huge weight on your chest. In addition to the unnerving sensation of breathing through a narrow pipe, now the chest movements are restricted and breaths are shallow. Even in less extreme cases, in people who are moderately obese or simply overweight, lung capacity is often compromised.

It is in the early stages of respiratory insufficiency that breathing exercises are most effective. There are other reasons for breathing exercises.

A Program for the Deconditioned

- Always remember *easy does it*!
- Do not rush to work out. Begin with centering and focus. Breathe and stretch for 5 minutes.
- Next: 10 minutes of warm up with gentle aerobic exercise.
- Now begin your session: aerobic session, resistance training, interval training, and so on, as planned.
- Keep your heart rate at a rate that allows you to have a conversation. Keep the resistance low enough so you can do 15 to 25 repetitions. Rotate the muscle groups every other day to avoid injury and burnout.
- Cool down for at least 10 minutes. Stretch, stretch, stretch.
- Use an affirmation, a smile, a new favorite song to reinforce the idea of change.
- Reward yourself with a nice bath, a steam shower, or a massage often.

They also soothe the mind and balance the body chemistry. Breathing exercises may be performed lying down, sitting down, walking, or even during slow exercises such as yoga and Pilates or lifting. Finally, one way to use breathing in all kinds of activity is to use it for timing. People who tend be anxious or jittery can use breathing to set the pace for exercise and simple activities of daily living such as walking. For the best results, try breathing exercises in the sitting position. Later on, when your body is toned and there is less excess fat, you can try doing the breathing exercises in different positions.

We tend to forget about breathing because to a large degree it is under the control of our autonomic nervous system. The first exercise is simple: it is breath mindfulness, sitting comfortably in the sitting position. As your chest and upper airways become used to these exercises, you can add more sophisticated routines and features. Finally, vary the duration of the exercise and the rhythm of breaths for different results.

Conscious abdominal breathing (CAB) in and by itself is a step in the right direction. It centers the mind and calms the nervous system while oxygenating the blood. It instantly raises body awareness. In the sitting position, without slumping, CAB begins with a relatively slow and deep inhalation. Using your abdominal muscles, inhale and slowly bring air into your lungs. Inhalation sould not be forced or rapid; it should feel natural. Your mouth should be closed, with fresh air flowing in through both nostrils. Follow the flow of air from your nostrils (which cool off a little), to the back of your throat, down your chest, into the base of both lungs, and down to your belly. As the breath is flowing in, notice how your neck tends to extend, moving the head back. This slight movement relaxes the neck muscles and releases upper back tension.

At the end of each inhalation, the diaphragm—a big muscle at the base of both lungs that is shaped like an umbrella—is completely relaxed, and its weight pushes out the abdominal wall as if air is flowing into the belly. It almost feels like reaching a summit. Enjoy that moment! Fresh air is now flushing the lungs, blood flow has increased, and the air pockets (alveoli) in the lungs are wide open. This is truly a moment of exhilaration. You may count up to 3 or repeat a saying in your head before you let go of the inhalation. Now, the exhalation is the key for relaxation and control of anxiety. Exhalation should be slow, heavy, and complete. It may feel like your chest is relaxing from the collarbone down to your lower back. Each muscle in the chest wall, shoulders, and upper back slowly collapses. Your upper body feels heavy, relaxed.

In general during CAB, exhalation takes twice as long as inhalation. Try counting again or repeating a saying in your head, beginning at the middle of exhalation, slowing even more at the very end before the next inhalation.

Sometimes the mouth is kept closed and the throat slightly locked by raising the back of the tongue in the pharynx. This narrows the windpipe just enough to create a prolonged and audible exhalation that helps to center and relax the mind even more. This type of slow, rhythmic, and conscious breathing is referred to as Ujai or "ocean" breathing in yoga. Each yoga posture is timed according to a number of Ujai breaths. Because Ujai breathing makes an audible sound (the flow of air in the back of the throat creates a flowing sound like a wave in the ocean), it also gives a clue as to how relaxed you are and whether you are straining or forcing a pose. CAB is also performed to prepare the body for activity while relaxing the muscles; in this case, inhalations are deeper and more active to energize the body. But if CAB is performed to calm the body after physical activity or to prepare the body for sleep, exhalations should be prolonged. CAB is a simple exercise that even the most out-of-shape and limited individuals can do and should do regularly before or during all physical activities.

Active expiratory breathing (AEB), "breath of fire" breathing, "bellows" breathing, and kapalabhati are variations of rapid, shallow inhalations with small but sharp and active contractions of abdominal and diaphragmatic muscles. The inhalations are often in the form of sniffing with the mouth closed ("breath of fire" or "bellows" breathing) or are simply passive inhalations. In all cases, the amplitude of the breath (referred to as the tidal volume) remains small in comparison to deep breathing, or CAB.

AEB is energizing, and if done long enough, such as 5- to 20-minute intervals, it becomes an aerobic exercise—especially useful for those who may have back, hip, or knee problems. AEB tones the abdominal muscles and strengthens the diaphragm, and even though the chest does not move, the thoracic muscles also contribute to the workout. The only word of caution here is the risk of hyperventilation. Fast, shallow breathing is not the same as hyperventilating. Hyperventilation, which causes alkalosis of the blood (too much carbon dioxide escaping too quickly from the blood and raising the blood's pH), is both dangerous and uncomfortable. It can result in nausea, dizziness, or even fainting. It can also increase the chance of muscle cramps in some people. If AEB causes any shortness of breath, it is best to slow down or catch a few normal breaths as opposed to breathing faster and deeper. In fast, shallow breathing, such as AEB or "bellows" breathing, inhalations are subtle, like sniffing. The mouth is usually closed and the sniffing is done through the nostrils after each quick abdominal contraction. Breathing should remain comfortable at all times, but the pace is increased to 60 to 120 breaths per minute for most people (normal breathing rate at rest is about 20 per minute). If breathing becomes tight, it is best to stop, take a few normal breaths, and resume. Sniffing air in is passive; exhalations are the active part of the breaths.

For some people, AEB is easier when the chest is somewhat inflated—meaning that exhalations begin after taking in half of a full breath. If after 20 or 30 sniffs the chest feels too full, the extra air may be exhaled or the pace may be slowed. This type of breathing is referred to as the "breath of fire" in yoga because it warms up the body and sharpens the mind. In our center, we also use this breathing for its aerobic benefits. For obese individuals who cannot exercise at submaximal capacity yet (because they are too heavy or have physical impairments), we use the "breath of fire" with isotonic routines (arms are raised above the head, or legs may be pumping)—a kind of *sitting* Kundalini yoga. The rhythmic contractions, when performed for more than a few minutes and in particular if combined with activation of muscles in upper body parts, result in a gentle aerobic exercise. You might even break a sweat without leaving your chair! The "breath of fire" tones the cardiorespiratory system and, by increasing circulation of blood in the lungs and training respiratory muscles for exertion, helps prepare the obese body for aerobic workouts. It also centers the mind and tends to perk up the spirit. People usually feel more alert and sharper after such a breathing session, just like they would after an aerobic exercise routine.

CAB and AEB are two breathing exercises that most people can do and benefit from. However, there is a world of breathing exercises, such as alternate nostril breathing, retention breathing, and suspension breathing, to name a few, and when practiced regularly, they produce amazing results. Still, the exercises we have focused on here—CAB and AEB—are two simple methods of achieving those goals. With a word of caution to those who may have heart or lung disease, I strongly recommend that everyone explore the power and depth of breathing.

Why Yoga?

Yoga is both a way of life and a form of exercise. In the West, and in particular in the United States, yoga has become a popular fitness choice. Among the books that delve into the philosophy and tradition of yoga, one of my favorites is *Yoga and the Quest for the True Self*, by Stephen Cope. I also recommend a different type of yoga book called *Yogi Bare*, by Philip Self, in which the author describes how the practice of yoga acted as a tool or a catalyst for change in the life of many famous yoga instructors. What I would like to discuss here is our experience at our center using yoga for fat loss, for overcoming psychological and behavioral barriers, and for relaxation and meditation, all in the context of metabolic syndrome.

Yoga is often associated with strength of core muscles. Strength of the muscles is just one of the many benefits of yoga and should not be the main goal. There are many other forms of fitness training that are more specifically designed for strength and power. At our center we use different styles of yoga for different mind-body profiles. In the context of metabolic syndrome and excess body fat, we use yoga for stress reduction, fat loss, and preparation for fitness training. We like to ease people into exercise using yoga.

Vinyasa yoga, or *flow yoga,* is ideal for strong and driven individuals. This type of yoga has a nice pace to it and keeps the body moving from pose to pose while calming the mind. Big bulky men like firefighters or construction workers are often strong in the limbs but not in core muscles. Because of power lifting or manual labor, they are top heavy and often have back problems because of a weakened core. Vinyasa yoga uses body weight against the strength of the core muscles (the upper buttock, deep abdominal, and lower spine muscles). As the body moves from pose to pose, the person heats up and begins sweating. People are often surprised by how much they can sweat from a slow flow yoga that may seem easy at first. They are also surprised the next day, discovering sore muscles they never knew they had! This gentle form of fitness works for most men and women because its power comes from the mind: relaxation, pace, form, focus, and centering are the main constituents of this program. As long as it is done gently and patiently—avoiding competition with self and others—Vinyasa yoga has a unique and valuable role in a weight loss program.

Kundalini yoga is a type of nonimpact aerobic yoga we find very useful for fat loss and lifestyle change. In this form of yoga, poses are not held, but each is a movement, repeated for short intervals of 1 to 3 minutes. Because Kundalini yoga uses repetitive isotonic routines—such as raising the arms over the head, making circles with the arms, bending and extending the spine as if riding a "camel," and twisting the spine with arms held in the air and elbows at 90 degrees—it raises the heart rate much like aerobic exercise. In addition, a lot of breath work, like the "breath of fire," discussed earlier, is built into the routines. Each set of poses is followed by a short period of rest. For people who are deconditioned, sets can be shorter and rest periods longer.

We recommend Kundalini for big people because it is a safe and easy form of aerobic exercise that they can do at home (or even in the office) no matter what shape they are in. During Kundalini yoga, the body's weight is often supported by a chair or the floor, so overweight individuals can reach a higher aerobic effort without putting too much pressure on their knees, hips, and lower back.

Benefits of Yoga for Ordinary People
(Not Athletes and Not Yogis)

- Improved breathing for better oxygenation, energy, and mindfulness
- Increased flexibility of back, hips, shoulders, and knees in particular
- Total relaxation of the mind, the nervous system, and all muscle groups
- Stimulation of nerves controlling sense of balance and position of limbs (that is, proprioception)
- Massage of internal organs and deep muscles
- Stretching and toning of muscles; complementary to other exercise routines
- Teaching the mind to center, focus, and appreciate the present moment; meditation.

Kundalini yoga is not just a form of aerobic exercise. It is an ancient form of yoga that from the beginning had a psychological bent: in ancient times, it was used to heal pain, suffering, and stress and now is used for a number of psychological and behavioral disorders, such as obsessive-compulsive behaviors, addictive and eating disorders, and depression. It is also used very effectively for stress management, to overcome fear, and to increase pain tolerance. The concept of *breaking barriers* or limits is inherent to Kundalini yoga and is a key part of each set of routines. Kundalini enhances mindfulness by always adding one more, then another, and yet another repetition. It uses many poses involving hands and fingers. Locks, positions, and movement and direction of fingers and hands require a high degree of neuronal integration. The Kundalini hand and upper body movements "rewire" the neuronal integration of body parts. The breath work, aerobic movements, and enhanced propriocep-tive stimulation together result in a complete mind-body exercise during which the mind is relaxed and the body is refreshed.

Restorative and gentle yoga emphasizes relaxation with a lot of stretching. Restorative yoga is a healing yoga that in our experience works best for people who have musculoskeletal injuries or who are burnt out and need lots of deep relaxation. Gentle yoga, which is the more commonly available form of yoga, is also very effective for relaxation, stress management, and general well-being. Restorative and gentle (Hatha) yoga does not help you lose weight in the sense that it does not incorporate strength exercises, nor is it aerobic. From a calorie expenditure point of view, this type of yoga is more like stretching or tai chi. However, as with other yoga styles, the purpose of yoga is not just toning and fat loss and should not be graded by number of calories burnt. Yoga is a wonderful life-transforming tradition that uses the body as a tool to reach a higher level of well-being, compassion, inner strength, and balance. All these characteristics of yoga are valuable for weight loss but are not related to calories per se. Self-respect, love, and anger and anxiety control are critical for healing and for the cure of behavioral disorders such as binging, stress eating, and eating out of loneliness and boredom. So, restorative and gentle yoga may not burn many calories, but it is a helpful tool for lifestyle change. For those who are exhausted, lacking stamina and inner strength, other types of yoga may seem out of reach. To them, restorative yoga represents hope—a light at the end of the tunnel—and a path to healthy living.

Add Play and Fun to Your Program

The key is to change your lifestyle while keeping your spirit up and your mind at peace. Change is the topic of this book, but change cannot be forced on a person. It has to be voluntary, desired, and embraced without too much upheaval. In the case of weight loss through lifestyle change, the process has to be realistic, organic to one's life, and joyful. Joy and pleasure are not limited to sensuous or lusty feelings. In my experience, the feeling of being "body proud" (that is, showing off your success by your new body) is rewarding and fun. But there are methodical ways to incorporate rewards, fun, play, and pleasure into a lifestyle change program. Doing so will increase the likelihood of success and the magnitude of change.

If you have ever been to a French café, perhaps you noticed that the waiter had a certain attitude. If you have ever taken a taxi in New York City, perhaps the driver had an attitude, too. And you expect your doctor to have a certain attitude as well—a bedside manner. These are all ritualistic roles. In the same way, I encourage my patients who are on a weight loss mission through lifestyle change to put on an attitude. The attitude is just that: role-playing based on a protocol. It may be called a meal plan, a diet, a twelve-step program, a spiritual transformation, or a fresh start. In all cases, for it to succeed, the individual has to have a certain perspective, a cool head, and a mission. That is where fun and play have a huge role to play.

Breathing Fear and Anxiety Away

Cecilia is a seventy-three-year-old grandmother. She is obese and suffers from most of the complications of obesity: diabetes, congestive heart failure, and respiratory failure. She also has bad kidneys and has had surgery on both knees. When I first met her, she wasn't doing well. She had just left the hospital where she had been admitted for shortness of breath. She thought she was going to choke to death and was frightened. She couldn't sleep at night. She would sit up in her bed, watching TV and
eating till her sleeping medications kicked in. Then she would wake up in the middle of the night and again eat and watch TV.

Cecilia's failure to lose weight was due to her overwhelming anxiety and fear of death from suffocation. So we had her do a weekly breathing meditation program, slowly increasing her respiratory capacity while comforting her and calming her fears. She has not lost weight yet, but she breathes and moves better and has now signed up for fitness sessions. And the TV is out of her bedroom. She sleeps well.

Without fun, healthy lifestyle change turns into boot camp. Dieters often have two negative attitudes that make change more difficult than it should be: first, they have the negative feeling of being a failure; second, they adopt an attitude of being "too hard on themselves," too critical and unforgiving. These attitudes discourage and disappoint the dieter and lead to relapse. Just like the spoonful of sugar that makes the medicine go down, adding a little fun to change makes it more likely to get traction. By not looking at this process as "torture," pessimism yields to pleasure—the pleasure of losing fat. The pounds of fat have accumulated over many years, and getting lean is not going to happen overnight. Joy and pleasure are as critical as focus, confidence, and "stick-with-it-ness" in the process of change.

But how do you make an exercise program into fun and play? The first order is to identify things not to do. Don't commit to a program that you don't want to engage in. If you hate aerobic exercise, then don't sign up for it. If you don't want to do yoga, then don't get talked into it. There are plenty of other ways to lose calories with physical activity, and they do not even have to be considered "exercise." Maybe at some point later in your life you will revisit these programs. For now, you may want to do outdoor activities, such as hiking or biking or just plain walking. You may want to plan for the recommended activities at a future time—perhaps when your friend or your spouse can take part. The important thing right now is to stay determined and to do something that works for you.

If you are not interested in competitive matches or team games or perhaps are not conditioned enough, there are ways you can make solo activities fun. Call a buddy to accompany you to the gym. If you go to the gym by yourself and feel isolated, make your session more fun by adding a reward to it. Add 15 minutes of sauna or a steam shower to the tail end of your gym session. If you like massages, get a massage after a week of disciplined workouts. If you work out at home in the evening, you may wish to take a nice aromatherapy or salt bath before going to bed. Or you may just want to relax and listen to music after exercise. Rewards are essential to change. Just remember that they cannot be food related.

In my experience, spontaneity in the exercise program is the most fun. If I wake up and I feel lazy and sluggish, I decide to do slow but powerful resistance training or perhaps yoga. If, during my warm-up and stretches at the gym, I decide that my upper body (shoulders, arms) are still sore from the previous session, I switch my workout so it includes more lower body routines. If I missed my morning yoga class, I try to go for a walk or a jog in the afternoon. If I have been traveling and breathing the airport/plane and conference hall air too much, I hike or kayak. The element of change has surprise built in it and as such is play and fun. Use the environment, the weather, and family and friends to bring variation and novelty to your program. If it is a gorgeous day, you may not want to go to the gym; instead you may want to go to the beach. If family is visiting, you may want to go for a bike ride with them or go camping for the weekend. If your spouse is down, you may decide to go out for a long walk instead of going to the gym. If you are a person in need of a structured and disciplined program, such as: MWF 6 to 7 A.M. at the gym, no ands, ifs, or buts, that's fine; then be more flexible on the off days. If you are on a mission to lose fat, you have to have physical activity somehow, somewhere, almost seven days a week. The key is what kind of activity. No one can sustain the same pace, the same routine, and the same schedule day after day for an extended period of time. If monotony and boredom do not lead to burnout, injury will. Doing the same exact routines day after day will not give great results and will most likely increase the risk of wear and tear or other injuries. An exercise program has to change based on the level of fitness and goals. It also has to vary with seasons, life events, and day-to-day changes in your spirit and in your body.

The Practice of Rewarding Yourself

Sometimes, a single event can be life transforming. But more commonly, lifestyle change requires a daily *practice*. You can take a yoga class or buy a bunch of yoga videos. But to get results, you have to integrate yoga *practice* into your daily life. Just like people practicing a religion, you must

An Ideal Exercise Program

Time of Day	M	T	W	T	F	S	S
Morning	meditation	yoga		yoga	resistance training		long jog or kayak 3 hours
Noon							
Afternoon	resistance training		jog 3–4 miles			massage	
Evening			hot bath				

commit to daily goals, the process, and all that is required for a successful lifestyle change. Goal setting is discussed elsewhere in the book. The
requirements or criteria for success are also discussed elsewhere. Here,
the process of change and its implementation are discussed in the context of commitment to exercise. Simply said, you know that in addition
to dieting and stress management, you have to exercise regularly. How
do you stay disciplined, motivated, and committed? The answer is to
have a personalized rewards system designed to reinforce regular exercise in a natural and organic fashion.

Rewards are very personal in nature. Nonetheless, in our experience,
successful reward systems appear to have similar patterns. Whether it is
riding an ATV in the forest or getting a pedicure, these rewards have to be
proportional to the effort made. As more fat is lost, the rewards can become
more meaningful and "bigger"—which does not necessarily mean more
expensive. We recommend daily, weekly, and monthly rewards. In addition, we recommend a meaningful reward to look forward to at the end of
the program or when the weight loss goals set at the beginning are reached.
Daily rewards can be as simple as putting a coin in a glass jar and seeing
them accumulate; it can be setting a dollar away to use in the future, or
knitting for 15 minutes, or even putting a checkmark on the wall calendar.
As days go by, each successful day is marked by a symbolic reward, a visual
presentation of "progress" and a powerful reinforcement of the dieter's will
and commitment to change. Visual reminders of successful days, such as
coins in a jar or checkmarks on a big calendar, are placed somewhere in
the house or at work where they are seen frequently.

Weekly rewards are a bit more significant. Here the strength is not in
numbers. These rewards have to be delicious and joyful enough to attract
the dieter like a lamp attracts moths. A session of physical pleasure
and/or relaxation is a good choice: a massage, a pedicure or manicure, a
nice long bath, or a yoga or dance class would qualify. Spending time
with your children or your partner or going out with a friend may be fun,
but keep in mind that the rewards have to be about you, reminding you
that you are on a mission entirely about you—not about your children
or your family. (So spending time with your family doesn't really count—

no matter how much you cherish it!) A self-rejuvenation session such as a delightful massage feeds your self-esteem and reminds you to be kind and generous with yourself. During my first interview, I ask every one of my patients to name a few of their favorite activities. People who have lost their self-esteem and their self-love often cannot come up with a list of favorite activities. By simply asking that question, I remind them that they have not been putting themselves first and that it is now time to reset their priorities.

Monthly rewards have one common characteristic: they are permanent. Daily rewards get their strength in numbers, weekly rewards are about pampering, and monthly rewards are here to stay. Effective monthly rewards include inspirational pictures, objects, or projects. Framing that picture of you when you were fit and placing it somewhere special; buying a special decorative object, such as a lamp for your bedroom or a piece of pottery for your office; or painting a room a nice color or working on a piece of antique furniture are examples. Of course, clothes (if your closet is not already full of clothes that you are dying to be able to wear again) are big monthly rewards. After a few months, these monthly rewards may become more ambitious, such as a trip for two to a favorite getaway destination. (Trips are not permanently displayed, so do not forget to take lots of pictures or bring back souvenirs.) Finally, even bigger rewards are reserved for the time when you reach your goals. These may include buying a new car, remodeling your house, or landscaping your garden. One interesting "big" reward is plastic surgery. It may appear at first that plastic surgery has no place in a healthy lifestyle change. After all, you are losing fat and reshaping your body through a natural process of eating healthy and exercising. However, men and women who lose a lot of body fat often have extra skin and some stubborn subcutaneous fat that may take years to completely clear. At the end of a long weight loss program, if all you see is the unwanted skin and fat, then consider taking it out. Consult more than one surgeon; initial consultations are often free of charge.

Healthy anchors and reward systems are not just useful for well-being and physical health. They help put in place a structure that is organic and suited to your life. With such a structure in place and the right attitude, your lifestyle change will be propelled forward without too much turbulence. There is no doubt that some fine-tuning and readjustments will be necessary as you go along. After all, the process of change here is a transformation in how you live your life, and that is very different from following rigid instructions. There are always surprises, setbacks, and events that will bring about new twists and turns. With the help of healthy anchors and rewards, lifestyle change does not have to be reinvented at every turn. As long as the health seeker is committed, the process of therapeutic lifestyle change will take its roots, and after shedding some body fat and gaining more energy and hope, it gets easier and easier.

6 The Healthiest Way to Eat

Let us briefly discuss two misconceptions about dieting. The first misconception is that there is a diet or a certain type of food that will *make* you lose weight. There is not a single diet or food that will *make* you lose weight, but there are plenty that will *help* you lose weight. *You can lose weight with almost any diet.* It is difficult to prove that a given diet, such as Atkins, works better than a balanced low-calorie diet or any other sound diet. Even if a diet is proven clinically to be superior for weight loss, it still has to work for *you*. As long as calories taken in are less than calories burnt, you can lose weight eating any food.

Early in any diet, restricting carbohydrates to less than 50 grams per day, depletion of glycogen stores, and elimination of protein waste products cause fluid loss. In obese people, this fluid loss can easily add up to 10 or 15 pounds. This weight loss, albeit not from fat loss, encourages dieters to continue. After a while, the fluid loss is balanced, and further weight loss is truly from fat. So, the first misconception is that a given diet or food has a magical power to shed weight for you.

The second misconception is that it is the *food* you eat that matters the most—when in fact what matters most is *you* eating that food. It is not about a diet you follow. It is about *you* dieting. The key is in your eating habits and the role food plays in your life. If eating and food have a healthy and balanced place in your life, it is unlikely that you will gain weight.

So let's focus on you. You are the person interested in losing body fat because you either have metabolic syndrome or are at risk for it. You could also be a person with insulin resistance and diabetes or other features of the syndrome, such as hypertension or heart disease. For best use of this book and in your best interest, you should consider consulting your physician and/or a dietitian, who may adjust the recommendations found in this book to your specific medical profile. If you have kidney disease, diverticulosis, gout, or other medical conditions, dieting can be harmful if you do not take the necessary precautions. My meal plan described here assumes that you are free of these risks or, if not, that you are medically monitored. Besides medical risks and possible side effects, you may also have personal limitations and/or preferences that make meal planning not feasible.

For example, you may not be able to prepare meals in an organized way at this point in your life because you do not have access to a kitchen or because you travel too often. Here, I assume that you are able to follow and implement a meal plan for an extended period of time. After all, if you want to go through a therapeutic lifestyle change, you have to prepare for it. And for this process to succeed, you need skills, stability in your life, and a vision of your future.

This chapter reviews both the basics of dietary science and popular diets of recent interest. It also lays out the rationale behind my meal plan. Finally, a number of delicious and simple recipes by the renowned chef and author Jacques Pépin are included for your use. These recipes can be easily integrated in your prescribed meal plan. Some are used in my clinic (which has a kitchen) for teaching purposes and to prepare frozen foods for my patients.

Having the right kind of prepared foods and snacks available at home and at work prevents cooking in a rush or eating foods that are not consistent with your meal plan. I always encourage my patients to be proactive, preparing foods in advance and always having backup alternatives. But as in the rest of this book, the emphasis is on designing personal strategies and solutions that work for you.

Basics of Nutrition: Calories and Macronutrients

You often hear doctors say, "A calorie is a calorie is a calorie." While this is certainly true, once ingested, calories are not equal. Fat and carbohydrate calories are efficiently stored, but proteins have to be broken down, resulting in a waste of calories by as much as 30 percent. Calories from fat, on the other hand, are so efficiently stored that only about 5 percent is wasted. So, 100 protein calories are really 70 once in your body, while 95 of 100 fat calories go straight to your fat stores!

By definition, 1 calorie is the amount of energy needed to raise the temperature of 1 gram of water by 1 degree Celsius (°C), from 14.5°C to 15.5°C. Although it is customary to use the term *calorie* as a measurement of food or dietary intake, we are really measuring the number of *kilocalories* (1 kilocalorie = 1,000 calories). So when we say that a 6-ounce serving of fat-free plain yogurt contains 80 calories, we really mean that it contains 80 kilocalories. Calories in food types are calculated based on the content of the four major macronutrients: sugar, protein, fat, and alcohol.

- Starches, sucrose (cooking sugar), and glucose (which is the breakdown product of carbohydrates and is the common sugar substrate in the body) all have approximately 4 calories per gram.
- Proteins also have 4 calories per gram.
- Fat has the highest energy density at 9 calories per gram.
- Alcohol has 7 calories per gram (or 5.6 calories per milliliter.

In practical terms and for calorie-counting purposes, all fats, from vegetable oils to butter and lard, can be grouped together. Similarly, all carbohydrates and different proteins are grouped. When grouped together and adjusted for serving size, these categories make the exchange lists used by dietitians to teach people about calories in meals or food items such as pasta, fruit, milk, and chicken. In the next chapter, food categories, alternatives, and calorie counting are discussed in more detail. Learning how to "see" food in terms of categories allows you to "eyeball" calories in food. But before we can do that, we need a primer on basic nutrition.

Carbohydrates, such as starches, are made of multiple sugar units. These units are either glucose or fructose (fructose is found in fruits). Disaccharides, like sucrose, lactose, and maltose, are made of two units of sugar. Oligosaccharides, found in legumes, have three to ten units. And polysaccharides, which include starches, have more than ten. In fact, starches contain amylose and amylopectin, which are made of thousands of units of sugar linked together. Glycogen, which is the storage form of sugar in our body, is also a polysaccharide.

As soon as we eat carbohydrates, the enzyme amylase present in saliva starts breaking down starches and complex sugars into smaller molecules. Other enzymes in the intestine further break down these sugars into single units before they are absorbed into the bloodstream. Some carbohydrates, like nondigestible fibers, cannot be broken down or absorbed. Recently, some food labels take into account the nondigestible carbohydrates and show a "net carbohydrate" content corresponding to the amount of carbohydrates digested in the body.

Once in the bloodstream, carbohydrates are in the form of glucose or fructose and are taken up by cells in the liver, muscles, and other organs for energy generation or for storage. When glucose is not immediately used as fuel, it is stored as glycogen. Sugars cannot be stored as fat. The fat deposits in fat cells originate from the dietary intake of fat, not sugar. In a fed state, hormones, mainly insulin, control blood levels of circulating glucose. After we eat a meal, our body stores carbohydrates as glycogen in the liver and muscles. At the same time, sensing high glycogen stores, our body stores the ingested fat in fat cells.

If we do not eat carbohydrates or if we fast, our blood sugar levels drop and our liver releases glucose from its glycogen stores. In very low-carbohydrate diets or in a state of starvation, glycogen stores in the liver are depleted and our hormonal system senses low reserves, stimulating fat cells to release their stored energy as free fatty acids. These fat molecules are then used as fuel instead of glucose. When this happens, the liver produces ketones or ketoacids. Almost all the cells in our body can use fat and protein to generate energy. The only cells that absolutely require glucose as fuel are the cells in our brain and central nervous system. The brain is estimated to require between 110 to 140 grams of glucose per day. So how are people who starve or are on a very low-carbohydrate diet able to think? Well, our brain has a backup system that uses ketones as fuel. In prolonged starvation, 80 percent of the brain's energy requirement is provided by ketones from the liver. Still, our brain needs about 22 to 28 grams of glucose per day to survive. In a prolonged fast, this amount of glucose is produced from the metabolism of fats and proteins.

Can we reduce dietary carbohydrates down to zero? The answer is yes—at least for a short time. If our liver is healthy, it will generate plenty of ketones to be used by our brain as fuel. The rest of our body has to use fatty acids and protein for energy. But after a few days, cutting the carbohydrates completely causes vitamin and mineral deficiency as well as dehydration. Ketones also make the blood acidic and may have negative consequences in the kidney. Elevated body ketones is called *ketosis*. Diets with very reduced carbohydrates (for example, 20 grams per day) are called ketosis diets. The Atkins diet is an example of a ketosis diet. Dieters can check their urine for the presence of ketones to see if they are following the diet correctly. There is, however, no firm evidence that reaching ketosis is necessary for weight loss. On a low-carbohydrate diet, most people lose weight without reaching ketosis, and ketosis should not be a goal for dieters. On the other hand, some individuals get used to ketosis to the point where it has little effect on their weight loss efforts.

Proteins are made of units, too. These units, called amino acids, are simple molecules that have an amino nitrogen group and a side chain attached to a central carbon. The differences in amino acid characteristics come from their side chains. Nine amino acids are considered indispensable for survival and have to be included in all diets because they cannot be produced in our body. Unlike sugar units, very little amino acid circulates free in body fluids. Amino acids are the building blocks of proteins, but they can also be metabolized to generate glucose when needed (a process called *gluconeogenesis*). When proteins are ingested, first they are cut by digestive enzymes into free amino acids, then absorbed from the intestine, and then transported in the circulation attached to carrier molecules. Some of the absorbed amino acids are used right away in the liver; the rest pass through the general circulation to reach cells in peripheral tissues.

Proteins have to be consumed in sufficient amounts to provide essential amino acids. Although most animal sources of protein, such as meat, eggs, and cheese, contain the nine essential amino acids, plant sources, such as legumes, grains, and seeds, are often deficient in one or more of these essential amino acids. About half of our body's protein is in our muscles, where there is not much protein processing. Other organs, such as bone marrow, liver, intestine, and skin, are responsible for most of the body's protein turnover and loss. A by-product of protein turnover is nitrogen, which is eliminated in urine and is sometimes measured to assess whether protein intake is adequate. When most energy stores in the body are depleted or when protein intake is less than protein turnover, muscle proteins are broken down. If this continues, some of the stores of essential amino acids become depleted, resulting in malnutrition and wasting.

Unlike carbohydrates, which can be completely cut out, protein malnutrition will ultimately disrupt critical body functions and lead to death from starvation. The lowest necessary intake of protein is about 50 grams per day, but the highest safe intake is not known. Most adults need between 0.6 and 0.8 gram of protein per kilogram (2.2 pounds) of body weight in a steady state. So an average 220-pound person would require 60 to 80 grams of protein to maintain muscle mass. But a muscular or very active body needs more. Bodybuilders, athletes, or people following a high-protein diet for weight loss typically eat 1 gram per kilogram of body weight or more. It is not unusual for a big athletic man to eat 200 grams of protein a day.

Is it healthy to eat a lot of protein? Hunters, explorers, and people living in extreme environments (such as Eskimos) eat considerable amounts of protein and remain healthy. The highest limit of safe protein intake is probably determined by the kidneys' ability to eliminate urea, the end product of protein breakdown. A protein intake of more than 250 grams per day (corresponding roughly to 40 ounces of "meat" products) may be the maximum safe level for an average man or woman. One thing is clear: people with even mild kidney failure or a history of kidney damage should not follow high-protein diets.

Fat, regardless of its source, is usually divided into three major categories: saturated, monounsaturated, and polyunsaturated fatty acids. Almost all the fats we eat are made of triacylglycerol, a glycerol molecule attached to three fatty acid chains. The rest of dietary fats are sterols and phospholipids, and they are not usually measured in food labels and diet. Fatty acids are essentially chains of hydrocarbons linked together. When the carbons are linked with double bonds, the fatty acid is said to be saturated. Saturated fats are solid at room temperature because they have high melting points. The more unsaturated a fatty acid, the lower its melting point. That is why butter, a saturated fatty acid, is solid, whereas vegetable oil, which is unsaturated, is liquid at room temperature. Saturated fats and *trans*-fatty acids are "bad" fats because they cause plaque buildup in blood vessels. *Trans*-fatty acids are unsaturated, but like saturated fats, they are solid at room temperature, and that is why they are used in cookies, chocolate, and candy.

Most dietary saturated fats come from animal meat and dairy, but they are also present in small amounts in some plants. Saturated fats are not used for energy production in our body. Like proteins, they are incorporated into the structure of cells. So when doctors advise against eating too much saturated fat, it isn't because saturated fat is a major source of fat calories, but rather because it is harmful to the body as a whole and the cardiovascular system in particular. Most calories from fat come from monounsaturated and polyunsaturated oils used for cooking. Most oils in food are used for energy, but our body needs some natural oils for other important functions. For example, linolenic acid (also called omega-3 fatty acid) and linoleic acid (also called omega-6 fatty acid) are two useful oils that cannot be produced in our body and have to be included in all diets because they are essential for health. Fatty fish is rich in omega-3 fatty acids, while vegetable oils and evening primrose are rich in omega-6 fatty acids. These essential fatty acids regulate complex processes, such as inflammation, platelet aggregation (or "stickiness"), and oxidative damage in cells. They are highly recommended in preventing complications of metabolic syndrome. If you are not eating fatty fish at least three times a week, you may take fish oil as a supplement. Other sources of these good fatty acids, such as flaxseed oil, are also available.

Once we eat a fatty meal, the pancreatic enzyme lipase breaks down all ingested fats to smaller molecules. These are then absorbed in the small intestine and are repackaged together with proteins to form large particles called chylomicrons. Most chylomicrons reaching our liver are processed there. Another lipase enzyme located at the surface of the walls of arteries handles the chylomicrons in general circulation. This enzyme releases packaged fatty acids into the bloodstream to be captured by fat cells, for storage as triglyceridess, or by muscles cells for energy. As reviewed earlier, the flow of free fatty acids is under the control of insulin. In insulin resistance and metabolic syndrome, eating too much fat results in excess deposits of fat in muscles. Muscle cells loaded with fatty acids have a sluggish metabolism and cannot use glucose efficiently. When muscle cells cannot use glucose, blood sugar levels rise, causing diabetes. That is one reason why a high-fat diet can make diabetes worse. Keeping in mind the high risk of heart disease in people with metabolic syndrome and the direct effect of fat on blood sugar level, I do not recommend a high-fat diet such as the Atkins plan.

What You Need to Know About Popular Diets

Atkins, South Beach, Sugar Busters, Protein Power, Zone. These and other popular contemporary diets share one common denominator: they are anticarbohydrate. These diets are rich in either fat or protein at the expense of carbohydrates.

Until recently, very few studies had carefully compared the success rate of popular diets. Most older studies that focused on the cardiovascular benefits of low-fat dieting (therefore higher carbohydrate intake) were conducted on individuals who were not overweight or who were only moderately overweight. Most of those studies failed to show that lowering fat intake results in any significant weight loss. However, some studies that lasted over a year showed that low-fat diets did indeed result in a modest weight loss, suggesting that overall, low-fat foods deliver fewer calories.

But low-fat diets that do not restrict carbohydrate intake often result in an unfavorable cholesterol profile—*low* HDL ("good") cholesterol, *high* triglycerides level, and *elevated* small dense LDL—associated with a greater risk of coronary heart disease. These diets also increase blood insulin levels and cause glucose intolerance, or prediabetes. Therefore, in the context of metabolic syndrome, low-fat, high-carbohydrate diets (such as vegetarian diets) are not recommended, even if they result in a modest weight loss.

Is there convincing evidence that high-fat (therefore low-carbohydrate) diets cause weight loss? Many studies have shown that a high fat intake results—at least in the short term—in an increase in the total caloric intake. High-fat foods are more palatable, often have a smaller volume-to-energy ratio, and as a result can be consumed in larger quantities. Increased fat intake—that is, more than 35 percent of total calories—may also result in a rise in the bad LDL cholesterol, increased insulin resistance, and poor diabetes control. But a high-fat diet that delivers fewer total calories by restricting carbohydrates (such as Atkins) can result in weight loss. Several well-conducted studies have recently shown that such diets are also safe and even improve the cholesterol profile in some people. In addition, high-fat, very low-carbohydrate diets cause mobilization and loss of body fluids, which early in the diet result in a rapid weight loss and encourage dieters.

In spite of all the positive news about the success rate of Atkins, most studies have not been able to demonstrate a clear advantage in high-fat, low-carbohydrate diets compared with other low-calorie diets. In a recent study conducted at the Tufts-New England Medical Center and published in the *Journal of the American Medical Association*, overweight and obese dieters were divided into four groups, each following Atkins, Ornish, Weight Watchers, or the Zone diet. After one year, the average weight loss in each group was surprisingly similar and ranged from 2.1 to 3.3 kilograms, or approximately 6 pounds. Given that no diet "won," the authors emphasized that dieters now have options and should try popular diets till they find one that "works" for them.

Taking together all the available data, it appears that neither low-fat diets delivering less than 25 percent of calories in fat nor high-fat intakes of more than 35 percent are recommended for people with metabolic syndrome. In the context of metabolic syndrome, the optimal fat intake should be about 30 percent of total calories. To reduce calories, carbohydrates have to be reduced to 40 or even 30 percent. Since fat intake is to stay relatively constant at 30 percent, the total protein intake has to increase to 30 or even 40 percent of calories. This kind of diet is referred to as a "high-protein" diet.

Is there any evidence that high-protein diets work better? There are only a few published studies showing the weight loss benefits of a high-protein, low-carbohydrate, low-fat diet. A high-protein intake may be more effective in increasing satiety and thus reducing hunger and cravings. Such a diet also provides enough amino acids to replace muscle breakdown caused by dieting. Maintaining muscle mass is important to preserve an adequate metabolic burn rate. There is no established upper limit of safety for protein intake, but it is known that eating too much protein can precipitate kidney stones and loss of minerals such as calcium, magnesium, and potassium as well as dehydration. These potential complications can be avoided by proper hydration and mineral supplementation. Recent examples of high-protein diets include the South Beach diet and our own meal plan described later in this chapter.

Contrary to the belief that calorie counting is not useful, we find that both dietary journals and calorie counting help educate dieters about food choices and portion sizes. In the long term, eating foods from a preselected list or from a commercially prepared menu is not realistic. Dieters have to be educated about portions, calorie counting, alternative choices, and ultimately healthy cooking. Finally, no matter what diet or meal plan is used, we find that regular exercise, mindfulness, and stress reduction are key parameters for weight loss and maintenance.

Diet, Blood Sugar Control, and Diabetes

Do carbohydrates cause obesity? All carbohydrates break down to glucose in the body, so the right question is: Does glucose cause obesity? The answer to this question has been elusive. Recently, investigators finally demonstrated that sugar added to processed foods causes obesity. For example, boys and girls who eat excessive amounts of sugar from candy or soda also eat more food and gain weight. It is suggested that added sugar releases more insulin, stimulates appetite, and delivers more total calories. In addition to weight gain, eating too much sugar precipitates diabetes in predisposed obese people.

For years, we have known that people with insulin resistance have an abnormal response to sugar even before the onset of diabetes. In the oral glucose tolerance test (OGTT), an individual with insulin resistance, or prediabetes, is given 75 grams of sugar, and blood sugar levels are tested every half an hour up to 2 hours. In such an individual, blood sugar spikes quickly to abnormally high levels and stays high for too long. This is called an *impaired glucose tolerance*, signifying a prediabetic state. If the OGTT results are frankly in the diabetic range, the test is diagnostic of full-blown diabetes. Is a person with impaired glucose tolerance predisposed to obesity? Or are obese individuals who eat too much sugar and starches at higher risk of diabetes? The answer is yes to both questions, the latter question being more relevant to our discussion here. Individuals with central obesity often have impaired glucose tolerance because of their underlying metabolic syndrome, and if they eat high-carbohydrate foods, they will develop diabetes. People with metabolic syndrome should avoid sugar to prevent diabetes and to lose weight.

High-glycemic-index foods refer to refined starches, sugar-rich foods that once ingested are rapidly absorbed, causing a spike in blood sugar levels. Islet cells in our pancreas sense this rapid rise in blood sugars and release large amounts of insulin. Once blood insulin level rises, glucose enters the cells and rapidly clears out of the bloodstream, resulting in a drop in blood sugar. This rapid peak followed by a dip is thought to stimulate appetite and hunger. It also causes other symptoms, such as headache, anxiety, and sometimes nausea and light-headedness. If there is insufficient insulin secretion, as in frank diabetes, blood sugars rise and remain high. Any dietary intervention that balances blood sugar levels is beneficial for diabetes control and prevention of its complications, including weight gain.

All dietary carbohydrates causing exaggerated or prolonged insulin responses are considered to have a high glycemic index. From a technical angle, glycemic index is defined as the area under the curve, when plotting blood sugar levels, as a function of time in response to consumption of specific food items. Glycemic index as a clinical concept is both intriguing and controversial. The idea that some sugars may act differently in the body and even cause weight gain more than others is very interesting. In general, foods that are slow to digest have a slower and smaller insulin response. On the other hand, refined starches, candies, and certain fruits are absorbed more quickly and have high glycemic indices. Although there is no evidence that foods with high glycemic indices promote weight gain in everyone, they are definitely harmful to people with diabetes and metabolic syndrome.

If a food rich in sugar, like a sweet fruit or a refined starch like white bread, is ingested alone, it causes a sharp rise in blood sugar level. But if the same food is consumed together with protein or fat, blood sugar does not rise as high or as fast. So the glycemic index depends to a large degree on the food mixture and how foods items are consumed. The glycemic index also tends to vary from person to person and even from day to day in the same person. All these variables have reduced the practical use of the glycemic index. But the concept is sound and well received: different carbohydrates raise the blood sugars to different degrees, and some have more impact on insulin resistance than simply based on their caloric content. Potatoes, white rice, corn flakes, jelly beans, table sugar,

Diets in a Capsule

- All diets cause short-term weight loss if total caloric intake is less than total energy expenditure or burn rate.
- Low-fat diets, such as vegetarian diets, are often high in carbohydrates and may aggravate the cholesterol profile in metabolic syndrome: they raise triglycerides and lower good (HDL) cholesterol levels. They also aggravate insulin resistance and blood sugar control.
- Low-carbohydrate diets may be high in fat or high in protein.
- High-fat diets, such as Atkins, may initially cause significant weight loss but are likely to worsen insulin resistance in individuals with metabolic syndrome, especially when strict carbohydrate restriction is lifted. Excess animal fat intake also raises bad (LDL) cholesterol levels.
- High-protein diets are safe and effective for most people (except in people with kidney failure). Lean high-protein diets improve lipid profile and insulin resistance in metabolic syndrome. Because a high intake of protein increases satiety, high-protein diets do not cause excessive hunger and thus help adherence to a weight loss program.
- High-glycemic-index foods, such as refined starches and sweets, should be avoided by individuals with metabolic syndrome because they predispose to diabetes and may also stimulate appetite.

white bread, carrots (and other root vegetables, such as beets), and sweet fruits (such as oranges, strawberries, and grapes) all have high glycemic indices. On the other hand, peas, beans, most fruits (for example, apples), and all bran cereal or other high-fiber, slow-absorbing carbohydrates have low glycemic indices. Most studies done to determine the glycemic index of foods have been performed on individuals with normal body weight and fat. People with metabolic syndrome are likely to have an even more exaggerated response to high-glycemic-index foods. In summary, it is generally accepted that foods with high glycemic indices cause impaired glucose tolerance, predispose to diabetes, raise triglyceride levels, and cause more hunger and cravings in individuals with metabolic syndrome.

Beware of Empty, Hidden, and Dense Calories

Empty calories are those that are neither necessary nor useful. These items are typically poor in nutritive value and should simply be eliminated from the diet. These include such items as muffins, scones, doughnuts, soda, and various high-calorie sweets and candies. Think about your choices.

- Would you rather have a delicious side dish with dinner or a can of soda?
- Would you rather exchange a scone for a piece of toast and save up to 1,000 calories? Most scones contain about 1,000 to 1,300 calories of carbohydrates and fat.
- Would you rather skip the chips before dinner and instead have a nice baked potato or a delicious side dish of steamed vegetables?
- How about replacing the ice cream after dinner with a sugar-free Popsicle? For every cup of chocolate ice cream, you could have a *dozen* (not that you would) chocolate-flavored sugar-free Popsicles.

Empty calories are symptomatic of a distracted mind and a poor planner. No one seriously committed to weight loss would prefer to eat junk food at 4 P.M. and then starve at dinner. Empty calories that haunt our children include junk food, candies, and soda. Even the so-called *power drinks* or nonsoda beverages are sources of empty calories because they do not add any nutritional value, do not satisfy hunger, and in fact often stimulate appetite. Committed dieters should look at empty calories as a waste of their efforts. They are just not worth it and are easy to avoid.

Hidden calories are typically found in items added to food for flavor, palatability, or presentation purposes. Most foods and drinks that contain these items are avoidable altogether. Sometimes these additional sources of calories can simply be replaced or removed without a significant change in the quality of the food but with a major reduction in total calories. High-calorie salad dressings, mayonnaise added to tuna or spread on a slice of bread, the batter covering low-fat meats, sugar added to a sauce or a stew—these are all examples of hidden calories. Food labels can be misleading when it comes to hidden calories. Fruit protein drinks, for example, post the amount of protein per drink on the front of the bottle. But the label on the back clearly says that the bottle contains two servings. When we compare the number of calories per bottle (usually we drink the whole 8- or 12-ounce bottle, not half of it), we realize that the protein in these drinks comes at a high caloric cost: 300 calories for 15 or 20 grams of protein.

A common source of hidden calories is the popcorn sold at movie theaters. When flavored with canola oil or butter, a large bucket of popcorn may contain as much fat (and therefore as many calories) as up to five hamburgers. That's about 1,500 calories! A Friday night Chinese dinner followed by a movie (with a large popcorn and a soda) could easily add up to 4,000 calories. That's almost three days of eating for a dieter!

Hidden calories are avoidable. Mayonnaise can be replaced with mustard. Salad dressings can be low calorie and low fat. Instead of a mashed potato, you can be similarly satisfied with a baked potato or a yam. Batters and other preparations that soak up oil can be eliminated. If you have to eat a doughnut, skip the glazing. If you have to drink a soda, choose a diet soda. If you crave chocolate, eat a dark piece instead of milk chocolate or (even worse) white chocolate. If you feel like a drink after dinner, have a glass of wine instead of sweetened liquor. All these steps count, and before you know it, you will be saving thousands of calories.

Dense calories refer to foods that have a lot of fat and sugar for their weight. Corn bread, Swiss cheese, cashew nuts, and trail mix are examples of foods that pack many calories into few grams. Here serving size can be deceiving. Some believe that calorie-dense foods, such as high-fat foods, actually cause weight loss because they are more effective in sending satiety signals from the gut to the brain. It is true that some of the satiety hormones released from the gut respond better to fat and protein. But during the time it takes for these signals to reach the brain—15 to 20 minutes—too many calories are consumed if the ingested food is calorie dense. Bacon and other high-fat meats are often added to a diet like Atkins exactly for their hunger suppression qualities. But someone who loves these foods can overcome satiety and gain weight. Overall, calorie-dense foods have to be consumed with great attention to portion size. Enjoy as much smoked turkey breast as you want, but watch out for that crab cake or pork sausage. When you think about portion size, remember to take into account calorie density.

Choose a Diet That Works for You

To calculate how many calories you need to consume to lose weight, you need to first know what your estimated burn rate is. At our facility in Connecticut, we measure our patients' estimated resting burn rate using a handheld device that functions like a breath analyzer and measures oxygen consumption. From the measured oxygen consumption, resting burn rate is extrapolated. If this test is not available to you, use the formula in Chapter 3 to calculate your estimated burn rate. Keep in mind that this formula was developed from studies done on lean, healthy men and women. In my experience, in obese and overweight people, this formula underestimates the actual resting burn rate by 300 to 500 calories. In any case, to lose weight at a rate of 2 pounds per week, you need to cut back your total caloric intake by 1,000 calories per day. To lose 1 pound per week, 500 calories have to be cut. If you are very active and exercise daily, you may credit your balance by about 300 calories per day. So, for example, someone with a total burn rate of 3,000 calories will have to eat 2,000 calories a day to lose 2 pounds per week. If that person decides to exercise daily, he or she can eat 2,300 calories and get the same weight loss results. Most people, in particular women with small builds, do not have high burn rates and have to settle with a 1,200- or even a 1,000-calorie diet. Therefore, most commercially available diet plans deliver about 1,200 calories a day.

Diets designed to deliver fewer than 1,000 calories are designated "very low calorie diets," or VLCDs. VLCDs require careful medical supervision, good general health, a high degree of commitment, and the use of food replacement products such as shakes and bars. The main danger with VLCDs is in causing deep deficits in micronutrients such as minerals (for example, zinc, iron, magnesium, calcium, and potassium), essential amino acids, and fatty acids. Long-term use of VLCDs is not advised because of health risks. In the long term, they are not sustainable and increase the risk of relapse and "yoyo" dieting and even eating disorders. VLCDs are quite challenging and are often used as a last resort for people who are refractory to low-calorie diets.

A 1,400-calorie diet for most women and an 1,800-calorie diet for most men is sufficient to lose weight at a healthy rate of 2 pounds per week. If possible, a 1,200-calorie diet is even better. But knowing how many calories you should eat is one thing; designing a practical meal plan is another. In the next few sections, recently popular diets will be reviewed. You will see that all diets can result in weight loss, but some are easier than others to follow. A balanced low-calorie diet often requires calorie counting and/or use of the exchange lists established by the American Dietetic Association. A balanced meal plan typically contains 50 percent carbohydrates, 30 percent fat, and 20 percent protein (50:30:20 for short). That means that 50 percent of total calories come from carbohydrates, 30 percent from fat, and 20 percent from protein. Balanced diets are easy, safe, and therefore ideal for weight maintenance. Good fats such as omega-3 and -6 fatty acids, which are sometimes rare in restricted low-fat diets, do not need to be supplemented here. Neither do vitamins, minerals, and trace elements, since the choice of food types is quite varied.

In high-fat or high-protein diets, a smaller percentage of calories comes from carbohydrates. When carbohydrates are severely restricted, such as in "low-carb" diets, the relative percentage of protein and fat are naturally increased. So a typical ratio of carbohydrate to fat to protein would now be 40:30:30. A very low carbohydrate but *high-fat* diet like the Atkins has a composition close to 30:40:30 (that is, 40 percent of calories are now from fat). As opposed to a low-calorie balanced diet, low-carbohydrate diets often have the advantage that they do not require calorie counting, exchange lists, or even a food scale.

A low-carbohydrate diet does not have to be high in fat. The rationale behind increasing the fat content of a diet is to increase satisfaction or satiety. It is true that a high-fat food is often perceived as more filling. But some people are able to eat unhealthy amounts of fat, increasing their risk of heart disease, insulin resistance, and diabetes without any weight loss. High-fat diets will forcibly increase the intake of saturated fats. Saturated fats have been shown beyond a doubt to increase the bad (LDL) cholesterol and thus the risk of heart disease. While there is a general agreement that low-carbohydrate diets improve insulin resistance and diabetes control, there are no clinically validated claims that such low-carbohydrate diets do better when they are also high in fat. In other words, a high-fat low-carbohydrate diet is not necessarily more effective than a lean low-carbohydrate diet. A low-fat, or lean, low-carbohydrate diet is also called a high-protein diet. Such high-protein diets may contain as much as 40 percent of total calories in lean meats and other sources of protein.

So let us design two 1,500-calorie diets and two 1,200-calorie diets, one balanced with a ratio of carbohydrate to fat to protein at 50:30:20 percent and the other with a high-protein composition and therefore lower carbohydrate at 40:30:30 percent (row 1 in Table 6.1). Once the number of calories from each macronutrient is determined (rows 2, 4, 6), the quantity of that food type is calculated by dividing calories into the number of calories per gram of food. This determines the total daily intake of that food type (rows 3, 5, 7). As shown in the summary (row 8), all four diets provide sufficient amounts of fat intake (30 to 80 grams per day). All diets provide plenty of carbohydrates. And all four diets may be supplemented with additional protein if needed.

TABLE 6.1: Basic Diet Design

	Total Calories: 1,500 per Day		Total Calories: 1,200 per Day	
	Composition: Balanced	*Composition: Low-Carb High-Protein*	*Composition: Balanced*	*Composition: Low-Carb High-Protein*
1	50:30:20%	40:30:30%	50:30:20%	40:30:30%
2	Carbs = 0.5 × 1,500 = 750 calories	Carbs = 0.4 × 1,500 = 600 calories	Carbs = 0.5 × 1,200 = 600 calories	Carbs = 0.4 × 1,200 = 480 calories
3	Total grams of carbs = 750/4 = 187.5 grams	Total grams of carbs = 600/4 = 150 grams	Total grams of carbs = 600/4 = 150 grams	Total grams of carbs = 480/4 = 120 grams
4	Fat = 0.3 × 1,500 = 450 calories	Fat = 0.3 × 1,500 = 450 calories	Fat = 0.3 × 1,200 = 360 calories	Fat = 0.3 × 1,200 = 360 calories
5	Total grams of fat = 450/9 = 50 grams	Total grams of fat = 450/9 = 50 grams	Total grams of fat = 360/9 = 40 grams	Total grams of fat = 360/9 = 40 grams
6	Protein = 0.2 × 1,500 = 300 calories	Protein = 0.3 × 1,500 = 450 calories	Protein = 0.2 × 1,200 = 240 calories	Protein = 0.3 × 1,200 = 360 calories
7	Total grams of protein = 300/4 = 75 grams	Total grams of protein = 450/4 = 112.5 grams	Total grams of protein = 240/4 = 60 grams	Total grams of protein = 360/4 = 75 grams
8	*Summary:*	*Summary:*	*Summary:*	*Summary:*
	187.5 grams of carbs (6.6 ounces)	150 grams of carbs (5.28 ounces)	150 grams of carbs (5.28 ounces)	120 grams of carbs (4.22 ounces)
	50 grams of fat (1.76 ounces)	50 grams of fat (1.76 ounces)	40 grams of fat (1.40 ounces)	40 grams of fat (1.40 ounces)
	75 grams of protein (2.64 ounces)	112.5 grams of protein (3.96 ounces)	60 grams of protein (2.11 ounces)	75 grams of protein (2.64 ounces)

Once the amounts of macronutrients are determined, by arranging macronutrient groups into food groups and serving sizes, you will design a meal plan. Note that the total number of grams or ounces of each macronutrient in row 8 corresponds to the weight of each macronutrient, not the weight of a specific food type. For example, each ounce of red meat or its equivalent contains 7.5 grams of pure protein, so to get 75 grams of protein per day, you have to consume 10 ounces of meat.

If you choose to eat six meals and snacks per day, you will then decide how to distribute the foods throughout the day. Here food choices are critical. Do not waste your caloric allowance with inappropriate foods. If you choose to have a bag of M&M's or a Mars bar for a midafternoon snack, you will consume calories equivalent to a lean meal in a couple of minutes but will be hungry an hour later. Advance planning can provide nutritious and satisfying meals while avoiding hunger. There is plenty of flexibility in the diets described here. Later in this chapter, an example of a low-carbohydrate high-protein meal plan will be described together with recipes and cooking instructions. For now, as a quick exercise, let us just take the 1,500-calorie 40:30:30 diet and make a schematic meal plan:

- *Breakfast:* Three egg white omelet with smoked ham and herbs, black coffee or tea. Total: 150 calories, approximately 20 grams of protein, and 5 grams of fat.
- *Midmorning snack:* One protein bar containing 15 grams of protein, 10 grams of carbohydrates, and 5 grams of fat, for 140 calories, and a fruit such as a small (4-ounce) apple containing 17 grams of carbohydrates, or 70 calories. Total: approximately 210 calories; 27 grams of carbohydrates, 15 grams of protein, and 5 grams of fat.
- *Lunch:* A nice, large garden salad with tuna (3-ounce can of tuna in water) with 5 olives and a low-cal dressing and a slice of bread. Total: approximately 285 calories; 35 grams of carbohydrates, 25 grams of protein, and 5 grams of fat.
- *Midafternoon snack:* A low-fat yogurt (no fruit or sugar added but it can be flavored) and a dozen roasted almonds. Total:

approximately 180 calories; 20 grams of carbohydrates, 8 grams of protein, and 7 grams of fat.

- *Dinner:* Three or four slices of roast beef, one sweet potato, and a small salad. Total: approximately 450 calories; 25 grams of carbohydrates, 35 grams of protein, and 20 grams of fat.

And don't forget to drink eight to ten glasses of calorie-free noncaffeinated fluids.

The total approximate calories and composition is as follows: 1,275 calories, 107 grams of carbohydrates, 103 grams of protein, and 42 grams of fat.

Add a little wine or an additional vegetable serving or a fruit or piece of cheese after dinner, and the grand total will be close to 1,500 calories with a 40 percent carbohydrate, 30 percent protein, and 30 percent fat distribution of macronutrients. This simple example demonstrates that 1,500 calories provides a range of satisfying choices and is by no means difficult to implement. Next, I will review the rationale behind our clinically tested meal plan.

A Choice Eating Program for Metabolic Syndrome

The rationale behind our meal plan is based on the recent understanding of the hormones that control eating and the mechanisms that regulate our metabolism. Eating patterns, food choices, stress, and exercise all influences the signals that regulate our body fat reserves. We are now beginning to understand how fat cells, the digestive system, and appetite centers in the brain integrate these signals using hormones. The discovery of a gut–brain axis regulating appetite and satiety has shed a new and fascinating light on the physiology of cravings, feeding, and energy storage.

Because these recent discoveries support the design of our meal plan and our entire approach to fat loss, I will review them here.

A key signal that acts on the hypothalamic neurons regulating food intake and energy expenditure is the hormone PYY, sometimes referred to as peptide YY. PYY was discovered in 1980 but has recently generated a lot of news. This hormone is released by the small intestine and acts as a satiety signal. Approximately 15 minutes after eating, the blood PYY level rises, then reaches a plateau in 90 minutes and remains high for several hours. The rise of PYY is proportional to the size of the ingested meal and the amount of fat and protein in it (not carbohydrates). In a recent and carefully conducted study published in the *New England Journal of Medicine*, investigators were able to show a 30 percent drop in caloric intake for 24 hours after an infusion of PYY in obese subjects. They also showed for the first time that obese individuals generally have lower than normal blood levels of PYY, raising the possibility of PYY replacement as a weight loss drug. Indeed, at least one pharmaceutical company is already testing PYY as a weight loss medication. Finally, it was shown that after administration of PYY, levels of another gut hormone, ghrelin, which acts in the opposite way, gradually rises.

Ghrelin, which was first discovered in 1999, also "talks" to the hypothalamic neurons, but (opposite to PYY) it induces hunger and prompts an increase in portion sizes. (Interestingly, the early studies on ghrelin were focused on this hormone's ability to stimulate growth hormone release; in fact, the name *ghrelin* was extracted from growth *hormone-re*leasing hormone. Also, *ghre* means "grow" in early Sanskrit language.) Recently, ghrelin was recognized as the first known "appetite" hormone secreted from the stomach. Ghrelin interacts on many levels with other key players that regulate our body's metabolism, such as insulin, blood glucose, growth hormone, cortisol, and leptin, as well as hypothalamic neurons, all to ensure that sufficient amounts of energy are available and stored in fat cells. Ghrelin levels rise when we fast, peak immediately before meals, and are typically higher during weight loss and in anorexia—as if the stomach is telling the brain to eat more. Before a meal, blood ghrelin levels can double, depending on the timing and size of the *previous* meal.

Skipping lunch would therefore trigger more appetite for a bigger dinner. After a meal, ghrelin levels drop for several hours. Ghrelin shifts the body's metabolism to an energy-sparing mode by slowing fat breakdown or oxidation and by increasing use of stored glycogen. It also reduces the body's core temperature and thus energy expenditure. Injection of ghrelin in laboratory animals causes increased food intake and a clear accumulation of body fat. These animals also show increased anxiety, suggesting that ghrelin-induced hunger also causes anxiety. Finally, in patients who undergo gastric bypass surgery, ghrelin levels are low (because the part of the stomach that secretes ghrelin is bypassed), explaining why these patients are not as hungry as dieters.

Our understanding of hormones like PYY and ghrelin that influence food intake helps us design a better dietary program for weight loss. For example, since it takes at least 15 minutes for the gut to release the satiety hormone PYY, if food is ingested too fast, we tend to consume a lot more calories before feeling full. Eating fast has indeed been shown to result in weight gain and insulin resistance. The composition and number of meals and/or snacks also influence the release of these hormones. More frequent meals containing higher amounts of protein and fat may reduce ghrelin-induced appetite while stimulating PYY to maintain satiety. Larger high-carbohydrate meals consumed far apart would increase hunger and cravings and tempt us to eat larger portions. This hypothesis seems consistent with the clinical experience of many obesity experts. In my experience, people who eat a high-protein meal or snack every 3 hours are rarely hungry and yet consume fewer calories in a 24-hour period. On the other hand, those who skip meals such as breakfast and/or lunch are always hungry, feel sluggish all day, and eat a lot of food through the night. We are beginning to understand the hormonal changes caused by various eating patterns and types of food. We have used this knowledge to design a clinically validated diet.

Another hormone released by fat cells called leptin directly influences our metabolism. Fat cells stop releasing leptin when energy storage is diminishing. Low blood leptin levels therefore imply low energy stores. Hypothalamic neurons sense low leptin levels, slow down energy expenditure (the burn rate) through a not yet fully understood process, and increase the appetite. When leptin levels drop, the brain gets an "eat, eat" signal, and when leptin is high, the brain senses a "fed" mode. Leptin therefore acts as an energy gauge, or a "fat-stat." Because women have higher body fat percentages than men, they have higher leptin levels. But in a recent study of nonobese young men and women, it was shown that the *more* abdominal fat one has (as in "apple-shaped" bodies with higher waist-to-hip ratios), the *lower* leptin levels are, resulting in *more* hunger. Could it be that apple-shaped women and men are more likely to feel hungry all the time? This study also showed that leptin levels rise as much as threefold during chronic overeating, but when overfeeding is mainly from carbohydrates, leptin does not rise as much—meaning once again that carbohydrates do not trigger a sense of fullness, even when we overeat. This, together with the finding that the satiety hormone PYY also does not respond to carbohydrate ingestion, can explain why high-carbohydrate meals and snacks are not as filling. In addition, carbohydrate-rich foods cause an exaggerated release of insulin, which also stimulates the appetite centers. Overall, a diet rich in protein and fat suppresses the appetite without turning down the metabolic rate. Such a diet is able to deliver low calories without triggering hunger or a slowdown in burn rate.

Food volume and fiber intake are also important factors that may control hormonal signals from the stomach. High-fiber carbohydrates like raw vegetables deliver fewer calories per portion size than low-fiber carbohydrate-dense foods such as starches in processed foods. The former contain significant amounts of indigestible fiber, causing a sense of fullness while delivering fewer calories, and because they are digested slowly, blood sugars do not rise as fast. This kind of food is preferred for people with impaired glucose tolerance, metabolic syndrome, or diabetes. High-volume foods that are rich in carbohydrates but poor in fiber, such as some fruits or starches, often cause a rapid rise in blood sugar and may stimulate appetite when sugar levels drop after they peak. Therefore, no matter what the composition of diet is, food combinations, portion sizes, and the speed at which an individual eats and digests food all have to be taken into account. In the remainder of this chapter, I will detail my dietary recommendations for metabolic syndrome that make up my meal plan.

Choose Your Foods Wisely

- Buy fresh and seasonal foods rich in antioxidants, vitamins, and trace elements. The more colorful your fruits and vegetables, the more they contain healthy flavinoids, lycopenes, and other antioxidants.
- Use herbs in your diet. They have no calories and contain minerals and other trace elements. They are good for you.
- Choose lean meats—preferably organic and free-range—as opposed to fatty meats.
- Reduce your consumption of high-fat premixed foods such as ground beef, pâté, and sausages.
- When possible, choose real cheese from a farm rather than processed cheese made in a factory.
- Cold-water fish such as salmon, herring, haddock, and white tuna are rich in good fats such as omega-3 fatty acids.
- Try different spices, condiments, and vegetarian spreads. They are usually low calorie and add excitement to simple dishes such as meats.
- Don't buy junk food or soda. Avoid artificially flavored and colored products.
- If you really have to have a sweet dessert, choose a thin slice of freshly baked fruit pie or tart.
- Buy and eat real and seasonal fruits, as opposed to canned fruit, fruit juice, or fruit-flavored products such as yogurt and drinks.
- Buy almonds, walnuts, and peanuts (not cashews) in their shells. Cracking the shells takes time and you will not overeat them as easily. Nuts are healthy snacks, but they are calorie dense. If you cannot stop eating them, preportion them in small bags or buy them preportioned and eat only one bag—put the rest away.
- Buy and learn to incorporate into your meals low-calorie products that are healthy and add flavor, such as herbs, shiitake mushrooms, garlic, soybeans, tofu, hummus, ethnic vegetables, legumes, and sprouts.

- Use only sparingly vegetable oils such as safflower, sunflower, or canola oil. These are rich in polyunsaturated fatty acids that may trigger inflammation and coagulation in the arteries. Olive oil is better because it has more monounsaturated fatty acids, which are healthful.
- Drink one glass of red wine daily if you're a woman, two glasses daily if you're a man, for the added protection that red wine offers against heart disease and diabetes. If you do not drink alcohol, you can buy grape-seed extract supplements.

Healthy and Efficient Cooking

- Plan and execute mindfully with a cool and committed head. Emergency cooking is often more oily, has energy-rich items like pasta, sausage, egg yolks, and potatoes, and does not necessarily taste good. Don't cook while you're very hungry.
- When cooking, play music or turn the TV to a calming channel. Your food will taste better and you are more likely to cook often if you enjoy it.
- Learn to cook simply. It is better to eat grilled meats, broiled fish, and roasted chicken with a side dish of vegetables than a pot roast or a complex saucy dish or a soufflé. The latter are often time-consuming to prepare and are very calorie rich.
- Learn about the fat content of different cuts of red meat, pork, chicken, and fish.
- Choose grilling, roasting, and broiling over sautéing and deep-frying. The latter two methods retain most of fat in the meat and absorb the oils used for cooking. The former methods help remove the fat and do not need much oil for cooking.
- People who live alone often say, "It's hard to cook for one person." So don't: cook, then pack and save the extra food (or give it to friends or family).
- You may take an afternoon and relax while you bake a turkey or roast two chickens. Cut them into serving-size portions. Set aside enough for two or three meals in the refrigerator. Freeze

the rest. You could always microwave a frozen piece (at work, for example) and add it to a salad or combine it with another dish. Be proactive and strategize.

- Use nonstick pans—for omelets, for example—to cut the use of cooking oil or butter.

- Avoid recipes that require batter with bread crumbs or flour. They soak up and retain oils, and the combination of starch and fat becomes very energy dense. These are examples of hidden calories, discussed earlier. Season and add flavor to the dish with herbs and spices.

- Organize your cooking so you can save some for the next day. Keep the leftovers for future use (your freezer will soon have no room for ice cream!). Save the side dishes (steamed vegetables and relishes, for example) to use in an omelet or salad. Grill fish steaks often and use them in salad for lunch the next day.

- Always have low-calorie, high-fiber vegetables, such as bell peppers and celery sticks, in the refrigerator. A guacamole dip with celery sticks or bell pepper slices is a healthy, nourishing, and filling snack. You do not need chips for dips!

- Learn to use alternatives to starches like pasta and potatoes. If you love pasta dishes, use them sparingly and as a side dish, not as the main plate. Obviously, rice, noodles, and potatoes deliver fewer calories when steamed or boiled than when fried.

How to Eat Healthy

- Be mindful of your eating. Are you eating because you are hungry? Or are you eating because you are distracted, stressed, or tired?

- Avoid hunger. Eat frequent lean and small meals. Always have a balanced approach. Do not eat fast-absorbing carbohydrates alone. Mix them with other foods, such as nuts, cheese, and meats.

- Eat with peace of mind. Try not to eat on the run. Taste the food and decide how much of it you will eat. Be in touch with your senses. Use your recollections, such as: "Last time I ate this, I got heartburn. This time I won't finish it." Be mindful.

- Do not eat the same foods over and over again. You will deplete your body of micronutrients, essential amino acids, and fatty acids, for which you need to eat a variety of foods. Variety is key when it comes to healthy eating.

- To lose weight, you have to plan not to get "surprise" hunger pangs. If you often get hungry at a certain time (like 10 A.M.), prepare a low-calorie healthy snack for that time—or eat a bigger breakfast, low in carbohydrates but rich in protein and healthy fats (for example, smoked salmon). Emergency scavenging will lead you straight to the vending machine or the doughnut shop.

- Sit down to eat a meal. Begin with protein and fat before eating carbohydrates. The French eat crudités (like tomatoes, cucumber, and lettuce in a vinaigrette dressing) before a meal to open up their appetite. If you don't want to stimulate your appetite, go directly for the chicken or the beef. Then try the side dish, which typically has more carbohydrates.

- You must eat slowly. Do not eat over the kitchen sink or in the hallway. It takes about 15 minutes for your brain to get the satiety signals from your intestine. If during that time you have already eaten too much of a calorie-dense food, regardless of its nature, the damage is done. Once the calories are *in*, their mission is accomplished!

- Avoid eating high-glycemic-index or fast-absorbing carbohydrates at the onset of the meal. You will get a sharp and short-lasting spike of insulin, which will stimulate your appetite even more. If you have to, eat high-glycemic-index carbohydrates with protein or fat (for example, fruits with yogurt or nuts).

- Eat and talk. Engage in easy conversations that do not stress you. Socializing while eating slows you down. In Asian restaurants, use chopsticks to slow you down. Learn to cut your meat as you eat as opposed to all at once (kids do that). Cut the slices in gracefully thin sizes you can eat slowly. *You do not want to eat fast.* It is shown that eating fast worsens insulin resistance and diabetes and causes weight gain.

- Learn to enjoy drinking water with lunch instead of sweetened drinks, soda, or even coffee and tea (if you use cream and sugar). Some people believe that if you drink a lot of water before and during a meal, you will feel full and not eat as much. Others argue that drinking fluids with meals accelerates gastric emptying and reduces the satiety effect. Let your body be the judge.

- Use smaller plates so that the portions look satisfying. If you eat small portions, you can eat anything you wish. Portion control is key to healthy eating.

- If you feel that you are still hungry after a meal, wait an hour. Then if you are still hungry, eat another small portion or another mixed-meal snack. Do not justify cravings for desserts or sweets by mistaking them for hunger.

- Keep a food journal. If you are still losing weight or trying to address a specific problem like hunger and/or hypoglycemia, you need to have a record of what you eat. If needed, you can consult a nutritionist to address your concerns.

Your Weekly High-Protein, Low-Carbohydrate Plan

- Consult your doctor before beginning such a meal plan.
- This meal plan is not suitable for people with kidney failure.
- Certain items may have to be replaced in case of food intolerance.
- This meal plan is to be used as an example. You may personalize your meal plan with the help of a dietitian.

- When useful, reference is made to the Jacques Pépin recipes included in the chapter.
- This meal plan delivers between 1,200 and 1,400 calories. Add one starchy vegetable per day if you are allowed to have a higher daily caloric intake.
- Once you have reviewed this meal plan, look for cooking instructions in Jacques Pépin's recipes, described below and in his other books.
- At the end of each of Jacques's recipes, nutrition information is followed by simple recommendations about different ways you can include these foods in your meal plan. For example, the salad dressing in a recipe may be used as a dip for a snack. A vegetable dish recipe may be used in a lunch or dinner menu or it could be used in an omelet or salad.

Tips for Healthy Eating

- Learn to choose foods wisely.
- Learn to cook simple dishes.
- Eat slowly and frequently.
- Begin meals with proteins and fats; then add the carbohydrates.
- Avoid high-glycemic-index or fast-absorbing carbohydrates.
- For weight loss: Choose a high-protein, low-carb, low-fat diet.
- For maintenance: Choose a balanced, low-cal diet rich in micronutrients.
- Avoid starches, sweets, and foods rich in saturated fats.
- Eat foods rich in omega fatty acids and antioxidants.
- Include foods rich in fiber in meals and snacks.
- Eat and move. Stay active after meals.

Monday

Breakfast	3 to 4 egg white omelet
Snack	2 ounces (4 tablespoons) low-fat (1 percent) cottage cheese or 1 low-carbohydrate protein bar or shake
Lunch	6 ounces roast beef or turkey, garden salad with $^1/_2$ tablespoon low-cal salad dressing
Snack	5 celery sticks with a low-cal, low-carbohydrate dip or with 12 almonds ($^1/_2$ ounce)
Dinner	6 ounces grilled or roasted chicken breast, no skin, $^1/_2$ yam, and steamed veggies, such as string beans
Snack	*Optional:* sugar-free gelatin or protein pudding

Tuesday

Breakfast	3 to 4 egg white omelet or 1 cup low-fat cottage cheese with chopped bell peppers and herbs
Snack	15 halves (1 ounce) walnuts or 1 low-carbohydrate protein bar or shake
Lunch	6 ounces of the grilled chicken from dinner with a tossed salad and $^1/_2$ tablespoon low-cal dressing; may add 1 sliced tomato or onion
Snack	Bell pepper sticks with 2 ounces smoked turkey or a protein shake
Dinner	6 ounces of grilled or roasted lean beef trimmed of fat: sirloin, tenderloin, or flank steak; roast with steamed veggies such as string beans or asparagus; green salad with $^1/_2$ tablespoon low-cal dressing
Snack	*Optional:* sugar-free gelatin or protein pudding

Wednesday

Breakfast	3 to 4 egg white omelet or 4 ounces smoked salmon or ham with 1-ounce slice of low-fat cheese, such as Gouda or Jarlsberg
Snack	12 almonds plus 5 celery sticks or 1 low-carbohydrate protein bar or shake

Lunch	6 ounces leftover meat sliced and microwave heated or 6 ounces roast beef, turkey, or ham; garden salad with $^1/_2$ tablespoon low-cal dressing; may add herbs and spices
Snack	A fruit from the fruit list with a protein bar or a shake
Dinner	6 ounces grilled salmon or tuna steak with steamed veggies and a large green salad with $^1/_2$ tablespoon low-cal dressing
Snack	*Optional:* sugar-free gelatin or protein pudding

Thursday

Breakfast	2 hard-boiled eggs and a fruit or a protein smoothie
Snack	1 low-carbohydrate protein bar or shake
Lunch	4 ounces salmon or tuna with 1 sliced tomato, onion, and 2 cups of any nonstarchy vegetables
Snack	Bell pepper sticks with 2 ounces smoked turkey or a protein shake
Dinner	6 ounces grilled chicken or turkey breast, no skin; $^1/_2$ yam and steamed veggies, such as string beans
Snack	*Optional*: sugar-free gelatin or protein pudding

Friday

Breakfast	3 to 4 egg white omelet or 1 cup cottage cheese with chopped bell peppers and herbs
Snack	1 ounce walnuts, 1 fruit, or 1 low-carbohydrate protein bar or shake
Lunch	6 onces of the grilled chicken from dinner with a tossed salad and $^1/_2$ tablespoon of low-cal dressing; may add 1 sliced tomato or onion
Snack	Bell pepper sticks with 2 ounces prosciutto or a dip or a protein shake
Dinner	6 ounces grilled or roasted lean beef trimmed of fat: sirloin, tenderloin, or pork tenderloin, with steamed veggies, such as string beans or asparagus; green salad

with $^1/_2$ tablespoon low-cal dressing; may add grilled
portobello mushrooms

Snack *Optional:* sugar-free gelatin or protein pudding

Saturday

Breakfast Tired of eggs? Try a veggie patty or 2 soy dogs with
tomatoes and feta cheese

Snack 1 ounce walnuts or 1 low-carbohydrate protein bar or
shake

Lunch A large salad with 4 ounces smoked salmon or ham
with 2 cups of any nonstarchy veggies (usually
leftovers)

Snack Bell pepper sticks with 2 ounces smoked turkey or a
protein shake

Dinner 6 ounces grilled salmon or tuna steak with steamed
veggies and a large green salad with $^1/_2$ tablespoon
low-cal dressing

Snack *Optional:* sugar-free gelatin or protein pudding

Sunday

Breakfast 3 to 4 egg white omelet or 1 cup cottage cheese with
chopped bell peppers and herbs

Snack 15 halves (1 ounce) walnuts or 12 almonds or
1 low-carbohydrate protein bar or shake

Lunch 4 ounces smoked salmon or tuna with 1 sliced tomato,
onion, and 2 cups of any nonstarchy vegetables

Snack Bell pepper or celery sticks with 2 ounces smoked
turkey or a protein shake; also 1 fruit

Dinner 6 ounces grilled or roasted chicken, turkey, or ham
with steamed veggies, such as string beans or asparagus; green salad with $^1/_2$ tablespoon low-cal dressing;
may add grilled portobello mushrooms

Snack *Optional:* sugar-free gelatin or protein pudding

Low-Calorie Recipes for Your Meal Plan by Jacques Pépin

During one of my walks with Jacques, I asked him if he would provide me with a week's worth of recipes to be used in my meal plan. He very graciously agreed, and the delightful results are included here. Most dishes described here can be used in several ways: as a side or main dish or even as a snack. Some can be used as leftovers to make sandwiches or be added to a salad. The dips or vegetables, for example, can be added to an omelet or salad. These recipes are not time-consuming and do not require a culinary degree. Use them in your meal plan and enjoy eating a variety of foods consistent with your dietary goals.

Salmon with Spinach and Tomatoes
Yield: 6 servings

This is an elegant dish for a special dinner party. If you can't find salmon, substitute grouper, striped bass, or another firm-fleshed fish—whatever variety is the freshest. Be sure that the thickness and size of the fish you select are about the same as what is called for below. If you have any leftovers, cut the fish into pieces, mix with any remaining sauce, season with lemon juice, and serve on salad greens. As part of your meal plan, this recipe can be used as a side dish in a meal, in a salad, or with eggs in the morning.

4	cups (loosely packed) spinach leaves
6	boneless, skinless salmon fillet steaks, each about 6 ounces and $^1/_4$-inch thick
$^1/_2$	cup peeled, seeded, and diced ($^1/_2$-inch) tomato
$^1/_2$	cup white wine
$^3/_4$	teaspoon salt
$^1/_2$	teaspoon freshly ground black pepper
$^1/_3$	cup sour cream

Spread the spinach leaves evenly in a large skillet, and arrange the salmon fillets in a single layer on top. Add the tomato, wine, salt, and pepper, and bring to a boil. Cover, and cook over medium-high heat for 3 to 4 minutes, until the salmon is barely cooked.

Heat the oven to 180°F. Using a slotted spoon, lift the spinach from the skillet and, still holding it over the skillet, press on it to extrude most of the moisture, letting it fall back into the skillet. Transfer the spinach and fish to an ovenproof serving platter, and keep warm in the preheated oven. Reduce the juices remaining in the skillet to 4 to 5 tablespoons. Add the sour cream, bring just to the boil, and spoon over the fish. Serve immediately.

Nutrition Facts (per serving of 290 grams): calories, 290; fat, 13 grams; cholesterol, 105 milligrams; carbohydrates, 29 grams; protein, 35 grams

Portobello Mushroom Grill
Yield: 4 servings

Large, meaty portobello mushrooms are juicy and flavorful. They can be baked as well as grilled, but grilling is my favorite way of preparing them. The stems are a bit tougher than the caps but are good oiled and grilled next to them. The mushrooms are a terrific garnish for steak, roast chicken, or turkey or served with a salad for a meatless lunch. Any leftover mushrooms can be cut into pieces and served as a garnish for any meat or fish or added to a salad. They are also good mixed with eggs for an omelet or added to soups as an enhancement. As part of your meal plan, this recipe can be used as a side dish in a meal, in a salad, or with eggs in the morning.

4   large portobello mushrooms, stems removed and reserved
1¹/₂ tablespoons good olive oil
¹/₄   teaspoon salt
¹/₄   teaspoon freshly ground black pepper

Heat a grill until very hot. Rub the top surface of the mushroom caps and the stems with the oil (which will be quickly absorbed), and sprinkle them with the salt and pepper. Place the caps top side down on the grill with the stems, and cook, for about 3 minutes. Turn them over, and cook them for 3 minutes on the other side. Serve immediately or set aside in a warm place until ready to serve.

Nutrition Facts (per serving of 62 grams): calories, 60; fat, 5 grams; cholesterol, 0 milligrams; carbohydrates, 3 grams; protein, 2 grams

Seviche of Scallops
Yield: 6 servings

Seviche is a South American—particularly Peruvian—type of marinated fish. The fish is "cooked" with citric acid from limes or lemons. Here we use scallops, which goes very well with the marinade, and we extend the recipe by adding diced tomatoes, cilantro, mint, and a julienne of lime skin, which give the dish a zesty and piquant flavor. Diced cucumber, added at the end, adds some crunchiness and contrast. This dish is excellent as a first course, served on a plate or in cocktail glasses with lettuce around it. You could extend the recipe by adding additional fish, perhaps a dice of salmon or cod, and for a fancier presentation, you can serve the seviche surrounded by ripe avocado slices. As part of your meal plan, this recipe can be used as a side dish in a meal, in a salad, or with eggs in the morning.

1	pound sea scallops, washed and cut into 1-inch pieces
1	cup diced ($^{1}/_{4}$-inch) red onion
$1^{1}/_{2}$	cups diced ($^{1}/_{2}$-inch) tomato
1	tablespoon seeded and finely chopped jalapeño chili pepper
$^{1}/_{4}$	cup coarsely chopped fresh cilantro
1	tablespoon julienned lime rind
$^{1}/_{4}$	cup (about) lime juice

1   tablespoon white wine vinegar
2   tablespoons coarsely chopped fresh mint
1   teaspoon salt
$^1/_2$ teaspoon freshly ground black pepper
2   teaspoons sugar
1   cucumber, trimmed and peeled

Combine all the ingredients, except the cucumber, in a bowl. Cover, and refrigerate for a couple of hours, stirring occasionally, so the mixture is well combined.

Cut the cucumber in half lengthwise, and scrape out the seeds with a metal measuring spoon. Cut the cucumber flesh into $^1/_2$-inch dice.

At serving time, mix the cucumber with the scallops, and divide the seviche among 6 plates.

Nutrition Facts (per serving of 100 grams): calories, 100; fat, 1 gram; cholesterol, 25 milligrams; carbohydrates, 10 grams; protein, 14 grams

Broiled Chicken on Vegetable Salad
Yield: 6 servings

This is a dish that could be divided, with the vegetables served separately from the meat, which is very flavorful served on its own this way. And for a meatless lunch, the vegetable salad alone is a perfect choice. Any leftover chicken can be sliced and served cold the following day on greens with a little mustard. The cold chicken would also go well with a jalapeño dip. As part of your meal plan, this recipe can be used as a side dish in a meal, in a salad, or with eggs in the morning.

2   tablespoons finely chopped fresh tarragon leaves
$1^1/_2$ tablespoons grated lemon rind
$^3/_4$ teaspoon freshly ground black pepper
6   6-ounce skinless, boneless chicken breasts

Vegetable cooking spray

6   cups (loose) shredded iceberg lettuce

$2^{1}/_{2}$ cups peeled, seeded, and diced ($^{1}/_{2}$-inch) cucumbers

3   cups washed and diced ($^{1}/_{2}$-inch) button mushrooms

2   cups diced ($^{3}/_{4}$-inch) tomatoes

2   cups peeled, diced potatoes, boiled in water to cover until tender

3   tablespoons extra-virgin olive oil

1   tablespoon red wine vinegar

1   tablespoon Dijon-style mustard

$^{1}/_{2}$ teaspoon salt

$^{1}/_{2}$ teaspoon freshly ground black pepper

2   tablespoons chopped chives or parsley leaves, for garnish

Combine the tarragon, lemon, and $^{3}/_{4}$ teaspoon pepper in a small bowl, and rub the mixture into both sides of the chicken breasts. Then spray the breasts lightly on both sides with the cooking spray.

Heat the broiler. Arrange the chicken breasts side by side on a broiler rack, and place the pan so the chicken is about 4 inches from the heat. Broil the chicken for approximately 4 minutes on each side. Set it aside to cool slightly while you assemble the salad.

Combine the lettuce, cucumbers, mushrooms, tomatoes, and potatoes in a large bowl. Toss with the oil, vinegar, mustard, salt, and $^{1}/_{2}$ teaspoon pepper. Divide the salad among 6 dinner plates. Cut each chicken breast in half on the diagonal, and arrange 2 halves on top of the vegetable salad on each plate. Garnish with the chopped chives or parsley, dividing it among the plates. Serve.

Nutrition Facts (per serving size of 435 grams): calories, 330; fat, 10 grams; cholesterol, 100 milligrams; carbohydrates, 17 grams; protein, 43 grams

Mushroom and Apple Salad with Cucumber–Yogurt Dressing
Yield: 6 servings

This is a great combination of ingredients, refreshing as a light lunch or as a garnish to a grilled piece of meat or a roast turkey. The cucumber–yogurt dressing works well on most green salads and tomato salads but is also good spooned over grilled chicken or fish or cold chicken. As part of your meal plan, this recipe can be used as a side dish, in a salad, or as a snack.

Cucumber–Yogurt Dressing

1	cup chunks of peeled and seeded cucumber
$1/4$	cup coarsely chopped scallions
1	tablespoon chopped fresh tarragon
1	clove garlic, peeled
2	tablespoons fresh lime juice
2	tablespoons virgin olive oil
$1/2$	teaspoon salt
$1^1/2$	cups plain nonfat yogurt

Salad

$2^1/2$	cups sliced ($1/2$-inch) button mushrooms
2	apples, halved, cored, and cut into $1/2$-inch dice
$1/2$	teaspoon salt
6	large romaine lettuce leaves

For the dressing: Put all the ingredients for the dressing, except the yogurt, in a blender, and blend until smooth. Transfer the mixture to a bowl, and stir in the yogurt. (You will have about 2 cups.) Set aside 1 cup of the dressing for the salad, and store the remainder, tightly covered, in the refrigerator for up to 10 days to use on salads or grilled meat or fish.

For the salad: Mix together the mushrooms, apples, salt, and reserved cup of dressing in a bowl. Arrange a lettuce leaf on each of 6 plates, and spoon a heaping cup of the salad into each leaf. Serve.

Nutrition Facts (per serving size of 189 grams): calories, 110; fat, 5 grams; cholesterol, 0 milligrams; carbohydrates, 15 grams; protein, 4 grams

Beef Burgundy
Yield: 6 servings

This classic beef burgundy is best made with either beef shank or shoulder blade. These cuts are lean and usually quite gelatinous, and they work well—much better than a piece of bottom or top round, which would be too dry. This type of stew is always good to have on hand; the meat can be cooked with the onion and wine and frozen, then heated at the last moment, with fresh vegetables added at the end. The stew is good served with most any starch, from pasta to potatoes. As part of your meal plan, this recipe can be used as a dinner or lunch.

$2^1/_2$ pounds beef stew meat from the shoulder blade or shank, cut into $1^1/_2$- to 2-inch cubes

2   tablespoons soy sauce

1   cup homemade chicken stock or low-salt canned chicken broth

$1^1/_2$ cups dry, fruity red wine

1   cup peeled and chopped onion

1   tablespoon peeled, crushed, and finely chopped garlic

$3/_4$ teaspoon salt

$1/_4$ teaspoon freshly ground black pepper

2   bay leaves

$1/_2$ teaspoon dried thyme leaves

18   medium button mushrooms (about)

2   cups peeled, halved, and diced (1-inch) carrots

18   small pearl onions, peeled

1   tablespoon cornstarch dissolved in 2 tablespoons water

$1/_2$ cup petite frozen peas, thawed

2   tablespoons chopped fresh parsley

Put the meat in a Dutch oven, and add the soy sauce. Mix well. Add the stock, wine, onion, garlic, salt, pepper, bay leaves, and thyme. Mix well. Bring to a strong boil over high heat, reduce the heat to low, cover, and boil very gently for $1^1/_4$ hours, or until the meat is tender.

Add the mushrooms, carrots, and whole onions to the Dutch oven, moving the meat in the pan with tongs to make room for the vegetables, and bring the mixture back to a boil. Reduce the heat to low, cover, and boil very gently for 10 minutes. Remove and discard the bay leaf, and stir in the dissolved cornstarch mixture and the peas. Bring the stew back to a boil, and serve, dividing the meat and vegetables among 6 plates. Garnish each serving with a little of the parsley.

Nutrition Facts (per serving size of 478 grams): calories, 380; fat, 8 grams; cholesterol, 75 milligrams; carbohydrates, 20 grams; protein, 46 grams

Creamy Eggs with Smoked Fish
Yield: 4 servings

The combination of smoked fish and scrambled eggs—whether served for breakfast, brunch, or as a light dinner—is a great favorite at my house. You can find smoked fish at many supermarkets and delicatessens now. I like to serve the eggs and fish on crunchy toast made from whole wheat, whole grain, or even country-style bread. The eggs are stirred with a whisk while they cook to ensure that the curds are small. Conventionally, they are finished with cream, but yogurt gives them a little acidity and creaminess and stops the cooking. The eggs could also be served with sautéed fresh tomatoes or mushrooms or spooned over salad greens lightly seasoned with olive oil and white wine vinegar. As part of your meal plan, this recipe can be used as a meal or a snack. The added salt is optional.

1   large smoked trout or white fish (about 10 ounces)
4   large eggs
$^1/_4$ teaspoon salt
$^1/_4$ teaspoon freshly ground black pepper
3   tablespoons chopped fresh chives
4   slices whole wheat bread (about 4 ounces total)
1   tablespoon good olive oil
3   tablespoons nonfat plain yogurt

Separate the flesh from the bones and skin of the fish, and break each fillet into pieces or flakes, following the natural lines of the fish.

Using a whisk, beat the eggs in a bowl with the salt, pepper, and chives.

At serving time, toast the bread. Place one piece of toast on each of 4 plates, and arrange the fish around the toast.

Heat the oil in a sturdy skillet or saucepan. When it is hot, add the egg mixture. Cook over medium to low heat, mixing continuously with a whisk to create the smallest possible curds. Continue cooking for about 2 minutes, until the mixture is creamy but still slightly runny.

Remove the pan from the heat, and add the yogurt. Mix well. The mixture should be moist and soft. Spoon onto the toast, dividing the eggs among the 4 plates. Serve immediately.

Nutrition Facts (per serving size of 166 grams): calories, 320; fat, 15 grams; cholesterol, 270 milligrams; carbohydrates, 15 grams; protein, 29 grams

Beef Steak with Herb Crust
Yield: 4 servings

The best steak for me is the New York strip, which is also called a *shell steak* or *loin steak*. It is important to let the meat rest in a warm place after cooking so it will be pink throughout. Cut into thin slices, a steak this size will serve 4 people with the addition of a salad and/or a couple of cooked vegetables. Any leftover steak is great sliced thin and served with a salad. As part of your meal plan, this recipe can be used as a meal.

1	teaspoon dried thyme
1	teaspoon dried savory
$1/2$	teaspoon freshly ground black pepper
1	large New York strip steak, about $1^1/2$ pounds, trimmed of all fat ($1^1/4$ pounds trimmed weight)
$1/2$	teaspoon salt
1	tablespoon good olive oil
$1/4$	cup homemade chicken stock or low-salt canned chicken broth

Heat the oven to 450°F. Crush the dried herbs between your thumb and finger, and mix them with the pepper in a small bowl. Pat the mixture on both sides of the meat.

When ready to cook, sprinkle the meat with the salt. Heat the oil on top of the stove in a heavy ovenproof skillet or saucepan. When hot, add the meat, and cook over medium to high heat for 3 minutes on each side.

Transfer the steak to the preheated oven, and cook for about 8 minutes for medium rare meat. Remove the meat to a platter, and let rest in a warm place for about 10 minutes before serving.

Add the stock to the drippings in the skillet, and bring to a boil. Cut the steak into thin slices, and serve with the skillet juices spooned over them.

Nutrition Facts (per serving size of 159 grams): calories, 320; fat, 16 grams; cholesterol, 110 milligrams; carbohydrates, 1 gram; protein, 41 grams

Roast Turkey with Mushroom and Raisin Stuffing
Yield: 8 to 10 servings

Roast turkey is certainly one of the least expensive and most delicious dishes to prepare for a holiday dinner. We always serve it for Thanksgiving, certainly, but also for Christmas and other holidays. Here, I prepare a stuffing with bread, raisins, and mushrooms to which we add the gizzard and neck meat of the turkey. Cold, thinly sliced turkey is, of course, delicious in sandwiches the following day, and the stuffing can be reheated and served as a bed for any type of roast—from chicken to pork to veal—or under pork chops or lamb chops. The stuffing can also be sautéed in a skillet and served with fried eggs on top, or it can be combined with any leftover meat and gravy and, with the addition of chicken stock or broth and a little pasta, transformed into soup. As part of your meal plan, full portions of the stuffing are not recommended. But tasting it in small portions is acceptable. Therefore, the serving size is reduced to $1/18$ of the whole stuffing (Jacques's recipe serves 8 to 10). The stuffing is useful for retaining moisture and flavor while cooking and should not be eliminated.

1	turkey, about 11 pounds
$1/2$	teaspoon salt
$1/2$	teaspoon freshly ground black pepper
2	cups peeled and diced (1-inch) onions
10	cloves garlic, unpeeled
2	tablespoons canola oil
2	tablespoons good olive oil
1	cup peeled and chopped onions
$1/2$	cup chopped celery
$1/2$	teaspoon *herbes de Provence* or Italian seasoning
2	teaspoons peeled, crushed, and finely chopped garlic
2	cups coarsely chopped mushrooms
6	slices wheat bread
$1/3$	cup golden raisins
$1/2$	teaspoon salt
$1/4$	teaspoon freshly ground black pepper
1	teaspoon potato starch dissolved in 1 tablespoon water
1	tablespoon soy sauce

Put the turkey neck, gizzard, and heart in a saucepan with 3 cups of water. Bring to a boil, cover, reduce the heat, and cook over low heat for about 1 hour.

Heat the oven to 425°F. Drain the turkey parts, reserving the parts and the liquid in separate receptacles. Pull the meat from the neck bones, dice ($^1/_4$ inch) the gizzard and heart, and return the parts to their bowl.

Sprinkle the turkey inside and out with the salt and pepper. Place it breast side up in a roasting pan, and bake for 30 minutes. Turn the turkey breast side down, and arrange the onions and garlic around it.

Reduce the oven temperature to 350°F, return the turkey to the oven, and cook for $1^1/_2$ hours. Add half the reserved liquid from the neck, gizzard, and heart, turn the turkey breast side up again, and cook for 30 minutes to brown the breast. Turn the oven off, transfer the turkey to an ovenproof platter, and return it to the warm oven to rest. Transfer the pan juices in the roasting pan to a saucepan, and set aside to rest for at least 5 minutes.

For the stuffing: Heat the oven to 400°F. Heat the oils in a large skillet or saucepan. When hot, sauté the onion and celery for about 3 minutes. Add the *herbes de Provence*, garlic, and mushrooms, mix well, and remove from the heat.

Toast the bread slices, and cut them into $^1/_2$-inch croutons. Stir the croutons and raisins into the mushroom mixture, and add the remainder of the stock. Add the salt and pepper, and toss gently. Pack lightly into a loaf pan, cover with aluminum foil, and bake for 30 minutes.

For the gravy: Skim off as much fat as possible from the reserved pan juices in the saucepan. Add the diced turkey parts, and boil very gently for a few minutes to reduce slightly. Stir in the dissolved potato starch and the soy sauce, and bring back to a boil. Set aside in a warm place.

To serve, carve the turkey, and serve with the stuffing and gravy.

Stuffing Only

Nutrition Facts (per serving size of 35 grams): calories, 70; fat, 5 grams; cholesterol, 0 milligrams; carbohydrates, 8 grams; protein 1 gram

Roast Turkey (Skinless)

Nutrition Facts (per serving size of 266 grams): calories, 370; fat, 7 grams; cholesterol, 155 milligrams; carbohydrates, 4 grams; protein, 68 grams.

When dark meat is included, fat increases to 11 grams per serving and cholesterol increases to 170 milligrams.

Chicken with Vinegar Sauce
Yield: 6 servings

This is a classic chicken dish from my home region of France, but I use skinless chicken legs to make the recipe less caloric. Notice that the acidity of the vinegar and wine reduction goes especially well with the chicken. If you have any leftovers, pick the meat off the bones, mix it with any remaining sauce, and serve as a type of ragout over pasta. You can also stuff an omelet with the leftover mixture and serve it with a green salad for a hearty meal. As part of your meal plan, this recipe can be used as a meal, in a salad, or even as a snack.

Seasoning Mixture

1	teaspoon dried oregano
1	teaspoon dried marjoram
$^3/_4$	teaspoon salt
$^1/_2$	teaspoon freshly ground black pepper

Chicken

6	skinless chicken legs (about $2^3/_4$ pounds)
$^1/_2$	teaspoon good olive oil

Sauce

$^1/_4$	cup balsamic vinegar
$^1/_4$	cup dry red wine
$^1/_2$	cup trimmed and minced scallions
2	tablespoons ketchup
$^1/_2$	cup homemade chicken stock or low-salt canned chicken broth
4	tablespoons peeled and thinly sliced garlic

For the seasoning: Combine the seasoning mixture ingredients in a small bowl.

For the chicken: Brush a large heavy saucepan or nonstick skillet with the olive oil, and heat it until hot. Add the chicken legs in one layer, and sprinkle the seasoning mix over them. Cook the legs, covered, over medium to low heat for 10 minutes. Turn the legs over, cover again, and cook them for 10 minutes on the other side. The chicken should be well browned on all sides. Using tongs, transfer the legs to a serving platter, and set them aside in a warm place while you prepare the sauce.

For the sauce: Add the vinegar and red wine to the crystallized juices in the saucepan, bring the mixture to a boil, stirring, and boil it for 30 seconds. Then add the scallions, ketchup, chicken stock, and garlic. Boil for about 2 minutes, until the mixture is reduced to about 1 cup of concentrated liquid.

To serve, discard any juices that have collected around the chicken on the platter, and drizzle the sauce over the legs. Serve.

Nutrition Facts (per serving size of 264 grams): calories, 290; fat, 9 grams; cholesterol, 175 milligrams; carbohydrates, 6 grams; protein, 42 grams

Cannellini Bean Dip
Yield: 2¼ cups

I use cannellini beans in this quick recipe, but feel free to substitute another variety of canned beans—anything from black beans to red beans. You can serve the dip on cucumber slices or melba toast instead of pita bread, if you prefer. This dip could also be used as a pasta sauce, extended with chicken stock for serving as a soup, or served lukewarm under a piece of poached codfish. As part of your meal plan, this recipe can be used as part of a meal, a salad, or as a snack.

1   cup (lightly packed) fresh cilantro leaves
3/4 cup (lightly packed) fresh parsley leaves
3   cloves garlic, peeled
1/2 teaspoon salt
1/4 teaspoon freshly ground black pepper
1   19-ounce can cannellini beans, drained
     A few drops Tabasco hot pepper sauce
2   tablespoons extra-virgin olive oil
     Pita bread or toast

Bring about 3 cups of water to a boil in a saucepan. Add the cilantro and parsley, and push the herbs down into the water. Blanch for 10 seconds.

Drain the herbs in a sieve, and spoon them into the bowl of a food processor. Add the garlic, salt, and pepper, and process for a few seconds to combine the ingredients.

Add the drained beans and process for about 45 seconds, stopping the processor a few times and scraping down the sides of the bowl with a rubber spatula, until the mixture is smooth. Add the Tabasco and olive oil, and process for about 5 seconds, until they are incorporated.

Transfer the bean dip to a serving bowl, and serve with pita bread or toast.

Nutrition Facts (per serving size of 71 grams): calories, 80; fat, 3.5 grams; cholesterol, 0 milligrams; carbohydrates, 9 grams; protein, 3 grams

Marinated Squid Vietnamese-Style
Yield: 4 servings

This dish, a kind of seviche, is inspired by a Vietnamese style of cooking. Notice that there is no oil in this dish; the combination of hot chili peppers (use whatever variety you prefer, and less or more, depending on your tolerance for spicy food), mint, and cilantro creates a very fresh taste that goes well with the squid. This recipe can be served as the main course for a light lunch or, in smaller portions, as the first course for a dinner; you can shred more salad greens than I use here and serve the squid on the greens. Leftover squid is also good spooned over sliced avocado or diced fresh tomatoes. As part of your meal plan, this recipe can be used as part of a meal, as a salad, or as a snack.

1	pound squid (body and tentacles), thoroughly cleaned
1	tablespoon peeled, crushed, and finely chopped garlic
1	teaspoon (about) seeded and chopped Thai hot chili peppers
$1^1/_2$	cups very thinly sliced onion
2	tablespoons lime juice
$^1/_3$	cup shredded fresh mint
$^1/_3$	cup coarsely chopped fresh cilantro leaves
3	tablespoons nuoc nam (Vietnamese fish sauce)
$^1/_2$	teaspoon sugar
4	large iceberg lettuce leaves

Bring 6 cups of water to a boil in a large saucepan. Cut the body pieces and tentacles of the squid crosswise into 1-inch slices. Add the squid to the boiling water, and cook for about 2 minutes, stirring occasionally until the water returns to the boil. Drain.

Combine the remaining ingredients, except the lettuce, in a large serving bowl. Add the hot, drained squid, and toss until well mixed. Let marinate for at least 15 minutes, stirring occasionally, so the squid can develop flavor. Serve on the lettuce leaves.

Nutrition Facts (per serving size of 199 grams): calories, 140; fat, 1.5 grams; cholesterol, 265 milligrams; carbohydrates, 10 grams; protein, 19 grams

Smoked Pork with Honey Glaze
Yield: about 10 servings

This is an ideal dish to prepare over a weekend when you are entertaining; it's easy to do and tasty, and the guests can help themselves. The cooking of the pork shoulder roast in water removes a lot of its salt and smokiness and preserves the moisture in the meat. The best part of the dish for me, however, is the leftovers. The meat makes a great sandwich filling with mustard, and it's delicious served alongside eggs in the morning. Also, there is nothing better than little pieces of the meat mated with vegetables or pasta and reheated in a gratin dish. Even the leftover bone can be reboiled to create a stock that you can freeze and use later to make a soup with split peas or beans. As part of your meal plan, this recipe can be used as a meal, in a salad, or with eggs for breakfast.

1 smoked picnic pork shoulder with bone (about 6 pounds)
2 tablespoons honey
2 teaspoons dry mustard
2 tablespoons Chinese hot chili and garlic paste
1 cup chicken stock

Put the pork shoulder in a stockpot, and add enough cold water to extend about $1/2$ inch above the meat. Bring the water to 180°F (just below the boil), and cook for $1^1/2$ hours at this temperature.

Meanwhile, make the glaze: Mix the honey, mustard, and hot chili paste together in a small bowl.

Heat the oven to 400°F. Let the pork cool in the cooking liquid, then cut off and discard the exterior fat and the rind from around the bones. Score the top of the ham, cutting intersecting lines about $1/2$ inch deep into it every $3/4$ inch. Spread the glaze over the surface.

Put the pork in a roasting pan, and bake in the preheated oven for 1 hour. The surface should be nicely browned.

Transfer the pork to a serving platter, and set aside in a warm place. Add the chicken stock to the pan juices, and stir with a wooden spoon to dissolve any solidified juices. Strain the juices over the pork shoulder, cut into slices, and serve.

Nutrition Facts (per serving size of 139 grams): calories, 270; fat, 15 grams; cholesterol, 105 milligrams; carbohydrates, 4 grams; protein, 29 grams.

Carbonnade of Beef
Yield: 6 servings

Beef cooked in beer is a national dish in Belgium. A very satisfying stew, this should be made with beef from the chuck or shoulder, so it is tender and juicy. As part of your meal plan, this recipe can be used as lunch or dinner.

$1^1/_2$	tablespoons canola oil
$1^1/_2$	pounds lean beef chuck, cut into $1^1/_2$-inch pieces
2	cups peeled and thickly sliced onions
1	teaspoon salt
1	teaspoon freshly ground black pepper
1	teaspoon *herbes de Provence*
2	bay leaves
2	cans (12 ounces) beer
1	tablespoon potato starch

Heat 1 tablespoon of the oil in a large, heavy saucepan. When hot, add half the meat, and brown lightly on all sides. Transfer the meat to a bowl. Repeat this browning process with the remaining oil and meat, and transfer the second batch of meat to the bowl.

Add the onions to the meat drippings in the saucepan, and cook for about 1 minute over high heat. Add $^1/_4$ cup water, and stir with a wooden spoon to loosen and melt any solidified juices in the skillet and to incorporate them into the mixture. Add the salt and pepper.

Return the meat to the saucepan, and add the *herbes de Provence*, bay leaves, and beer. Bring the mixture to a boil, cover tightly, reduce the heat to low, and boil gently for $1^1/_2$ hours. Remove and discard the bay leaves. Mix the potato starch with 3 tablespoons of water, and add to the stew, stirring well to thicken the liquid. Serve.

Nutrition Facts (per serving size of 242 grams): calories, 270; fat, 10 grams; cholesterol, 80 milligrams; carbohydrates, 10 grams; protein, 27 grams

Stew of Beans and Ham
Yield: 4 servings

There are many types of ham on the market that are quite good and quite lean. This recipe can also be made with cooked and smoked breast of turkey. As part of your meal plan, this recipe can be used as lunch or dinner, or it can be used in a salad or with eggs.

1	teaspoon corn or canola oil
1	teaspoon unsalted butter
$1^1/_2$	cups chopped onion
$^1/_2$	cup minced scallions
1	tablespoon all-purpose flour
$1^1/_2$	cups low-fat chicken stock
$^1/_2$	pound string beans or snap beans, cut into 1-inch pieces
$^3/_4$	teaspoon salt
$^1/_2$	teaspoon freshly ground black pepper
$^1/_2$	teaspoon Italian seasoning
2	cups sliced (1-inch) zucchini
1	pound lean ham, cut into 1-inch pieces
1	tablespoon chopped fresh parsley

Heat the oil and butter in a saucepan, add the onion and scallions, and sauté for 2 minutes. Stir in the flour, and then add the chicken stock and bring to a boil. Add the beans, salt, pepper, and Italian seasoning, return to a boil, and boil for 2 minutes.

Add the zucchini and ham cubes, and boil gently for 2 minutes, or until thoroughly heated through. Transfer to a serving bowl, sprinkle with parsley, and serve.

Nutrition Facts (per serving size of 316 grams): calories, 190; fat, 7 grams; cholesterol, 40 milligrams; carbohydrates, 16 grams; protein, 15 grams

Irish-Style Lamb Stew
Yield: 6 servings

Leg of lamb is ideal for this stew; tender and quite lean, it produces a very gratifying dish. Conventionally, the sauce is thickened with the puree of some of the vegetables. If you want the sauce slightly thicker, mash some of the vegetables with a fork or by forcing them through a food mill to give some viscosity to the juices. As part of your meal plan, this recipe can be used as lunch or dinner.

$1^1/_2$ pounds lamb from the leg, well trimmed of all fat and cut into
      $1^1/_2$-inch cubes
2   cups onion pieces (1-inch)
3   tablespoons coarsely chopped garlic
2   sprigs fresh thyme
2   bay leaves
1   teaspoon salt
$^1/_2$ teaspoon freshly ground black pepper
2   teaspoons Worcestershire sauce (preferably Lea & Perrins)
$1^1/_2$ pounds jicama, peeled and cut into 2- to 3-inch pieces
2   cups celery rib pieces (1-inch)
1   tablespoon chopped fresh parsley

Put the lamb in a sturdy casserole or Dutch oven. Add $2^1/_2$ cups water, the onions, garlic, thyme, bay leaves, salt, pepper, and Worcestershire sauce. Bring to a boil over high heat, reduce the heat, and boil gently for 45 minutes.

Add the jicama and celery, and continue cooking for 10 minutes longer, or until the vegetables are tender. Spoon onto a platter, sprinkle with the parsley, and serve with the natural juices.

Nutrition Facts (per serving size of 342 grams): calories, 310; fat, 7 grams; cholesterol, 75 milligrams; carbohydrates, 18 grams; protein, 24 grams

Poached Chicken with Vegetables Stew
Yield: about 6 servings

There is nothing better than a poached chicken for a winter Sunday dinner. Poached this way, the meat is juicy and succulent, and the savory stock has a minimum of fat. As part of your meal plan, this recipe can be used as lunch or dinner. The serving size as described is quite generous in vegetable portions.

1	whole chicken, about 4 pounds, skin removed
4	large, dried shiitake mushrooms
1	large sprig thyme
1	sprig rosemary
2	bay leaves
2	teaspoons salt
1	teaspoon black peppercorns
4	small leeks
4	medium onions, peeled
1	small Savoy cabbage, quartered
2	cups broccoli florets
1	small butternut squash, peeled, seeded, and quartered
	Dijon mustard
	Cornichons

Place the whole chicken in a deep, narrow stockpot, and add 4 quarts of water, the mushrooms, thyme, rosemary, bay leaves, salt, and peppercorns. Bring to a boil over high heat, then reduce heat to very low, and simmer gently for 30 minutes. Remove the chicken from the stock, and set it aside in a dish.

Strain the stock, reserving the mushrooms. Remove and discard the mushroom stems (which are tough), and return the caps to the stock with the leeks, onions, and cabbage. Bring to a boil, and continue boiling for 15 minutes. Add the broccoli and squash and boil for another 5 minutes.

Meanwhile, remove the meat from the chicken breast, legs, and carcass, and arrange it on a large, dark platter. Using a slotted spoon, remove the vegetables from the stock and place them around the chicken.

Serve with Dijon mustard and cornichons.

Nutrition Facts (per serving size of 524 grams): calories, 350; fat, 6 grams; cholesterol, 103 milligrams; carbohydrates, 38 grams; protein, 37 grams

Chicken in Red Wine Sauce
Yield: 4 servings

This is a simple but elegant way to prepare chicken with a minimum amount of calories and a maximum amount of flavor. As part of your meal plan, this recipe can be used as lunch or dinner. Any leftovers (the serving size is quite generous) can be used cold in a salad or added to an egg omelet the next day.

$1^1/_2$　tablespoons good olive oil
12　　small pearl onions, peeled
$^1/_2$　　teaspoon sugar
8　　　medium mushrooms, quartered

$^1/_2$ cup finely chopped onion

1   tablespoon finely chopped garlic

1   sprig fresh thyme

1   bay leaf

$1^1/_2$ cups robust, fruity red wine

4   boneless, skinless chicken breasts

2   teaspoons dark soy sauce

$^3/_4$ teaspoon freshly ground black pepper

1   teaspoon potato starch dissolved in 2 tablespoons water

Heat 1 tablespoon of the oil in a skillet, and add the pearl onions, sugar, mushrooms, and $^1/_2$ cup water. Bring to a boil, cover, and boil for 3 to 4 minutes. Remove the cover, and keep cooking over high heat until the water has evaporated. Continue cooking until the onions and mushrooms take on a dark brown color. Remove the mushrooms and onions from the skillet, and set them aside in a bowl.

Add the chopped onion, garlic, thyme, bay leaf, and wine to the skillet. Place the chicken breasts in the wine mixture in the skillet so they do not overlap, and bring to a boil. Reduce the heat, and simmer very gently for 7 to 8 minutes.

Add the soy sauce, pepper, and dissolved potato starch, and mix well. Return the mushrooms and onions to the stew in the skillet, heat gently for 1 minute, and serve.

Nutrition Facts (per serving size of 414 grams): calories, 430; fat, 10 grams; cholesterol, 135 milligrams; carbohydrates, 12 grams; protein, 56 grams

II

Your Plan of Action

How to Undo Metabolic Syndrome in Six Months

Therapeutic lifestyle change (TLC) is a gradual process that has to become an organic part of your life. Similarly, the processes of TLC coaching reflected in this chapter cannot be forced and have to take root in the depths of your aspirations and goals. As a day-by-day coaching guide aimed at reversing metabolic syndrome, this chapter guides, educates, motivates, and reinforces healthy change at a realistic and safe pace. Key concepts, such as motivational engagement, accountability, reward structure, self-love, self-care, and relapse prevention, are combined with education and useful information.

Most people gain weight gradually. But at certain times, like during pregnancy, menopause, a knee surgery, or other life-changing events, weight gain often accelerates. Sometimes, though, these triggers can initiate a lifestyle change and weight loss. *Triggers* are real, and they happen often, but there is no formula as to how they cause weight gain or weight loss. Triggers that cause stress eating, binging, or relapse for some may be used to initiate change or to reinforce commitment to exercise and diet by others. We are often so busy in our day-to-day routine that we are not mindful of how triggers influence us. If we do not pay attention to these life-changing events and experiences, we lose control of our life, mind, and body. Once we understand this subtle process, we can make decisions, change course, self-motivate, and make progress in spite of negative triggers and obstacles. But understanding this process does not necessarily guarantee success. To succeed, we need a healthy structure in our daily lives.

We have all had periods in our lives when we thought we had no control over our destiny. These periods are not necessarily negative in nature. The first time you fell in love, your life was probably dominated by your passion. Everything else—your job, your school grades, your bank account, eating, exercise, and even sleep—were all of a lesser priority than spending time with that special person. The same applies to life during divorce, grief over recent loss of a loved one, or a natural disaster. Therapeutic lifestyle change requires a period of stability to allow for meal planning, exercise routines, active relaxation, and stress management. In addition to stability, these all require concentration, focus, and commitment. In other words, change needs structure; it cannot be random. TLC is not possible if life is unpredictable, choppy, and uncontrollable.

A *structure* that fits one person may not be useful or realistic for someone else. A stay-at-home mom with small children has to reorganize her day planning differently than a full-time nurse or a traveling executive. You have to come to terms with what kind of structure you need in your life. To design your own plan, use this chapter as if it were a clinician coaching you along. Busy doctors do not typically focus on planning and strategizing a preventive lifestyle change program, so you can use this chapter as your lifestyle guide while you are under your doctor's care.

By carefully following this lifestyle planner, you can draw the blueprint of a new healthy life structure—one that reflects your organizational skills for time and meal planning, a detailed exercise program, and your use of active and passive relaxation techniques. Once your structure is designed, it needs to be implemented and fine-tuned. The easiest way to facilitate the implementation of change is to incorporate healthy *rewards* and healthy rituals or *anchors* into the fabric of your new lifestyle. Rewards and healthy anchors were discussed earlier and are also reviewed in the planner. Basically, you set goals, reach them, and reward yourself with health-promoting rewards. The Six-Month Plan on page 191 can serve as a guide.

What If There Is No Trigger Anytime Soon?

Joe was only thirty-five years old, but he weighed almost 300 pounds when I met him. He knew a lot about complications of weight gain: he already had diabetes and had a few admissions to the emergency room for chest pain. He told me that he had no trouble losing 150 pounds when he was twenty-two years old. At that time, Joe (who is still quite handsome) was trying to win the heart of a young lady. One day on a date with her, he overheard some tough guys make fun of the "fat boy" dating the beautiful blonde. He was so bitterly shocked that he used that "trigger" to lose weight, and he did. He lost 150 pounds in the year that followed. Unfortunately, the weight came back. My question to him was, What if there is no trigger like that anytime soon? Joe needed to find the motivation to change with or without a trigger.

Accountability and reinforcement are also key required elements of therapeutic lifestyle change. For example, hold yourself accountable for the three common sources of unaccounted for excess caloric intake: hidden calories, like the commonly ignored mayonnaise in a sandwich; excessive portions and serving sizes; and those forgotten calories consumed while distracted and stressed. The latter is a big source of error and frustration. Exercise can also become a source of dietary indiscretion: "I worked out, so I can eat that extra energy drink or the extra ice cream after dinner." So good record keeping goes hand in hand with accountability. Just as the accountant requires a close tracking of expenses, the dieter has to keep a careful log of calories consumed and spent.

Reinforcement is not a theoretical matter; it is an hourly and daily drill. I tell my patients to check their plan for the day before they even get out of bed: What does the day look like? What is my schedule? How much traveling am I doing? When and where am I going to eat? How does my body feel today? Am I sore or do I need to be energized? How is my stress level or my mood? I call this a "systems check." I ask my patients to do this before getting out of bed and then every hour to check that they're staying with the program. If you stay on track, you also stay assured and confident that you will get results.

With success comes *responsibility*. As you lose weight, acknowledge your success and be appreciative of your newly regained sense of control. There is indeed a lot of pleasure in weight loss. The waistline is shrinking, the cheekbones are once again prominent, and energy and libido are back up to where they were decades ago. People start to notice. You are *body proud* and you know it. Pleasure from success in your health enhancement mission is the best reward of all.

How long should you go on? Once you have reached your goal—the summit of the mountain, so to speak—you are no longer looking up; you are looking down. So, should you climb back down? Should you stay put at the top? Is that possible? Should you go on? Of course you should go on.

In fact, to avoid *relapse*, you have to explore and understand your new feelings and emotions related to your success. If, by controlling your life, your body, and your mind, you have become alienated and lost sight of your initial goals, you will have to do some soul searching and reassess your priorities.

Adopt a positive attitude, relax, and have a larger perspective of things. Life is not just about control and success. I remember talking to one of my successful patients about the dangers of the "eating season" (Thanksgiving to the new year). She had transformed her lifestyle in her own way, had lost weight, and had learned to exercise. We were talking about the art of eating just the "right amount." It just happened that same evening I was having a small dinner party at my house. I used that as an example. I told her I was cooking a low-calorie but tasty and festive meal, and I described it to her. I told her that I was going to cook a cod fillet and spray a little white truffle-infused oil on the dish just before serving it because it would make it special. That is when her eyes sparkled all of a sudden. She quickly said, "That is the kind of stuff I want to learn now." She had graduated from "Fat Loss 101" and was ready for the next course on "Better Living."

The Six-Month Plan:
Redesign Your Body and Rewire Your Mind

Month 1

Week 1	Gaining Momentum
Week 2	Finding Your Motivation
Week 3	The Foods You Eat
Week 4	Learning About Food Categories and Alternatives

Month 2

Week 5	Your Body Composition
Week 6	Making Progress
Week 7	Coping with Stress and Change
Week 8	Food and Energy

Month 3

Week 9	Getting Support
Week 10	Preventing Relapse (1)
Week 11	Liberalizing Breakfast
Week 12	Liberalizing Lunch

Month 4

Week 13	Liberalizing Dinner
Week 14	Preventing Relapse (2)
Week 15	Beginning to Exercise
Week 16	Yoga

Month 5

Week 17	General Exercise Information
Week 18	Finding Inspiration
Week 19	Time Management
Week 20	Mindfulness

Month 6

Week 21	Breathing and Relaxation
Week 22	Exercising to Rewire Your Brain
Week 23	Secondary Benefits of Your Weight Loss
Week 24	Maintenance

Maintenance does not mean staying still. After weight loss, maintenance means setting new goals. These goals may be body related: you may now wish to tone more or change your posture by developing your upper back muscles. Or your goal could be to become fitter, prepare for a marathon, or go rock climbing or kayaking. Alternatively, you may now wish to learn more about healthy cooking, learn and consume healthy gourmet foods without gaining weight. Perhaps your next goal is to master spiritual energy and your mind's power. After years of stress eating and battling weight gain, you have finally reached serenity and peace of mind. So you may wish to explore deeper dimensions of mindfulness, meditation, relaxation, and spirituality. Whichever path you choose, do not stay still. At the end of this planner or once you have reached your weight loss goals, you will find yourself at a stage commonly referred to as the "maintenance phase." Just as in the rest of this book, my approach to maintenance is also based on constant and healthy change. Stagnation is a source of illness, and healthy *change* is a natural part of life. So your journey will not end with this planner. Your journey will take on a different path.

Week 1: Gaining Momentum

Week 1, Day 1

Congratulations on making the commitment to our weight balance program. You have taken a step that will pay enormous benefits in health, happiness, and well-being. Pardon the cliché, but today is indeed the first day of the rest of your life.

Give yourself credit for taking this strong and important first step. You may be anticipating the months ahead with dread—but the reality is, most of our patients have experienced this time of change as rich and invigorating. Expect to enjoy this experience! If you follow the program, you will not only look and feel better physically, you will also regain control of your life.

Buy a notebook or a blank journal and write down your most desired health-related goal today on the very first page. It can be to lose a certain amount of weight. Go back to that page frequently and review your goal.

Week 1, Day 2

When you make an initial commitment to changing your life—no matter how strong—you need to also take practical steps toward achieving this goal. Your priority right now is to organize your schedule, your household, and your family around this new commitment to *optimizing your health*. Keep in mind that to reach your goals, you will have to make changes in your life. For instance, food-related pleasures like cooking and eating—at least as you have been used to them in the past—may have to be put on hold for the foreseeable future. Remind yourself that this is a trade-off: As you will soon see for yourself, your new lifestyle and the rewards that come with it will bring you even greater pleasures. Here are tips to keep in mind:

- Shop smart. Limit the supply of high-calorie foods in your home.
- If others want foods you find tempting, enlist their help in reaching your goal. Store forbidden foods in hard-to-get-to locations; put them in opaque containers. Try to find substitutes that satisfy them but don't tempt you as much.
- If you must prepare food for others, have a warm beverage while cooking or keep a bowl of cut-up fresh veggies nearby to help prevent sampling.
- Minimize kitchen time. Avoid recreational cooking or baking. If you must contribute to a party or bake sale, purchase a type of dessert that you can eat without feeling compromised.
- When serving dinner, keep serving dishes off the table to avoid being tempted to take seconds.
- To facilitate cleanup, bring trash cans to the table when the meal is finished so you don't find yourself nibbling leftovers. Better yet, have someone else take responsibility for cleaning up after meals.

Be totally honest with yourself. What habits of yours—such as picking food off the plates of others or tasting while cooking—contribute to overeating? Be creative in thinking of how to avoid those situations or overcome temptation. Write your thoughts in your journal.

Week 1, Day 3

You have goals in mind. They are the reasons you have committed yourself to following our program for therapeutic lifestyle change.

Now it's time to think about why these goals are so important to you and identify the different factors motivating you to work hard to change your life.

Ask yourself these questions, and write down your answers in your journal so you can refer back to them at those times you need a reminder of how important these changes in your life will be.

1. What are the specific things I hope to accomplish by losing weight and taking charge of my life? (List all that are relevant.)
2. Who am I that these goals are so important to me? (For example, a parent, an aspiring athlete, a person who wants to live a longer life?)
3. What else can I change in my life to reflect the relative importance of these goals? (This is a chance to evaluate whether you need to make a career change, to reevaluate relationships, or to find new interests.)

Week 1, Day 4

To be successful at this weight loss program, you must reprogram yourself to think of food as a source of nutritional sustenance aimed at weight loss—not a reward, not a source of solace or creative outlet or social pleasure or any of those other roles it may have played in your life thus far.

Make a plan to eliminate temptation as fully as possible and write it down in your journal. Use these thoughts to get ideas flowing:

- How to avoid the kitchen unless you are fixing or eating a meal

- How to keep food without displaying it in dishes around the house or in easy reach
- How to change your driving patterns to avoid fast-food outlets and other places you find tempting
- How to socialize and enjoy the company of your friends doing non-food-related activities
- Pleasurable activities to replace snacking: for example, taking a walk, reading the newspaper, enjoying a warm cup of herbal tea
- A list of foods that tempt you (Circle the ones that you should stay away from to reach your weight loss goals.)

Always be mindful of how you feel and what situations set you up for nervous eating or overeating.

Week 1, Day 5

As you work to build a lifestyle where food becomes less important emotionally, think about how you can create new routines and rituals that bring other sources of comfort and pleasure into your life.

Analyze your day and evening routines and identify the times of day you find yourself vulnerable to temptation. Rework your schedule and routine as necessary. This will be a process of trial and error. You may find yourself tweaking new routines as you go. Reevaluate and revise as often as you need, until you find that your life is flowing smoothly, comfortably, and easily.

The goal is to eliminate inappropriate food behaviors and self-sabotage from your life. Then you won't have to rely on willpower to resist overeating and inappropriate eating. Common sense and self-nurturing will ensure that you keep excess weight off for good.

Often, when we are tired or anxious, we resort to eating as a temporary fix. Stay in touch with your feelings at all times. What feelings might you be interpreting as hunger? How are you going to respond to these feelings and emotions other than by eating?

Week 1, Day 6

Today you should take the time to reflect on the last six days. Review your notes, and write down questions and comments. And think of one of your favorite things in life you would like to reward yourself with.

Choose a favored symbolic reward and describe it here. Write a schedule for rewards. Example: quiet time for listening to music or an audio book every day at your chosen time; a massage or a pedicure at the end of each successful week.

Week 1, Day 7

Reward day!

This concept is more important and more relevant than it might seem. One common reason people become overweight and unhealthy is because they have learned to substitute food—which may seem dependable—for other sources of pleasure and satisfaction. *Our system of regular rewards is intended to help you focus on other ways to feel good.*

Every week we will suggest a way to reward yourself for the progress you have made. The specific choice of a reward is always up to you. If you prefer to schedule a massage each week, for instance, go ahead and do so. The point is that you deserve to feel good and take care of every part of yourself. This program is not about deprivation but about learning how to feel good.

Since this week's topic is motivation, we suggest that you buy, find, or make a visible symbol of your commitment to changing your life. Choose an object or symbol that has meaning to you, one that will enhance your environment, one that you will enjoy looking at. Display it in a prominent place, and when your energy for the program begins to flag, spend a few minutes reflecting on why you chose this particular symbol.

Week 2: Finding Your Motivation

Week 2, Day 1

Motivation comes from many different sources. To succeed at this program of therapeutic lifestyle change, it is critical that you understand *why* you are doing this and exactly *what* it is you hope to change about your life.

Each day this week, you will answer a series of questions. A "yes" answer to these questions indicates that this factor is an important motivator for you.

Reflect and list your motivators in your journal. Review them. Remember to use this as a motivator list frequently and you will get there.

Week 2, Day 2

Ask yourself these questions:

- Do I avoid warm-weather vacations and summer activities because of the way my body looks in a bathing suit or shorts?
- Do I dread social gatherings because I feel like I don't look good dressed up?
- When I watch kids play sports, does it trigger nostalgia for the body I used to have?
- Do I miss the way I looked and felt and were able to move when I was younger and/or fitter?

If you answered yes to one or more of these questions, then you are unhappy with your body image. Improving your appearance is an important motivator for you. Though it may seem a cosmetic issue, this may actually represent the more active lifestyle you wish you had and can therefore be used as a motivating force in your effort to lose weight and optimize your health

When you need a push, visualize yourself thin and in shape, fit and strong, wearing the clothing you wish you could wear.

Write in your journal why your body image is important to you and how you wish to change your physique.

Week 2, Day 3

Ask yourself these questions:

- Are there sports—such as kayaking, skiing, or cycling—that I wish I could do but am unable to because I'm out of shape?
- Do I wish I were stronger so I could keep up with my family on walks or bike trips or other activities?
- Do I lack the stamina to enjoy outdoor activities with my friends and family?
- Do I feel out of shape, despite devoting time to fitness?

If you answered yes to one or more of these questions, then you are disappointed at being overweight and out of shape.

Focus on becoming strong and fit. What are you doing to gain strength so you will feel good when you exercise? Depending on your body type and preferences, it may be a good idea to seek advice from an exercise expert about a routine that will work well for you. For motivation, envision yourself doing sports you know you would enjoy. As you lose weight, begin to participate in activities as a reward for your progress and also as a way to help you reach your goal.

Planning to start an active lifestyle is the first step you may be taking— and it is already a big step! Write here a provisional plan to increase your exercise activity level (for example, I plan to walk 20 minutes every day after lunch).

Week 2, Day 4

Do you dread social activities, such as dinner parties and cookouts, because you fear you will overeat? Ask yourself these questions:

- Do special events like holidays trigger my anxiety about gaining weight?
- Do I feel so overwhelmed by everything I'm responsible for that I have lost my sense of focus?
- Am I frustrated by the fact that I work out regularly (or fairly regularly) but still feel more like the "before" picture than the "after" one?

"Yes" answers indicate a fear of being out of control. You feel that you are "lost" in your roles and responsibilities as parent, spouse, worker. A lack of control over your eating and your life may be at the root of your problem.

As I tell my patients, if you are gaining weight, you probably already feel out of control. Quick fixes that just take off weight won't really solve your problem, because they aren't rewarding you in the same way as the sense of achievement you get when you successfully accomplish true lifestyle change.

By committing to our program of therapeutic lifestyle change, you will derive great satisfaction from the knowledge that you have taken charge of your health.

When you feel that you are losing control, take a moment to focus- intensely—on your power to make decisions and to shape your own life. Take satisfaction in the steps you've already taken. Look forward to a greater sense of control and enjoyment of your ability to impact your own health and well-being.

Try to remember a time when you felt like you were going to lose it and you were able to regain your sense of control. Describe it in your journal for future use.

Week 2, Day 5

Ask yourself these questions:

- Do I wonder why I don't have enough stamina to get through the day?
- Am I worried about a medical condition that I have or am at risk for, such as heart disease or diabetes?
- Is sex and performance anxiety on my mind much of the time?
- Are big events, like graduations and weddings, an uncomfortable reminder of my own mortality?

If you answered yes to any of these questions, you have deep concerns about your health. You feel a lack of energy and focus in your life. This is sometimes linked to other health issues; midlife hormonal shifts and depression are two common causes.

Instead of stressing over activities that don't work for you, consider alternative routines that increase energy while helping you to get fit-such as yoga, which we often use at our center as a way to ease into fitness.

A key motivating factor is that you are finally taking strong, meaningful steps toward addressing your health issues. You will feel better and in more control now that you are committed to making yourself as healthy as you can be.

Write a list of self-care activities, such as fitness training or yoga, and health-related services, such as a bone density or a coronary scan or a massage, that you wish to have done in the upcoming weeks. Be creative and imaginative.

Week 2, Day 6

Ask yourself these questions:

- Does it seem like I'm the only one around who isn't enjoying life?
- When I'm around people who are happy, am I more acutely aware of my own unhappiness?
- When everyone around me seems enthusiastic, festive, and celebratory, do I wonder where my self-confidence and joy have gone?
- At romantic times and special events, do I wonder what's up with my own sex life (or lack thereof)?

If you answered yes to these questions, depression is an issue for you. You are worried about your unhappiness. The phrase I often hear from patients is, "I don't feel like myself anymore."

You can use this feeling as a motivator for change. If you aren't happy, something isn't working in your life. It may be that you are not meeting your health goals, or it could be related to your job or an important relationship. But it is important to put time and thought into evaluating the obstacles to personal happiness in your life *or your weight loss efforts will fail.*

It is important that you focus on your feelings and learn to recognize what makes you feel good and what makes you feel bad. Taking control of your physical health is a step toward improving your emotional health. Committing yourself to doing what it takes to feel better in every way will help you stay motivated.

Week 2, Day 7

Today, reward yourself by taking the time to indulge—really setting aside time for it—in something you enjoy that neither costs money nor has calories. Look back at the questions you answered on the first day of this week, and focus on what your most important personal motivating factors are. Then choose a reward accordingly.

Whether your reward means that you take a few minutes to sit quietly and enjoy the company of a grandchild (a good choice for someone motivated by concerns about his or her own poor health), read for an hour in the middle of the day (perfect if you have been feeling frustrated by your loss of mental focus), or take a walk in the afternoon (good for someone who wants to become strong and fit), do it.

Really, truly, do that thing that will make you feel good and happy.

Focus on how it feels to do what you want to do—the sensory delights, the pleasure you experience. Think about why you don't do this more often. Is it an issue of time? Of feeling that you need to get other things done first? Do you question whether you *deserve* to indulge yourself in this way?

Identifying the obstacles—and the benefits—is important. Everyone has responsibilities, but everyone also deserves to have a life that feels good and is enjoyable!

What stops you from moving forward? Name one obstacle, mental (such as being fearful of failing) or physical (such as pain and aches) or environmental (such as a demanding schedule), and write next to it a brief plan for solving that problem. Then write a realistic reward value you assign to the solution—if accomplished. Use this approach for all challenges you face.

Obstacle	Solution	Reward Value Examples
Fear of failing again	Plan day by day	Reward good days
Spouse loves desserts	Antitemptation strategy	Reward each time
12-hour workdays	Learn active relaxation	Feel great!

Week 3: The Foods You Eat

Week 3, Day 1

This is your third week. You have completed fourteen days of the program. How is it going? How are you feeling? Energetic? Tired? In control? Or frustrated?

Focus on how these changes are affecting your days in terms of mood, energy, and hunger. Consider how your relationships with family and friends are impacted by your changing relationship with food. Think about how these variables are shifting and changing.

But try not to overanalyze or overevaluate yourself. Paying too much attention to details, focusing on every shift in mood, berating yourself for every small transgression—such practices are both discouraging and self-defeating. As soon as you realize you have lapsed, acknowledge it—and move on. What is important is that you are taking responsibility for changing your life, one step and one day at a time.

Write in your journal your feelings and your thoughts about how you have progressed in the program up to this point.

Week 3, Day 2

Planning is the most critical element in a successful weight loss lifestyle. The best way to approach food shopping is to make a list in advance. A few minutes of preplanning is efficient, economical, and effective in helping you to meet your weight loss goals.

Think about the twenty-one meals you eat each week and the foods you like best, find easiest to prepare, and are most satisfying to you. Keep plenty on hand.

A good strategy for shopping is to type up a master computer list and circle items you need to replenish before you shop.

Consider carefully whether clipping coupons is really in your best interest. Many money-saving offers are for high-calorie, low-nutrient items.

A smart shopping strategy is to buy as much of your food as possible from the perimeter of the supermarket, where you will find the least processed foods, including fruits, vegetables, meats, and dairy products.

Review in your journal the foods you eat now for breakfast, lunch, and dinner.

Most people do not shop for food every day. In your journal, make a master shopping list of foods you must have at home or at work so as not to resort to unplanned and erratic eating; then copy this list to a separate sheet that you take with you. Revise this shopping list to reflect your new habits as you advance through the program. Each time you add or remove an item, ask yourself, Why am I making this change?

Week 3, Day 3

Examples of foods to keep in the house:

- Frozen meat and poultry
- Canned tuna in water
- Preportioned frozen fish steaks
- Low-fat cold cuts
- Soy foods
- Canned broth
- Bouillion cubes
- Precooked frozen shrimp
- A selection of herbal teas, diet sodas
- Artificial sweeteners
- Frozen fruits and vegetables
- Diet gelatin, low-fat popcorn
- Nuts and seeds
- Fresh vegetables
- Fresh fruit

You just reviewed food items you should have available at home. To make room for these items, you have to clean up your kitchen and throw away items that you will no longer eat. Here all the kinds of items you need to get rid of:

- Junk foods, such as candy and cookies
- Soda and other sweet drinks
- Baked goods such as muffins and sweet rolls or cakes
- Potatoes, corn, beets, and other starchy veggies
- Breads, crackers, chips, pretzels, and other high-carb snacks
- Calorie-dense items such as sausages, hard cheeses, and high-fat meats

What should you do if you have children and other family members at home who are not dieting and want these food items? Make a plan for getting their support and/or keeping their treats boxed up or out of sight.

Week 3, Day 4

There are four "macronutrients" in our foods: carbohydrate, protein, fat, and alcohol. Calories are a measure of energy. Energy is both taken in (as food) and used as calories. All food calories provide the same amount of energy. In that sense, "a calorie is a calorie." But foods have to broken down, digested, and used as energy or stored in our body in the form of glycogen, protein, or fat. Up to 30 percent of calories from protein are wasted during digestion. Approximately 10 percent of calories from carbohydrates and only 5 percent of calories from fat are wasted. Therefore, fats and carbohydrates are more efficient fuels for energy storage. Whereas 1 gram of protein or carbohydrate yields 4 calories each, 1 gram of alcohol yields 7 calories, and 1 gram of fat provides 9 calories. So keep in mind that fats are very calorie-dense foods, and while carbohydrates provide the same number of calories as protein, they are more "fattening."

One way to categorize foods is to use the exchange list. Foods on this list are grouped together based on their macronutrient content. Therefore, foods in each category may be "exchanged" as alternatives. According to the exchange list, foods are divided into meats, fats, and carbohydrates. Carbohydrates include starches, fruits, nonstarchy vegetables, and milk. Fats include nuts, oils, and animal fat, such as butter. Meats are divided into very lean, lean, medium, and high-fat categories.

This list is available at the American Diabetes Association and the American Dietetic Association websites. You do not have to use exchange lists to categorize food items. But this list is used by many nutritionists and is a useful tool for your education and for a quick estimate of daily food intake. Foods in the same exchange category are alike, such as meats, vegetables, and fruits. But some foods, such as dairy products, may belong to different categories, depending on their fat content.

Understanding food items and the categories they belong to is just one key to sound eating habits. You need to be informed in other ways as well. See which of the following statements apply to you. Then educate yourself here, in the other chapters of the book, or ask a nutritionist.

- I am confused about the very basics of nutrition. For example, I do not know what a protein is. Where can I find some reading material to educate myself?
- I am not sure I understand food categories. How can I learn more about it?
- I do not want to weigh foods. Is there a way I can diet without weighing?
- I do not know how to read food labels. How can I educate myself?
- I understand that portion control is important. How do I know what the right portion size is?
- I know that the timing and number of meals and snacks is important. How can I learn more about meal planning?
- I have never cooked a meal in my life. Where should I start?

Week 3, Day 5

Nutrition labels provide useful information but may be confusing. If you use them often, you will avoid large caloric intakes and you will also make more intelligent choices. Here are some key pointers about labels:

- First understand what a serving size is. There is often more than one serving size in prepared food items. Calories per serving corresponds to the calories in the defined serving size, such as a certain number of pieces, ounces, cups, or glasses. Be careful with the serving size listed; it is often arbitrary, and you may consume more than the indicated serving size.
- Look at the grams of carbohydrate in the serving size. Usually, if a food item provides 15 grams or more of carbohydrates per serving, it is categorized as a "carb." More important, you should pay attention to the amount of sugar in the serving size. Sugar is of course a carbohydrate. But because it is absorbed fast, the more sugar in the serving size, the faster and higher blood glucose levels rise. This is not good for dieters and it is even more harmful to people with metabolic syndrome and/or diabetes. Finally, when people follow a diet plan restricting carbohydrate intake, they can use labels to count the grams of carbs and the calories from carbs in their diet. Some labels specify the amount of "net carbohydrates." By doing so, they are taking nondigestible or poorly digestible fibers out of the calculation to make the item look like a "low-carb" item. While it is true that some carbohydrates are not easily digested, the critical indicators are total calories from carbohydrates and the number of grams of total carbohydrates and in particular sugar.
- Now look at the grams of fat. Fat is rich in calories, so a high-fat item is high in calories, regardless of the nature of fat in it. Almonds, for example, have healthy fat and are very satisfying as a snack. However, you can certainly get fat eating almonds all day! In a food label, you also want to know how many of the fat calories are bad fats such as hydrogenated or saturated fats. You also want to know the number of milligrams of cholesterol in the item. In a low-calorie diet that provides 1,200 calories a day, the total fat intake is usually no more than 400 calories (corresponding to 30 percent of total calories), or roughly

45 grams of fat. By paying attention to the fat content in food items, you avoid eating too much fat and therefore exceeding your caloric allowance.

- Finally, look at the protein content per serving size. In most weight loss diets, there are no upper limits for daily protein intake. In our meal plan, we recommend six meals and snacks, each providing 15 to 30 grams of protein. According to the exchange list, each meat exchange provides 7 grams of protein, and this corresponds to 1 ounce of lean meat. So in our meal plan, a snack should contain 15 grams of protein or more. This could be 2 ounces of deli meat (with veggies, for example) or a prepared food item such as a soy patty or beef jerky. It could also be a combination of almonds and cottage cheese (see our meal plan).

Week 3, Day 6

Are carbohydrates bad?

Carbohydrates include starches, sugars, and fibers. Carbohydrates give us energy, and if we eat too much of them, we store energy as glycogen and fat. Hunters, gatherers, and Eskimos live quite well on a very low carbohydrate diet. Therefore, to cut down your total daily caloric intake, carbohydrates can be safely reduced. On the other hand, diets that are very low in fat and protein intake are not healthy. In other words, eating fewer carbs is the easiest and perhaps the safest way to diet. Some foods that are rich in carbohydrates are healthier than others. Fresh vegetables, fruits, and grains are considered "carbs" but are certainly much better for your health than refined sugars and starches or junk foods such as candy or soda.

Starches are molecules that are made of sugars linked together. They are not sweet. Foods like potatoes, grains, and legumes contain most of their calories as carbohydrate in starch form. When these foods are consumed in their "whole" (unprocessed) form, they also provide many other valuable nutrients, like fiber, vitamins, minerals, and some protein. When starch-containing foods are refined and adulterated with sugar and fat, they become sources of "empty calories."

Sugars come in many chemical forms, some sweeter than others. For example, lactose (milk sugar) is not sweet at all, but fructose (fruit sugar) is very sweet. Table sugar is called *sucrose*. In food processing, "high-fructose corn syrup" is often used to provide sweetness and texture. Sugar is rapidly absorbed into the bloodstream. Some people believe they feel a sugar "high," while others feel sick. Blood sugar levels are controlled by insulin, the main pancreatic hormone that regulates glucose metabolism. There is some evidence that when blood glucose and insulin levels drop quickly, our appetite center gets turned on and we crave more sugar. Therefore, in addition to providing "empty calories," fast-absorbing sugars also stimulate appetite and cause overeating.

Fibers are carbohydrates that are not broken down for energy. They provide no calories and do not affect blood sugar levels. Some fibers, like wheat bran, are beneficial to the digestive tract. Others, like oat bran, improve the cholesterol profile. Whole grains, including brown rice, whole wheat, and kernels of corn, provide a lot of fiber. Refined grains, such as white rice, white flour, and refined corn meal, have had the fiber removed. Refined grains are digested faster than whole grains and therefore raise the blood sugar faster and higher.

In summary: The best recommendation is to consume lots of vegetables and fruits, eat a few servings daily of "complex" carbohydrates, and consume as little refined carbohydrates as is tolerable.

Week 3, Day 7

To lose weight, you have to limit your carbohydrate intake. To know which foods are considered high carb in your current diet, circle the number next to the item(s) and think of an alternative.

1. Orange, grapefruit, and other citrus fruits or juices
2. Melons, pineapple, pears, peaches, and bananas
3. Dried fruits, such as dates, figs, and raisins
4. Grapes, grape juice, or other fruit cocktails or drinks
5. Strawberries and cherries

6. Corn, potatoes, yams, carrots, beets, or other root vegetables

7. Crackers and snacks, such as pretzels, rice cakes, chips, matzoh

8. Beans, lentils, and peas

9. Starchy foods prepared with fat, such as French fried potatoes, mashed potatoes, corn bread, croutons, muffins, taco shells, pizza crust, or different pasta or rice dishes

10. Baked goods such as breads, bagels, cakes, muffins, and scones

These foods have different amounts of total carbohydrate and sugar content. In addition, they contain various amounts of fat and protein per serving. Those items that are denser have more fat and sugar and therefore have higher calories per serving. For example, one scone may have up to three times the calories that a muffin has.

Many of us love carbohydrate-rich foods because they are comforting and satisfying. The emotional value of a food item is often not discussed in nutrition writings or even in most diet books. By reducing your carbohydrate intake, you are naturally taking away some of your favorite foods. Instead of depriving yourself of this kind of emotional release, plan a reward system to replace a potential (but temporary) void in your life. This week's reward should focus on satisfying your appetite for life.

Would you describe yourself as a person who loves adventure? Then go have one. Do something you have always wanted to do but have never actually tried.

Are you a person who derives your greatest satisfaction from relationships? Then schedule time with someone you love, but with whom you don't spend enough relaxed time.

Is time alone what makes you feel whole and happy? Then head out on your own for a few hours—or send everyone else in the house out, and enjoy the time at home.

Your reward for this week might be to take a class in kayaking or a long walk with a good friend or to spend an hour at a gallery or to take a hike. But find something that makes you feel lighthearted to do, and then do it—and enjoy it!

Week 4: Learning About
Food Categories and Alternatives

Week 4, Day 1

When you are following a meal plan, you are essentially guided and told what to do. However, at some point you have to make food-related decisions by yourself. These decisions go beyond meal planning, calories, and macronutrients. So how are you going to safely navigate your eating choices and plans through the maze created by the food and nutrition industries? There are many ways to eat healthy. People count fat grams, calories, and carbohydrates. Portion sizes and timing of eating are also important. Practical and healthy recipes come in handy. The best way to start is to take small steps. Elsewhere in this book you were given a meal plan to follow. That meal plan provides you with a 1,200- to 1,400-calorie intake. Since most of the foods in the meal plan are lean protein sources and vegetables, you can alternate the same food types for variety. If you have access to a nutritionist, you may wish to run your choices and your changes by her or him.

In planning a low-calorie menu, your nutritionist will calculate your total caloric intake while making sure you get enough protein, good fats, vitamins, minerals, and fluids. Then he or she will figure out the appropriate number of servings from each exchange list or other similar food categories, with consideration given to your personal preferences. There is often room for flexibility.

If someone does not like dairy products, for example, that group may be eliminated, and provisions for adequate calcium and protein will be made from other groups.

Using the exchange list system eliminates the need to count up separate nutrients and makes planning easier. As discussed previously, there are three main categories of foods: carbohydrates (vegetable, fruit, milk, starch), meats, and fats. Foods are in the same group if they have similar nutrient value. Portion sizes are also important; when attended to, there is no longer a need to count calories or the number of grams of carbohydrates, protein, and fat in each item.

Generally, there is no limit to consumption of items on the vegetable list. During meal planning for weight loss, foods in the starch category are usually avoided. It is important to provide feedback to your coach at each session so that your meal plan works well for you. Meat portions are similar when comparing different types of lean meats, such as chicken, turkey, or lean beef. The same is true with meats that have higher fat content. Naturally, you can eat more lean meat than fatty meat for the same calories. This is one reason we prefer lean meats. People who like eating fatty meats can actually gain weight while following a low-carbohydrate diet.

The next step is to use the meal plan provided to you to assign alternatives for each food. For example, breakfast might include one serving from the milk list, one serving from the fruit list, and one serving from the meat list. You can use the exchange list or the table on pages 208–209 to choose different foods with similar calories and protein content. Some people like to vary their meal pattern daily, but the easiest way is to keep the pattern the same for a few weeks at a time. Eventually, "mixing and matching" becomes easy.

Week 4, Day 2

Study the tables on pages 208–209. Note that the macronutrient that provides the greatest number of calories per serving usually defines the category each food item belongs to.

Do not feel discouraged if at first you are confused about food categories. With practice, you will find it easy and practical in most situations.

Week 4, Day 3

Before we look at two food groups, vegetables and fruits, let us do an exercise with food categories.

From yesterday's food category list, make up the following breakfast:

- A food item with 15 grams of protein (example: 2 ounces of meat or meat equivalent of your choice)
- A milk of your choice (example: 1 cup of 1 percent milk)
- A fruit of your choice (see page 210 for serving sizes)

Food Categories Based on the Exchange List

Food Item or Group	Category	Approximate Calories/ Serving Size	Protein Content (Grams)	Carbohydrate Content (Grams)	Fat Content (Grams)
Milk (low fat 1% or less)	Carb	90/cup	8	12	0–3
Milk (med. fat 2%)	Carb or fat	120/cup	8	12	5
Milk (whole)	Fat	150/cup	8	12	8

Serving size for milk is usually 1 cup. Low-fat yogurt serving size is 6 ounces. Cheeses belong to fat or protein categories.

Food Item or Group	Category	Approximate Calories/ Serving Size	Protein Content (Grams)	Carbohydrate Content (Grams)	Fat Content (Grams)
Fruit	Carb	60 to 100	0	15 to 20	0

Serving size for fruits are described elsewhere in the book.

Food Item or Group	Category	Approximate Calories/ Serving Size	Protein Content (Grams)	Carbohydrate Content (Grams)	Fat Content (Grams)
Veggies	Carb	25	2 or less	5	0

Serving size for nonstarchy veggies is usually 1/2 cup cooked, 1 cup raw. Most low-carb high-protein meal plans do not limit the amount of nonstarchy veggies.

Food Categories Based on the Exchange List, *continued*

Food Item or Group (Grams)	Category	Approximate Calories/ Serving Size	Protein Content (Grams)	Carbohydrate Content (Grams)	Fat Content (Grams)
Starch	Carb	80 to 100	Less than 5	15 to 20	Less than 5
Only cereals, grains, and beans are allowed in most low-carbohydrate diets. If necessary, $1/2$ yam, $1/2$ baked potato, rice, or beans may be added to your meal plan. A serving for rice or baked beans is $1/2$ cup. One serving size of beans is also one serving of lean meat because beans contain protein.					
Very lean to lean meat	Protein	35 to 55/ounce	7/ounce	0	3 or less/ounce
Medium-fat meat	Protein	75/ ounce	7/ounce	0	5/ounce
High-fat meat	Fat or protein	100/ounce	7/ounce	0	8/ounce
Most poultry, fish, seafood, low-fat cheeses, and egg whites belong to the first category. Serving size for egg whites is two. Most lean steaks, ham, and fatty fish, such as salmon or tuna, belong to the lean meat category. The medium-fat category includes whole egg, most soft cheeses, beef, pork, and lamb, as well as dark chicken meat. Ribs, chops, sausage, and hot dogs and hard or dry cheeses, such as American or Swiss, belong to the high-fat meat category, and their intake should be limited.					
Oils and nuts	Fat	45/teaspoon or 6 to 10 nuts	0	0	5

Once you have chosen the food items, add the total amount of protein, carbohydrate, fat, and calories in your breakfast.

The fruit list includes all fruits—fresh, canned, frozen, dried, and juiced. Whenever you can, try to eat the real fruit as opposed to juice or canned fruit. Real fruit has more nutritional value, is more filling, but often has the same number of calories per serving. A "fruit" portion provides 60 calories (15 grams of carbohydrate). Fruit portions differ depending on the caloric density of the item. Generally, a fruit serving size is one small fruit (4 ounces), $1/2$ cup of juice, or $1/4$ cup of dried fruit, such as dried apricot or peach. Just like other foods, the density of each fruit item makes a difference as to how much a serving size is. Watermelon, for example, has a lot of water in it, effectively spreading out the calories in a larger volume. A serving of watermelon is $1^1/4$ cup of cubes. Raisins have their calories compacted into a very small volume because the fruit is dry. A serving of raisins is 2 tablespoons, very small.

Fruits	**Serving Size According to Exchange List**
Apples, pears, peaches, bananas	1 small or $1/2$ large (4 ounces)
Oranges, grapefruit, tangerines	1 orange or $1/2$ large grapefruit or 2 tangerines
Blueberries and other fresh berries	$3/4$ cup
Cherries, grapes	3 ounces: roughly 12 cherries or 17 grapes
Cantaloupes, melons, watermelon	10 to 13 ounces or 1 to $1^1/4$ cups of cubes
Canned fruit	$3/4$ cup
Unsweetened fruit juices	Usually $1/3$ to $1/2$ cup

Week 4, Day 4

When referring to vegetables, or veggies, we often mean green leafy vegetables, such as celery, lettuce, or asparagus. We also think of colorful vegetables such as bell pepper, eggplant, and broccoli. Veggies are good for you and are not usually limited in most weight loss diets because they are not rich in calories but provide lots of healthy nutrients, such as vitamins and fiber. However, this category also includes root vegetables, such as carrots and beets, and starchy vegetables, such as potato and corn. In low-calorie or low-carbohydrate diets, starchy and root vegetables are not allowed or are limited to one meal per day. Each serving of starchy vegetables contains 80 calories and 15 grams of carbohydrate. Each portion of nonstarchy vegetables is approximately 25 calories and 5 grams of carbohydrate. A "portion" of nonstarchy vegetables is defined as 1 cup raw, $^1/_2$ cup cooked, or $1^1/_2$ cups of salad leaves. Because vegetables are so low in calorie and provide valuable nutrients and bulk to the diet, we do not ask you to religiously measure vegetable portions. The more the better. Try to eat at least five servings of different veggies daily. Even if you have to be on a very low calorie diet (800 to 1,000 calories), you should still be able to eat lots of healthy vegetables.

Sometimes people do not know what starchy vegetables are. Review this list, and try to remember the serving sizes.

Starchy Vegetables	Serving Size (80 Calories)
Potatoes/yams	$^1/_2$ baked or $^1/_2$ cup
Beans	$^1/_3$ cup
Peas	$^1/_2$ cup
Corn; corn on the cob	$^1/_2$ cup; 1 small or $^1/_2$ large
Squash	$^1/_2$ cup
Peas and lentils	$^1/_2$ cup

Because starchy veggies are plant parts (usually roots) that store energy for the plant or its seeds in the form of concentrated sugar, they are calorie rich and should be limited. We also recommend that you cut back your consumption of starchy vegetables because they raise blood sugar levels. For this reason, people with diabetes or metabolic syndrome should avoid or limit root starches such as carrots, potatoes, and beets even if they are not following a weight loss diet. If you really like to eat some of these vegetables as a side dish, then pay attention to portion sizes and do not add butter, cream, or lots of oil. In general, steamed, baked, or boiled vegetables have fewer calories per serving size than sautéed or grilled veggies.

Week 4, Day 5

Starchy foods include starchy vegetables but usually refer to starches that are cooked or processed. This list contains the most diverse range of foods, including breads, crackers, cereals, pasta, snacks, starchy vegetables, and grains. Because most of these foods are solid and dense foods and often have added oil and sugar, they are very rich in calories and are usually completely eliminated from low-calorie diets. Since foods such as cakes, cookies, and noodles are not rich in healthy nutrients, by eliminating or limiting them in your diet, you are not missing much other than unwanted calories. It is best to consume little if any foods from this list while you are trying to lose weight or if you have diabetes. If you cannot cut these items out of your diet, then at least monitor their intake accurately because calories quickly add up. If such food items are "trigger" foods for you, which tend to cause you to overeat, it is best to avoid them entirely until you feel more confident about controlling the portions.

Starchy foods that you should eliminate from your diet include chips, cookies, crackers, scones, muffins, waffles, pancakes, French fries, cakes, doughnuts, and most refined, white, or processed bread products. Pasta, rice, and potatoes are either completely eliminated or limited to one serving size per day (usually as a side dish with lunch or dinner).

In your journal, note these categories and answer them honestly.

Starchy foods I still eat: *Amount I eat:*

Week 4, Day 6

The food group for today is milk.

The milk list is subdivided into three sections, based on the fat content of the milk product. The fat-free/low-fat list provides 90 calories per serving (12 grams of carbohydrate, 8 grams of protein, 0 to 3 grams of fat). The reduced-fat list provides 120 calories per serving (12 grams of carbohydrate, 8 grams of protein, 8 grams of fat). The whole-fat list provides 150 calories (12 grams of carbohydrate, 8 grams of protein, 8 grams of fat).

It is preferable to use the fat-free/low-fat list whenever possible. Foods and beverages in the milk category provide dietary calcium. To meet dietary calcium needs, you need to consume three or four servings daily. Most people do not wish to consume so many portions of high-calorie dairy products, and therefore need to take calcium supplements. Here are some milk and calcium facts:

- Soy milk does not contain calcium unless it is fortified. (A food is *fortified* if nutrients are put into it that do not naturally occur in the item. A food is *enriched* if nutrients that normally exist in the item, but which were removed during processing, are put back after processing.)
- Cottage cheese does not contain significant calcium either unless it is enriched. It is categorized with meats rather than milk.
- Most cheeses are not on the milk list but on the meat or fat list because their macronutrient profile is more in line with protein- or fat-containing foods.
- Foods on the milk list are rich in calcium and typically provide one-third the daily calcium requirement.
- A calcium supplement that is well absorbed is calcium citrate, preferably with vitamin D.

Write down all the dairy products you like to eat—and review them with your nutritionist. Some foods may appear rich in calcium, but it is not as easily absorbed in some foods as in others. Other foods, while dairy products, may be very rich in carbohydrates or fat.

Week 4, Day 7

There are four sublists within the meat and meat substitutes food group. The lists vary in fat content. Poultry, beef, and pork may belong to different categories, depending on the amount of fat in particular parts.

The very lean meat and meat substitutes list contains items with 7 grams of protein, 0 grams of carbohydrate, 0 to 1 gram of fat, and 35 calories per gram. Poultry, fish, most shellfish, low-fat cottage cheese, and egg whites are in this group.

The lean meat and meat substitutes list contains items with 7 grams of protein, 0 grams of carbohydrate, 2 to 3 grams of fat, and 55 calories per gram. Beef, pork, some poultry, lamb, veal, cottage cheese, and fatty fish are in this group.

The medium-fat meat and meat substitutes list contains items with 7 grams of protein, 0 grams of carbohydrate, about 5 grams of fat, and 75 calories per gram.

The high-fat meat and meat substitutes list contains items with 7 grams of protein, 0 grams of carbohydrate, about 8 grams of fat, and 100 calories per gram. Pork ribs, sausage, hot dogs, and all hard and regular cheeses are in this group.

The difference in calories between sublists is significant and is due entirely to the calories from fat, since protein and carbohydrate content is the same. It is best to restrict most meat and meat substitute choices to those from the first two sublists to keep calories and fat lowest.

The last food group is fats. One serving from this list provides 45 calories (5 grams of fat). Serving sizes are very small, since fat provides the most concentrated source of calories in our diet. Fat imparts flavor and texture to our food. It is important to consume some fat daily to prevent boredom and a sense of deprivation. The healthiest choices from this list are those with fat that is monounsaturated or polyunsaturated.

Here is a list of "good" fats: avocado, olive and canola oil, olives, nuts, peanut butter, sesame seeds, tahini, and seeds.

"Bad" fats include bacon, butter, coconut milk, cream or cream cheese, sour cream, and shortening, or lard.

Week 5: Your Body Composition

Week 5, Day 1

Many people are confused by the concept of body type—in terms of what it means to them as individuals and how it affects their metabolism. For example, terms like *endomorph* and *ectomorph*, *apple-shaped* and *pear-shaped*, and *strong-boned* and *petite* are descriptive. We are all born with a predisposition to a particular body type. It is important to realize that our body type changes throughout life. For women, three critical times when the body undergoes change are puberty, pregnancy, and menopause. For men, there may be some fat gain around puberty, but the male body type tends to be more stable.

What does this mean to you? Your body type and hormones definitely affect your metabolism, which means that two people with very different body types may need to eat and exercise differently in order to reach their goals. For instance, a woman who has excessive deep abdominal fat (an apple-shaped woman) may lose weight more easily because her "burn rate" is higher. In contrast, a woman who carries fat in the lower body typically has a lower burn rate and may find it more difficult to lose weight. A successful weight loss program needs to take into account your body type and its implications. Most overweight men are apple-shaped and have excess abdominal fat. They may or may not have adequate burn rate. Measuring burn rate and body composition is a good way to profile individuals. Those with a lower than expected burn rate have to follow a more aggressive weight loss program.

Review the text of the book, and in your journal, summarize your body composition and burn rate test results (or estimates) and review them with your doctor at your next visit. How can you change your body composition? Do you understand the difference between lean mass and fat mass and their impact on your burn rate? Write down your answer and have it reviewed by your doctor.

Week 5, Day 2

The term *body composition* refers specifically to your unique measurements of body fat mass, lean mass (muscle), and bone density. While there are many ways to "measure" body composition, only x-ray techniques (such as DXA and CT scan) can determine specifically where and how much lean mass versus fat an individual has in his or her body.

This matters not only as an indicator of your metabolism, but also in ascertaining what kind of exercise program will work best for you. For example, an overweight person with very little lean mass in the upper body but strong legs may benefit from resistance training and lean mass development in the arms and torso. Walking and other lower body exercises, such as aerobics, may not have much impact on metabolism because they may not build additional lean mass and may not burn a lot of calories.

Based on your body composition and physique, design a test exercise program for yourself and ask your trainer or your doctor to check its effectiveness. Write a diverse list of routines to avoid boredom and injury.

Week 5, Day 3

What are the implications of your body type and body composition? Here are some facts to keep in mind:

- Merely continuing the same sort of exercise you did in your twenties may not help you reach your goals later in life, when your body type and your metabolism may require a different program.
- In our experience, women who are apple-shaped and under stress (whether it be physiological or psychological) tend to gain visceral fat but have a higher burn rate. These women would benefit more from a fat-burning program, which would include a low-calorie diet and whole-body exercise routines, such as interval training (there is more information to come on this subject later in the program).
- Women who are pear-shaped tend to carry more fat on their hips and have slower metabolisms; tend toward depression as opposed to anxiety; and have a harder time losing weight.

These women benefit from a program that would increase their burn rate with a high-protein diet and resistance training to build more lean mass.

- Most women have a tendency to be pear-shaped earlier in their lives and to increase their abdominal girth in their perimenopausal years because of an imbalance of estrogen, testosterone, and other related hormones. In our experience, women who are overweight have to pay attention to the specifics of their body composition and metabolism and its implications. No single solution fits all.

For women: A "pear" has a waist-to-hip ratio less than 0.85, and an "apple" has a waist-to-hip ratio higher than 0.85. Even though this measurement is not perfect, it is a good marker of hormonal balance in women.

For men, it is a lot simpler. If waist-to-hip ratio is higher than 1, then the risk of metabolic syndrome increases significantly.

Using a cloth tape measure, measure your waist at your belly button and then your hips. Divide your waist measurement (for example, 43 inches) by your hip measurement (for example, 47 inches). This is your waist-to-hip ratio. Write it down.

Week 5, Day 4

What does it mean to tailor an eating program to your body type? Here are some tips:

- *Be preventive, prepare for change.* If you are approaching menopause, you need to understand that your eating habits should change. If you are postmenopausal, your eating habits should again be changed to recognize your metabolic changes.
- *Gender affects the way you metabolize foods.* Men who do a lot of resistance training and do not change their diet tend to "buff up" without impacting their body composition; they continue to put on fat and lean mass and just get bigger.

Young men who are overweight have an easier time losing weight because they have higher lean mass and a higher burn rate. The key is learning to understand the source of excess calories, such as alcohol, portion control, and junk food.

Middle-aged men who are overweight tend to have excess visceral fat and inadequate lean mass as a result of a sedentary lifestyle. These men benefit from a high-protein, low-calorie diet for weight loss.

Elderly men (over sixty-five) who are overweight may have other medical conditions, such as heart disease or kidney failure. A low-calorie, balanced diet or at times even a low-fat or vegetarian diet may be indicated. Ask your doctor about these concerns.

For women the situation is more complex: Young "pears," or young women who are overweight, often have a sluggish metabolism. Unless they are very athletic, they have excess body fat and not enough muscle mass. They need to cut calories and increase protein intake.

Young "apples," or premenopausal women with excess visceral fat, should cut calories and in particular avoid stress-related eating, because this body type appears to be more prone to fat buildup related to stress hormones such as cortisol.

All women tend to become "apple-ish" in their perimenopausal years. Relative estrogen deficiency promotes a less feminine body shape, meaning you begin to lose your curves. Therefore, all perimenopausal women should avoid excessive caloric intake and chronic stress.

Week 5, Day 5

Later in the program, you will learn specific exercise routines designed for you. We typically do not ask people to start exercising in the first two months of the program, unless they are already physically active, for the following reasons:

- Most people who are overweight and sedentary are "deconditioned" and would benefit more from shedding some 10 to 15 percent of their body weight first, which will reduce the risk of injury and facilitate conditioning.

- Starting a strict dietary program can be stressful in its own right, and adding exercise to that might lead to frustration and a sense of being overwhelmed.
- Dehydration is a concern when someone is on a strict diet and in fact may be a complication of any exercise program, even a moderate one.

However, mild exercise activity, such as walking, stretching, and breathing techniques, are useful and are recommended as a preparatory step to committing yourself to fitness training.

Write a list of exercise activities you like, and mention where and how you plan to do them.

Week 5, Day 6

Your body type and your body composition measurements are useful in designing exercise routines for weight loss. However, any exercise you end up doing should be safe and enjoyable.

If your body composition shows that you have good lean mass (you are strong overall), then exercise routines should focus on fat-burning programs, including interval training and aerobics. (We will provide more specific information on this later in the program.)

If your body composition shows that you have good lower body lean mass (strong legs), then walking on the treadmill, for example, may not be as effective for burning calories. You require upper body lean mass development by resistance training (which you will learn later on), in addition to a fat-burning program such as interval training.

If your body composition shows that you have good upper body lean mass and excess fat (you are "top heavy"), our experience indicates that cardiovascular exercise routines, such as nonimpact aerobics or distance walking or jogging, is most appropriate.

If your body composition shows that you have very little lean mass at all, then whole-body weight training is the way to go. Emphasis should be put on large muscles, such as upper leg and core muscles, as opposed to smaller muscles such as the arms. (More on this later.)

In addition to all of these, exercise routines must take into account your specific preexisting conditions, such as history of injury, flexibility, back pain, and cardiovascular risks. As we get to know you better in the program, we will be able to carefully address these issues. We may recommend yoga, for example, as a way to prepare you for fitness.

Have you figured out how to change your physique yet? Now that you know so much about yourself, what exercise routines would you do? Write it down and have it reviewed by your trainer and your doctor.

Week 5, Day 7

We are all physical beings. In our experience at the center, we have found that many people who use food in place of other pleasures have become disconnected from their bodies: Eating becomes the primary source of sensory satisfaction.

So this week, reward yourself by choosing a very physical pleasure, one that makes your body feel cherished and cared for.

Spend an hour in a hot bath, or take a ridiculously long shower. If you have the means, schedule a massage or a facial. Take a yoga class.

Whatever it is, find and do something that celebrates you as a physical being.

And while you are doing this, be mindful of how you feel. Experience what you are doing as deeply as you possibly can, and figure out how these sorts of feelings and experiences might be incorporated into your life on a more regular basis.

Week 6: Making Progress

Week 6, Day 1

By now, it is certainly clear that what you are taking on—nothing short of changing your life—is a monumental task. Some days will be better than others. In this, as in all aspects of your life, you can expect to have ups and downs.

Remember to savor the journey. What you learn about yourself as you work toward your goal will be important in staying healthy in the future.

Week 6, Day 2

While you should always carry an awareness of your long-term goals, it is optimal at this stage to focus on the immediate short-term goal you have set for yourself: getting through this one day without slipping, or losing 1 or 2 pounds this week, or whatever it is that you have been working for over the next several days.

Don't allow yourself to be overwhelmed by the big picture.

Here is a tough one! We often make reference to the past: "I used to be able to . . ." or "I used to look like. . . ." Or we may project too far into the future: "I want to lose 50 pounds by next summer . . ." or "When I change my job, I will start to exercise. . . ." Think now and live in the present! Reassess your planning for time management, meal planning, exercise, and active relaxation so that you stay with the program today, tomorrow, and generally speaking in the here and now.

In your journal, write these headings and your thoughts on each:

My plan for this week is:
How will I reach my goals for this week?
How am I going to reward myself once I reach my goals for this week?

Week 6, Day 3

Celebrate your incremental progress. Give yourself time to notice and permission to feel really proud of how far you have come.

At our center, we do not insist on before and after pictures as a way of measuring success. Before and after pictures are so abused in the media that they have lost their true meaning. Losing weight (especially in an artificial way using crash diets or medications, without actual lifestyle change) does not necessarily translate into "happiness" or "joy" or even "success." Losing weight feels best when it results from a true and profound lifestyle change. In that sense, weight loss represents a true personal accomplishment.

So, think hard and figure out how you would want to measure your progress. Obviously, your weight on the scale or how your clothes fit provides you with direct measurements of your progress. But there are other ones:

energy level, self-esteem, pride, medical benefits such as lower blood pressure or sugar levels, better sleep, and so on. What would you like to use as your personal measure of progress? Write your own ways to measure progress in your journal, and use them often.

Week 6, Day 4

Accept each day in your life as it is, bad or good, successful or less so.

On the bad days, we have an opportunity to learn what it takes not only to get through, but to feel better! On the good days, we get a chance to remind ourselves how great it feels to be happy, healthy, and in control. Write down some of your emotions, reactions, and behaviors in your journal.

Write down how you would feel and behave on a "bad day" and a "good day." (A "good day" here is defined as a day when you could stick to your plans completely. A "bad day" refers to a day when you could not reach your daily goals.)

Compare the two. Do you see a pattern?

Week 6, Day 5

How are you doing?

With four and a half weeks behind you, you have certainly lost some weight. How much? You should be noticing some distinct physical changes in how your body looks and in how it feels. What are they? Take notice of the benefits. Do you have more energy? Do you enjoy the fact that some of your clothes are fitting more loosely?

You have probably noticed that some weeks have been easier than others. Is there a pattern to your lapses and setbacks that you can learn from? Are some regularly recurring situations more likely to lead to temptation than others? If so, write them down in your journal.

How might you rearrange your life to avoid those situations? What strategies might be helpful in circumventing a lapse in the weeks and months ahead?

Taking the time to evaluate your progress helps ensure your success.

Week 6, Day 6

Change is not a straight arrow. Often, with progress and change comes a certain degree of uncertainty, insecurity, fear, and at times even chaos.

You are taking proud steps, but your feet have to stay firmly grounded. You have to remain alert to unexpected situations. Think of it as reaching turbulent waters after an easy ride down a river. *Be ready.* These unexpected "roadblocks," or challenges, could be as simple as a remark someone makes, or it could be friction at work or at home. You and your plans for the rest of your life go beyond these obstacles. You are doing this for yourself, and every day you progress, you are making your "self" stronger and richer. Enjoy your new sense of determination and power.

Describe in your journal how you have improved your inner sense of self in the last six weeks.

Week 6, Day 7

Our theme this week has been "Making Progress." It is important that you make it a priority to notice, take credit for, and celebrate the progress you have made.

This week's reward is to choose a symbol of your success and find a way to mark your progress on your way to your goal.

Here are some ideas on how you might do that:

- Purchase a tall glass vase and some decorative marbles. Drop one into the vase for each pound you have lost, and make a weekly ritual of adding marbles.
- Keep a pair of slacks from when you were your heaviest, and put them on periodically so you have a visual reminder of how you are shrinking.
- A pound of butter is a good visual for picturing what a pound of fat looks like on your body. Another way to do this is to pick up a free weight, a dumbbell, weighing as much as you have already lost. Feel the weight. You have already lost the equivalent of that weight in fat (mostly from your belly).

- Buy candles to symbolize your weight loss—one for every 5 or 10 pounds. Keep them together on a coffee table and use them, enjoying the symbolic light you are shedding in your life.

Describe your chosen rewards.

Week 7: Coping with Stress and Change

Week 7, Day 1
People who successfully navigate the process of lifestyle change go through a predictable series of stages in their personal journey:

- *Awareness* of the need to change is the first step toward making it happen. You finally admit to yourself that the way it is no longer works for you and that you need to make changes in your life.
- *Contemplation* of the nature of change is the second stage. It is not enough to just decide to change your eating pattern or to stop smoking, for example. You have to also figure the "when," the "how," and the "where" of your decision making.
- *Decision* is the time when you reach a point of certainty about what you have to do to reach your goals.
- *Commitment* is the hardest stage. This is the part where you keep putting one foot in front of the other, step by step, knowing that each small victory along the way brings you closer to meeting your goals.

Since you are already in week 7 of the program, you have gone past the first three stages. Commitment is the stage you will live in until you reach your goals.

Most of us can easily remember periods in our lives when we were fully committed to a project. Describe one project that represented a high degree of commitment on your part. Analyze what it took for you to stay committed during that process: the changes you had to make, the sacrifices you made,

the hard work you did to move the project to completion. Also analyze the ful-
fillment and reward you felt for being committed.

Week 7, Day 2

Mindfulness is a term that reminds us to live in the moment and to experience our lives as we live them. Our lives are busy, our calendars are
full, our days are packed with things we need to get done, and it may be
easy to fall into the trap of looking at this program as one more thing that
you need to squeeze into your list of obligations.

Try, instead, to focus on the satisfaction that comes with taking control of your life. Remind yourself that your time on earth is meant to be
savored and that by committing to this program for lifestyle change, you
are slowing down and promising to take better care of yourself, with the
goal of improving your life. This works as a short-term goal (focus on
enjoying *this* moment, right now) and as a long-term goal (the habit of
mindfulness brings satisfaction within our reach).

Most people associate *mindfulness* with a psychological state of mind that
requires formal training such as Zen meditation. Although these (mostly
Eastern) philosophical schools have mastered the art of mindful living, the
basic elements of mindfulness are simple. Here are two examples:

If I hug and kiss my children every morning because I am afraid I may
never see them again, I probably suffer from an anxiety disorder! However, if I hug and kiss my children every morning because I appreciate
the love we share, I am being mindful of the present moment. But if I am
so busy or distracted that I am unable to take a moment and communicate my love to them, or if I hug them without really paying attention to
what I am doing and feeling, then I am mindlessly wrapped up in a world
of tasks, obligations, and other chores I have created for myself.

In a similar fashion, if I realize that the reason I am putting food in
my mouth is because I am stressed, tired, or frustrated, then I am mindful and I will learn to deal with the root of nibbling and grazing mindlessly. If I reach for food because I am truly feeling hungry (even if it is
not the right kind of food), I am also mindful of my hunger. Most of the
hidden or unaccounted-for calories come from mindless eating.

How we *feel* at any given time is an essential step toward mindfulness and thoughtful action. You do not have to be a meditation expert to benefit from mindfulness.

Describe how you feel and how you are now!

Week 7, Day 3

Stress is an inevitable part of our lives, even when things are going generally well.

When you are involved in a major life change, you will have days when you feel energized and terrific about all that is happening, and other days that test your ability to persevere. It is helpful to think about how you react to stress so you can become familiar with your personal pattern.

- Are you a person who loses your temper when you feel stressed, or do you bury your feelings in activity and efforts to solve the problem? Do you express or repress?
- Are you a person who is energized and motivated by stress, or do you tend to shut down?
- Do you sleep less or sleep more when under stress?
- Do you eat less or eat more? Is your typical response to stress a weight loss or a weight gain?

Stressors are usually related to relationships, work, finances, body, or the mind.

What are your top three stressors currently? Think about these and write how each affects you in your journal:

- *Relationship* (for example, marital problems or family illness):
- *Work* (for example, too demanding or conflicts):
- *Finances* (for example, lack of money or too complex):
- *Body* (for example, body image or medical concerns):
- *Mind* (for example, anxieties, regrets, or loneliness):
- *Other*:

Recognizing your stress response is the first step to developing a healthier response. *Ask yourself the following questions, and record your answers in your journal:*

- How do I respond to stress? (Not coping mechanisms: How do I actually feel when I'm stressed?)
- Do I get bodily symptoms, such as tension headaches or cramps?
- Do I get psychological symptoms, such as sadness, anger, seclusion, resentment?
- Do I get behavioral symptoms? Do I overeat, smoke, or drink? Am I too agitated to sleep at night?

Week 7, Day 4

While we do not always have as much control as we'd like over the *external* events of our lives, we do have more control than many of us realize over our *internal* life—our state of mind. In others words, while we cannot control what happens, we can control how we react to what happens.

Your individual stress level has less to do with what is going on in your life than in how you choose to respond to the things that happen.

You can train yourself to react calmly to stressful events. You can stop your habitual response to stress—the dialogue that begins to play in your head—by becoming conscious of what you say to yourself (adding fuel to the fire of your agitation) and changing the script to something calming.

"Affirmations" are a tool with which to accomplish this change. When you find yourself reacting negatively to an event—a person who cuts you off in traffic, a supervisor who speaks rudely to you at work—take a moment to take a deep breath, commit yourself to remaining calm and cool, and repeat a phrase that helps you remain centered.

Some examples of affirmations:

- I am calm and relaxed—and I can choose to stay this way.
- I am breathing *in* calm energy and breathing *out* tension and anger.

- I am in control of my mind, my emotions, and my body.
- I can choose to live my life in a way that is easy, effortless, and peaceful.

If you have a favorite affirmation, write it in your journal. If you do not have an affirmation that you like, try to write one and test it out. Ask your psychologist or very good friends to discuss it with you and to give you more affirmations to work with.

Week 7, Day 5

For seven weeks now, we have been discussing ways for you to tune in to what you feel, take better care of yourself, and take control of your own health. Even if these behaviors are totally new to you, it is likely that by now you have learned some useful things about how to keep yourself feeling calm, energetic, and satisfied.

It is helpful to have a basic plan for taking care of yourself. It isn't realistic to think that every day can be handled perfectly, but it is useful to know what your ideal is.

Ask yourself the following questions to lead you to a better understanding of the basics of self-care, and write your ideas on each in your journal:

- What morning routine works best for me? Do I need to make any changes in order to feel better or function more effectively? If so, what are they—and are they realistic?
- How do I like to pace my food intake throughout the day? What advance planning should I do to make this eating plan work for me?
- Is there time during the day for me to rest and regroup? A midmorning and midafternoon break of just a few minutes to move around can be helpful. Can this be structured into my day?
- What is my plan for handling stressful events?
- If there is a predictable pattern to stress—for example, my daily commute? Is there something I can do to change my reaction (such as listening to audiobooks on tape)?

- Does my schedule allow for physical activity? For planning and preparing healthy foods?
- Are my evenings relaxing and satisfying?

Week 7, Day 6

A way to refocus yourself during periods of stress is to pull into yourself, breathe deeply and relax, and remind yourself of the many things in your life that are good. Follow these steps:

1. Breathe deeply. Focus on your breathing, bringing your attention to each part of your body, moving from your toes to the top of your head.
2. Make a mental list of things for which you feel grateful in your life—starting with the most simple, such as your sensory abilities. Make a list of the people you love, the people who love you. Try to come up with one aspect of your life that you've never contemplated with gratitude—and try also to find a reason to be grateful for something that is posing a challenge in your life.

Week 7, Day 7

Stress is an inevitable part of life, and it is useful to accept that and to have a plan for how you will handle stressful feelings and situations so that when you feel overwhelmed, you know how to take care of yourself.

Here are some things you might do:

- Schedule a massage or a manicure/pedicure or some other personal service that relaxes you and makes you feel cared for.
- Listen to a particular CD or type of music (classical, meditation music).
- Take a walk or go for a run.
- Rent a humorous movie.
- Call a friend.
- Lean on your spouse or partner; ask for some nurturing.

For this week's reward, take a few minutes to make a list in your journal of the stress-relieving alternatives that you find appealing—and try them out, one by one (all in one day, if you have the time—you'll feel great!).

Copy this list onto a note card, and keep it with you. Next time you feel stressed, figure out which alternative is most satisfying and best fits into your life at the moment—and do it.

Week 8: Food and Energy

Week 8, Day 1

The connection between energy and food is well documented. Foods affect your energy level and mental state in many ways. Depending on your age, hormonal status, and possible medical conditions, such as diabetes, certain eating patterns can reduce your burn rate, increase drowsiness and fatigue, and affect your stress response. Here are some facts about food and energy to remember:

- Overweight, pear-shaped women tend to have excess ambient estrogen levels, causing high levels of a binding protein called SHBG. For such women, a high carbohydrate diet further elevates the level of the binding protein, causing the steroid hormones, such as thyroid hormone and testosterone (which are energizing hormones) to bind to the protein, making them unavailable to the body. *For these women, weight loss attained through a high-protein diet would prove energizing by making more steroid hormones available to the body.*
- Intake of carbohydrate-rich snacks, such as bagels and chips and other "junk foods" results in high blood sugars with spikes in insulin level. This is usually followed by low blood sugars, or hypoglycemia, and a feeling of fatigue, as if you were about to "run out of energy." *Avoiding refined carbohydrate-loaded snacks can rev up your energy level.*
- Large meals loaded with fat and carbs result in what we call "postprandial tide," meaning changes in digestive hormones

and blood contents such as free fat particles, amino acids, sugar, and other compounds that cause drowsiness and fatigue. *Eat smaller meals more frequently and avoid fats and carbs so that your energy level doesn't sag.*

- People with certain medical conditions, such as diabetes or heart disease, may need to pay more attention not only to their eating patterns but also to their use of additional supplements such as antioxidants, which help combat metabolic stress and may improve general well-being. *Ask your physician whether any medical conditions you may have will affect your energy level, and if so, what you can do to improve the situation.*

Week 8, Day 2

For those fit enough to exercise safely, physical activity is known to be energizing. If your movement is limited because of excess weight or other conditions, there are still ways to use movement, breathing, and stretching (for example, tai chi and yoga) as an uplifting, energy-generating routine.

Different types of exercise affect your physiology in different ways:

- Resistance training with short rest intervals raises the growth hormone level—a hormone that not only helps build muscle but also optimizes metabolism.
- Aerobic exercise started vigorously brings about an immediate rise in the stress hormones cortisol and catecholamines (although this effect diminishes as the body becomes better conditioned).
- Upper body resistance training raises your blood pressure and is therefore not advisable for patients with diabetic retinopathy or out-of-control hypertension.
- On the other hand, lower body aerobics, such as biking, improve the circulation and are recommended for patients with diabetes.

- Exercises that work the core balance muscles not only activate big core muscles and kick-start your metabolism but also enhance your sense of balance and "rewire" your nervous system.
- Breathing techniques are used in different types of yoga to generate body heat and sharpen the mind.

Think about your exercise-related goals in the short term and in the long term. Write down both short-term and long-term goals in your journal.

Week 8, Day 3

It is important to realize that increasing your level of physical activity will have a positive impact on virtually every aspect of your mind and body. Not only does exercise improve your physical health, but it has an immediate and lasting beneficial effect on your mood and state of mind. Remember:

- Exercise induces certain hormonal changes—namely, the secretion of endorphins and growth hormone—which boost mood and relax the mind.
- Aerobic exercise performed longer than 30 minutes releases the "feel good" hormone endorphin.
- Physical activity is uplifting because it increases oxygenation in the brain.
- Exercise helps overcome stress by relaxing the wandering and distracted mind. It improves concentration and self-esteem. It also reduces muscle tension.
- Body toning and fat loss, both of which are evident within just a few weeks of beginning a regular exercise program, provide a visible "reward" that provides continuous motivation for lifestyle change.

Most experts recommend some form of exercise daily. In your journal, make a preliminary exercise schedule for the week and discuss it with your fitness trainer. Try to complement different routines, as shown in the example below:

Monday	Early-morning walk
Tuesday	Weights plus bike at the gym
Wednesday	Early-morning walk
Thursday	Yoga class
Friday	Conditioning at the gym
Saturday	Afternoon walk or hike
Sunday	Yoga video at home

Week 8, Day 4

Exercise will prove immediately helpful to individuals who sleep poorly. Especially if your sleep problems are related to snoring and/or sleep apnea related to weight gain, you should find that exercise makes an enormous difference in the quality of your sleep.

Regular exercise is critical for cardiorespiratory health. It improves circulation, lung capacity and ventilation, upper airway muscle tone and compliance, as well as brain oxygenation, all of which are important in treating sleep disorders.

Exercising in the evening—particularly if it is a relaxing form of exercise, such as yoga or tai chi—calms the mind and burns off the accumulated stress and tension of the day. It releases muscle tension and helps to settle the mind and the body for sleep.

If you have trouble relaxing in the evening, write in your journal some ideas about relaxation techniques that may work for you. If you have no trouble relaxing in the evening, what do you attribute this to?

Week 8, Day 5

The way we breathe affects our energy levels in many different ways.

Yoga, in particular, provides useful instruction and experience in how to use breathing techniques for improved respiration. Ask your clinicians whether yoga breathing might be useful to you.

Most of us are not mindful of our breathing during the day. As a result, we often are not making optimal use of our thoracic muscles and lung capacity. Over time, our breathing becomes restricted because of poor chest compliance and minimal flow of air. By actively stimulating chest muscles and the airways, our breathing becomes more efficient, whether we are awake or asleep.

Yoga teaches breathing techniques, expands and loosens the rib cage, and increases spinal mobility—all of which are helpful for better oxygenation. Yoga also teaches how to use breathing techniques for relaxation, which facilitates sleeping.

Other forms of exercise improve breathing and also serve to reverse the obstruction of air caused by fat buildup in the neck. Obesity has a direct neurological effect on the brain causing sleep apnea—in addition to obesity's role in poor chest compliance and obstruction of the airways.

All respiratory problems improve with weight loss, regardless of the form of exercise used to accomplish it.

Week 8, Day 6

An important aspect of healthy weight loss and lifestyle change is learning to recognize the source of your "hunger." Sometimes you are, in fact, hungry for food. If that is the case, address that hunger in an appropriate way—eating a meal, if it is time, or a healthy snack if it is between meals. Make healthy food choices so you feel more energetic and like you are taking good care of yourself.

But often you will find that what you are craving isn't "food" so much as it is "feeling good." By learning to identify what you need and filling that need in a healthy way, you will almost certainly achieve success in your efforts to change your life.

If you are tempted to eat but aren't actually hungry for food, are you:

- Lonely? Call someone. Talk to someone in your office or your home. Go to the library, the mall, take a walk at a park.
- Bored? Pick up a magazine, newspaper, or book. Watch a movie you've wanted to see. Make spur-of-the-moment plans with a friend. Do something creative.
- Tired? Do something restful or rejuvenating, or something fun that makes you feel young again.

- Feeling empty? Connect with your spirituality or with someone you love, or do something for someone else.
- Worried about the future? Do one small thing to make your future better—read a book on writing résumés, make a commitment to attend a networking event, look at the classified section of your local newspaper.

There are many ways to feed your emotional hunger other than with food. Tune in to what you need, and fill that need. It is an important part of learning to take good care of yourself.

Identify those emotions that you may feel and deal with as "hunger," and write in your journal the time and situation you may feel those emotions. The example below shows one way to do this:

Emotion	Situation	Time of day	Frequency
"exhausted"	at home with the kids	3 to 6 P.M.	often

Week 8, Day 7

Each day this week we have talked about a different aspect of boosting your energy—through exercise, sleep, breathing, and meeting your emotional needs. Rest and relaxation are a vitally important aspect of this mix. Your bedroom and bathroom and the way that you care for yourself in these rooms should reflect your commitment to taking care of yourself. If you have the resources, you may choose to purchase some new linens or decorative items; or you may wish, instead, to simply use your energy to clean up and reorganize these rooms to make them more pleasing to the eye and soul.

This week's reward is to put some time and effort into making these spaces reflective of your commitment. Set aside a few hours to focus on improving the atmosphere in your bedroom and bathroom so that these rooms can truly become a retreat and sacred space.

Here are some ideas:

- What are your favorite "grace notes"? These are colors or fragrances or images or sounds that add to the texture of your life, that make you feel comfortable and happy. Use them in your bedroom and bathroom. If classical music relaxes you, put a small stereo in the bathroom. Lavender is an herb known for its relaxing properties; hang a sachet from your bedpost.
- Is your bed beautiful and comfortable? Is it a retreat for you? If not, consider what needs to be changed—new linens to make the room beautiful, a down comforter so you are warm at night, a few more pillows to surround you while you sleep.
- Is your bathroom merely functional, or is it a room with character of its own? This is the place where you care for your physical self. Equip it with the right tools and decorate it in a way that gives respect to this process. Something as simple as a small print with an inspirational quote or an image you find appealing can make a big difference.
- Eliminate clutter as much as you can. Get rid of the stacks of magazines, newspapers, and books you don't have time to read. Aim for an atmosphere of serenity.

Week 9: Getting Support

Week 9, Day 1

The relationships in your life shape who you are and how you function. As you continue through our program of life change, it is important to evaluate how the people in your life affect your ability to stay on track.

Take a few minutes to make a list of the people in your life who are affected by your new lifestyle, and think about what their reaction has been thus far. Are they supportive, or not? How have *their* lives changed as a result of the changes you are making in yours? If they have reacted negatively (because you no longer prepare the same sorts of foods or share the same recreational eating patterns), think about that reaction. Do you sometimes believe that their feelings are more important than your commitment to yourself?

You need to clearly communicate your commitment and goals to the important people in your life. Any friend or family member or coworker with whom you spend a lot of time can be considered "important." These people need to know how much time and effort you will be spending on yourself—which may well mean devoting less time and effort to them, because you need to allocate your resources differently. Assure them that their needs remain a priority but that you have moved yourself onto the list of people you take care of. (Many people with weight issues have totally discounted their own needs for the sake of others, so this is a vitally important step to take in your life.) *In your journal, or just in your thoughts, if that makes you more comfortable, do the following activity:*

- Identify people (at work, at home, or elsewhere) who support your lifestyle change.
- Identify people who may purposely or unknowingly undermine your efforts.

Week 9, Day 2
"I feel. . . ."
  "I need. . . ."
  "Would you please. . . ."

These are phrases that can be considered the building blocks of effective communication among family members. They are clear, nonjudgmental, and can be applied to most any situation. Experiment with using this format for making requests; do you notice a difference in how you feel? You should. It is validating who you are and the importance of your own feelings and needs in the family. Do you notice a difference in how others respond? Probably. It is unlikely that you have been expressing yourself this clearly.

The other side of the coin is that this is a positive way to enlist the help of others. Rather than putting people on the defensive, this gives them an opportunity to be helpful and supportive.

You can also use these phrases when talking to yourself. As we've discussed previously, many people with "food issues" aren't attuned to what they really feel. Every discomfort gets addressed with food, rather than taking the time to identify the real feeling and come up with a solution that solves that particular craving—which may be for rest or companionship or activity for distraction, rather than ice cream.

How do you assess your communication skills? Are you often compromising and giving in to others, or are you assertive and stubborn? Discuss one area where you feel your communication could improve (for example, talking to your elderly parents or your children about the choice of restaurants when you go out).

Week 9, Day 3

Clear communication with your doctor is a vitally important part of the process of true lifestyle change. We ask our patients to keep careful track of food intake, both in terms of quantity and type of foods they eat. This is as much for their own education so they can develop the habit of self-monitoring (which has been proven scientifically to help people keep weight off) as for our purposes in supervising their lifestyle change program.

Research has shown that people who are not on track tend not to keep careful records of food intake and that unless people measure their portions, they tend to underestimate how much they are eating. You need good records to make sure that what you are doing is safe and effective. You need to develop your self-monitoring skills so that you learn how to take care of yourself forever.

In our experience, many patients want to please us and therefore bring us "edited" versions of their food diaries. Many people with weight problems are "pleasers" who are inclined to want others to like them, and they don't want to cause any extra work for others. But remember, you are doing this for yourself, and you are following this guide to help teach you how to take care of yourself.

In reality, few patients are 100 percent compliant. We don't expect perfection, and you should not be disappointed in yourself when you lapse. Being honest with yourself may be an important step in developing assertiveness and communicating clearly with others.

Communicating your issues with others has a healing effect in and of itself. When you see your cup as "half empty," your friends and family may be able to remind you that it is "half full." When you are upset and frustrated, they can help you regain perspective. When you feel that you are a failure and a bad person, this guide and your counselor teach you to see beyond the black-and-white view and to pick yourself up and start again. This requires a two-way communication channel between you and your support structure. Now, try to establish this type of communication with yourself.

Write in your journal a recent example of how you were able to change your mind or put things in perspective by reasoning with yourself.

Week 9, Day 4

The "buddy system" can be a great way to enlist support for yourself—and many people enjoy having an opportunity to be helpful. Asking for help can be a compliment. It lets people know that you value them and their opinion.

Here are some guidelines on how to ask for help effectively:

- Be specific about what help you would like. If you want someone to go to when you are feeling tempted, say that. If you would like someone to commit to walking with you every day, say so.
- Don't expect your buddy to police you. Ask instead for your buddy to offer alternative food or activity choices.
- Ask for help from appropriate people. A friend who hasn't addressed her own weight issues may not be the best person to turn to right now.
- Remember the "I feel . . . I need . . . Would you please . . ." paradigm in asking for help. It really works!

Do you have buddies? If not, how would you go about asking friends to get involved with your efforts?

Start by making a list of people with whom you share common interests. Setting up a system that works for you requires active participation of all buddies involved. Here's a sample buddy list. Enter yours in your journal.

Buddy List	Activity	Time	Contact Info
Sally	Walk at lunch break	12:30 P.M.	Extension 1234
Mary	Shopping for food	Evening	Home phone
Jane	Call when frustrated	When needed	Cell phone

Week 9, Day 5

Others in your life may be affected by your decision to change your lifestyle and become as healthy as you can be, and they may not always react with enthusiasm. In particular, those individuals you've always shared recreational eating with may be unhappy, even threatened by your new lifestyle. People who are inactive may resent your new enthusiasm for physical activity.

Here are some strategies for dealing with these situations:

- Be creative in coming up with non-food-related activities you can enjoy together. Instead of going out for a meal, go to a bookstore or for a walk. Take a class together.
- Be proactive in choosing the venue if you are dining out. Choose restaurants that offer healthy alternatives.
- Don't be judgmental of their choices or expect them to change along with you—although you can, of course, be supportive if they do show an interest.
- Avoid individuals who sabotage your efforts and are not sympathetic to what you are trying to accomplish.
- Be prepared for the fact that some relationships in your life may undergo dramatic change. Know that taking care of yourself is important and valid, even if it means letting go of destructive relationships.

Week 9, Day 6

You need to figure out what it means to be always giving to others and not giving to yourself.

Are you afraid that this, then, will mean you are no longer a good wife/mother/employee? Do you fear that others won't like you as much if you don't give as much? Is your concern that you aren't really worth all that much time and attention?

For instance, a mother may feel that her homemade cookies or lasagna represent love to her family—and in fact they do. But the reality is that if her relationship with her family is a good and healthy one, they should understand that she needs to take time to exercise and that her need to avoid those sorts of foods is important, too. Why should she be the only one who arranges her life around the needs of others? If she is a loved member of the family, it is reasonable to expect them to accommodate her needs and wishes as well.

In your journal, write real-life examples of "food" used by you and others to express love, gratitude, and care. Analyze each one and look for nonfood alternatives.

Example: *Food expectations*—I need to cook my mom's favorite food (a risotto dish!) and take it to her. I know she is going to prepare my favorite dessert for me. I do not want to hurt her feelings and not go.

Nonfood alternative—I can explain to my mom that because I am on a weight loss diet, instead we are going to see a great movie together.

Week 9, Day 7

Our suggestion for this week's reward is to reward someone who has been especially helpful and supportive by thanking them.

Set aside time to write a note thanking this person for all they have done for you and for how much their support has meant.

Use beautiful stationery or purchase a lovely card for this purpose. Your note may be long or short, but do take the time to plan what you want to say in a very specific way to this person. Put enough time and effort into composing the note and making the presentation attractive that you find the experience rewarding as well; it is an opportunity to reflect on the value of this person in your life.

Some people choose to write more than one note. Some go on to make it a habit to thank people formally for their love and friendship. Most people find the experience of putting careful consideration into who should be thanked and why helps them to appreciate their circumstances more fully.

If it helps you to write down the steps, record them in your journal:

People I will thank
When I will buy cards
When I will write cards

Week 10: Preventing Relapse (1)

Week 10, Day 1

You have now completed two and a half months of your lifestyle change program. Not only have you undoubtedly made progress, but you have also had ample opportunity to experience setbacks of varying severity. (*Everyone* has setbacks!)

Take a few minutes to look back over your food journal. Think about the days and weeks that didn't go so well for you.

Ask yourself the following questions and answer them in your journal:

- Was there a precipitating event—such as a party or special event, a crisis, or a major change in my life?
- Can I detect a pattern to my setbacks? If so, what is it?
- Do I tend to eat when I'm tired? Stressed? Overworked? Underappreciated? Premenstrual? Or when I'm feeling rebellious, perhaps self-destructive or even resentful?

The key is learning from how you have reacted in the past and building a new repertoire of behavior. If you can anticipate a challenge and prepare for it with a strategy that has proved effective, you will be better armed to resist temptation.

You should still expect that there will be times when you do not perform perfectly. Don't be too hard on yourself. Just get back on the program as soon as you can, and move forward with confidence in your ability to succeed.

Week 10, Day 2

What we hear from our patients is that the most common cause of lapses is stress—a catchall term into which we toss a wide range of issues, including interpersonal strife, overscheduling, frustration, professional anxieties, travel, illness, major life change, and family life.

In reality, stress is more accurately defined as our reaction to a situation, not the situation itself. Of course, you are bound to experience negative emotions, but this doesn't mean that your behavior has to spin out of control.

Identify the specific situations that have felt "stressful" to you. How have you reacted? (By overeating, of course.) Instead, find an appropriate response for each situation. For instance, if you are feeling anxious about a major presentation the next day, it would be better to practice again, work out, or see a movie or visit with friends to distract yourself. Eating might feel better in the short run, but it doesn't solve your problems.

There are several common *stressors*, which are discussed elsewhere in this book. However, since this week's topic is *preventing relapse*, try to identify which stressors are more likely to result in your quitting or deviating from your meal plan. *List those stressors in your journal, and write down potential responses or coping mechanisms that will help you prevent relapse. Discuss this strategy with your clinicians.*

Example:

My biggest stressor at this point is my relationship with my daughter (who is going through tough times). When she rejects my help, I feel hurt, and every time I feel rejected and hurt, I get cravings. Since I have lost weight and I am changing my life, I can't stand that I can help myself but am unable to help her. So I want to just stop.

Week 10, Day 3

Social gatherings and special events present their own challenges. Food is often the center of activity and the main focus of an event. There may be all sorts of related issues, such as not wanting to hurt someone's feelings by not eating a meal they have prepared. Or you may be drinking alcohol, which reduces your resolve. Special holiday foods may have deep-seated, maybe even unconscious, associations. Or you may simply not feel like depriving yourself.

Food that is prominently displayed is often a trigger—the sight, the smell, other people's enjoyment are all factors that may lead you to overeat. And people tend to eat more when confronted with a wide variety of foods. Here are some coping strategies:

- Offer to contribute a dish, and prepare something in keeping with your food plan.
- Survey all the foods before putting anything on your plate, so you maintain control.
- Don't go back for seconds unless you can have veggies or lean protein in accordance with your meal plan.
- Position yourself as far from the food as possible, especially in the case of a buffet.
- Focus on the nonfood aspects of the gathering.
- Keep a glass of water filled and on hand so you have something to put in your mouth.
- Limit alcohol intake. If you have wine, add equal amounts of seltzer.
- Go for a walk before and/or after dining.
- Don't "bank up" calories for the event; this makes people more likely to overeat.
- Drink lots of noncaloric fluids, especially water.
- You may wish to eat a small meal in accordance with your diet before you go to such events. Avoid going to parties hungry so you can make wise choices.

Always remember that others (your coworkers, friends, and family members) respect you more when they see you in control. Stay away from people who "push" drinks and food on you.

Week 10, Day 4

Many people are dismayed to find that they gain weight after suffering an injury or undergoing surgery, such as a knee replacement. In addition to dealing with the emotional rigors of recovery, your physical activity is also curtailed. Not only are you not exercising; you may be barely moving.

During the period of recovery, come up with a plan to maximize what you can do physically while adjusting your food intake to the decrease in caloric expenditure. A nutritionist can help you plan the calorie adjustment while keeping the nutritional content of your menu as high as possible.

Recovery from injury or from surgery is a time when risk of relapse is very high. You will need additional support both from your medical provider and from your loved ones.

Here are a few scenarios to think about:

- *Example 1:* You hurt your knee during the program and you may have to cancel all your fitness sessions. Learn to cut back on your caloric intake until you are able to resume exercise. Cutting back 200 to 300 calories a day makes a difference. Meanwhile, learn to do upper body exercises that do not strain your knee.
- *Example 2:* Your back pain has flared up again. You do not know what to do. You are frustrated that in spite of your weight loss, your back pain came back. Put things in perspective. There are many physical and psychological benefits resulting from your weight loss. Weight loss and proper back exercises are always beneficial, regardless of your chance of recurrence. So continue what you are doing and talk to your trainer and/or yoga instructor to modify your routines.
- *Example 3:* In spite of great improvements in your health and energy, you will still have to undergo a surgery that you wished you could avoid. You are disappointed.

Think how much better an outcome and quicker a recovery you will have now that you are in better shape. Visualize getting back on track after surgery and remain strong. Ask your doctors about continuing with your lifestyle change after surgery.

Week 10, Day 5

Major personal illness is another factor that may affect your weight loss plan. Obviously, if you are diagnosed with a severe illness, your first priority must be becoming healthy—and diet should take a backseat to that effort. That said, this is not a license to overeat and throw caution to the wind—which will only make you feel more depressed and discouraged. Feeling good about yourself is a key to recovery. Negative thoughts and poor self-esteem will further hurt your chances of recovery.

Here are some ideas on getting through this time:

- Acknowledge the negative feelings you are having. Helplessness, hopelessness, frustration, uncertainty about the future, and resentment are common emotions.
- Nutritional adequacy must be balanced with a commitment to keeping your caloric intake within a healthy range. If you cannot eat certain foods on the meal plan, ask a nutritionist for alternatives.
- Exercise may be impossible—or may at least need to be scaled back. Discuss with your doctor how you should proceed and what, if anything, you can do so that you don't lose too much momentum.
- Some medications may increase your appetite, but this doesn't mean that you should overeat. Choose foods carefully and pay close attention to portion size. Talk with your doctor about how your medications are affecting your eating.
- When people want to bring gifts, encourage them to choose fresh fruits and vegetables instead of candy and baked goods. Flowers are even better. If your loved ones bring you foods you should not be eating, acknowledge their care but give away those foods. Seek comfort in the love and care you are getting,

not in foods. Be organized. Make a list of healthy foods you could request if someone offers to buy you something.

Week 10, Day 6

Life sometimes presents challenges we don't feel up to meeting—the death or illness of a loved one, divorce, or loss of a job, to name a few. Most of us meet crisis in the kitchen in one way or another.

Typical eating patterns during traumatic times include:

- Unpredictable schedule
- No time or resources to plan meals
- No time to cook or shop
- Lack of hunger followed by uncontrolled eating
- Craving sweets or salty foods in response to emotional roller coasters
- Drinking alcohol or use of other pacifiers

As soon as you are able to focus—which should be fairly quickly—try to plan for healthy eating. If you are away from home, locate a store where you can buy healthy, convenient foods (like yogurt). Ask your nutritionist for advice on what to order in fast-food outlets and restaurants and coffee shops. Never let yourself get overly hungry; keep fruit, cut-up vegetables, and protein shakes and bars available for use as directed.

You may not at this very moment be suffering from any setback as described above and in the last several pages. However, you may be able to imagine how you would (or would not) be able to handle an emotional trauma.

In your journal, write how you think you would try to handle a serious emotional trauma (or have done so in the past) without reaching out for food. Write down strategies, and think which one would most likely work for you. Consider the following examples.

Trauma: Loss of a loved one.

Strategy: Ask a family member supportive of your efforts to come and stay with you. Ask her/him to be mindful of your risk of relapse.

Trauma: Diagnosed with serious disease.
Strategy: Learn and use stress management techniques such as meditation, music, and yoga to relax, refocus, and regain your resolve.

Week 10, Day 7
This week's curriculum may have been largely theoretical (unless, of course, life managed to present some challenges, as we all know it sometimes does). However, you may still benefit from thinking over the past few months and analyzing how you have successfully circumvented temptation, focusing on the positive feelings that ensued.

To motivate yourself for next time, take a few minutes to chronicle this experience in your journal. Emphasize your impulses to slip from the program, and identify what motivated you to stay focused. Write it up for easy reference in the future. This will be an invaluable motivating tool.

Week 11: Liberalizing Breakfast

Week 11, Day 1
Regardless of the type of meal plan, we eventually need to increase the range of food choices available to you, while still allowing you to feel in control of your food intake. Many people come into the program feeling that they can't stop eating certain foods or that certain foods stimulate their appetite. We want you to feel confident learning to eat a wider variety of foods—partly because we don't want you to feel bored, but also because a wide range of foods provides a better nutrient base.

In your journal, list some typical breakfasts you've had each day for the last two weeks. Don't judge what you eat; just record it and notice patterns.

Week 11, Day 2
Not everyone eats breakfast at the kitchen table each morning. If you can, great. If not, it is still possible to make healthy choices. In general, strive

to keep breakfast between 300 and 400 calories to prevent midmorning cravings. Remember that anything you add to beverages (to your milk, coffee, or tea, for instance) counts toward your calorie allotment. Include some protein with each breakfast to keep your blood sugar stable.

If you are a person who eats on the run, here are some suggestions:

For eating while commuting:

- A protein shake that you make at home and bring in a commuter mug, with or without a protein bar (consult your nutritionist on good options for your eating plan)
- A container of sugar-free yogurt and a piece of fruit
- A whole wheat half bagel or other whole grain bread product, spread with light cream cheese
- Two ounces of low-fat cheese and six to eight whole grain crackers with no trans fats.

For eating in a diner or restaurant:

- An egg white omelet
- A serving of oatmeal or cold cereal with skim milk
- Cottage cheese and fruit
- A piece of whole wheat toast (no butter) and a poached egg

Week 11, Day 3

Skipping breakfast is a behavior common to many people who are overweight. Some believe that if they eat breakfast, they will overeat all day. Others believe that they do better to save those calories for later in the day. And many people simply say that they have neither the time nor desire for food in the morning. Some eat so much at night that they simply are not able to eat in the morning.

It is nonetheless vitally important to eat a healthy breakfast, however small it may be. This is because it stimulates your metabolism so that you more effectively burn calories all day. After a long night without food, your blood sugar is low, and you will not get through the morning with mental and physical energy if you don't fuel up. Additionally, skipping a meal often leads to out-of-control eating later in the day.

So don't skip breakfast.

There must be healthy and low-calorie breakfasts you like!

As an exercise, write in your journal healthy options for seven days of the week and run them by your nutritionist. Include everything you want to eat, including any juices, coffee, or other beverages.

Option (example): Egg white omelet with blueberries and coffee

Option (example): Half a bagel, low-fat cream cheese with lox

Week 11, Day 4

You have probably been eating very limited carbohydrates thus far. It is time to consider introducing more carbs into your diet, and breakfast can be a good time to do so—though a common error that people make is eating *only* carbohydrates in the morning, which results in all-day food cravings. For example, an English muffin with jelly is pure carbohydrate. Adding cottage cheese or an egg to the meal will make it more satisfying.

If you choose to start with a high-protein, low-carbohydrate diet, as in our meal plan, then you have started your day with foods such as eggs, egg whites, cottage cheese, or a protein shake. Now, in a controlled fashion, we will begin to reintroduce some carbohydrate foods to your morning.

We begin with a limited variety of carbohydrate-containing foods that do not stimulate cravings or appetite and devise a menu of two or three options to be rotated throughout two weeks. But some people prefer not to introduce carbohydrates at breakfast time, and if that works for you, there will be other opportunities during the day to round out your menu.

Some possible additions are oatmeal, whole grain bread, and whole grain cereal.

Week 11, Day 5

Many people report that eating certain foods "trigger" their appetite, especially for carbohydrates and sugars. There is not yet any scientific evidence supporting this, but it is common nonetheless. It is valid to pay attention to how your body has historically responded to specific foods.

At breakfast time, begin to increase your variety while still avoiding foods that trigger or stimulate your appetite. If certain carbs, such as cereal or bread, seem to make you hungrier later, replace them with other carbohydrate foods that don't seem to have the same effect. Many people find that foods like oatmeal and whole grain cereals, especially cooked grains, do not stimulate their appetite. These may be better options for you.

Adding protein and a small amount of fat, such as nuts, may sustain the period of time that you feel satisfied from your breakfast.

If there are foods that you feel stimulate your appetite, identify these, write them down in your journal, and learn to control your intake of those foods, or find other foods that provide the same nutritional value so that the offending foods may be safely eliminated from your diet.

Week 11, Day 6

Another helpful "trick" is to make your breakfast from foods that are naturally portion controlled. For instance, use a packet of oatmeal instead of preparing oatmeal from the big container. Single-sized cereal boxes and prepackaged peanuts are other examples.

This may be a less economical way to eat, but some people feel that the benefit of not overeating outweighs the additional expense. You might consider making your own individual packets by measuring out $1^1/_2$ ounces of cereal or $^1/_2$ cup of oats if expense is an issue for you. If you do this, choose a time when you aren't hungry—such as immediately after dinner—and measure out and package the entire box so that you aren't tempted to snack. Better yet, ask someone else to do this task for you.

Here are a few appropriate ways to divide foods into appropriate servings:

- Divide a can or jar of nuts and dried fruits (for example, trail mix) into small plastic bags.
- Cut a full-size bagel into two or even three slices, freeze, then toast just one piece at a time and spread lightly with cream cheese.

- Put a serving of breakfast cereal into a plastic bowl with a lid the night before. In the morning, add milk.

Week 11, Day 7

People tend to be quirky about their breakfast routine—perhaps more than about any other meal of the day. Some people want to sleep as late as they can, so they are accustomed to packing a quick meal they can eat in the car or on the train. Others cherish the opportunity to connect with family before the day begins, while many people appreciate quiet time by themselves.

What is your favorite part of your breakfast routine? Is it having a quiet cup of coffee while reading the paper? Eating with your family?

This week's reward is to purchase something—a special ceramic mug for your morning tea, a commuter mug to take on the train, a set of cheery bowls for cereal with your children—that connects you to the start of the day and to your commitment to treat yourself well all day long. If you prefer not to purchase something, see if you can find something in your cupboard that you haven't used in a while.

Week 12: Liberalizing Lunch

Week 12, Day 1

For people who work outside the home, lunchtime can present logistical challenges—especially if you are accustomed to buying lunch at a deli or restaurant. Portions are large, choices are tempting and generally high in fat, and there are all too often hidden calories in salad dressings, mayonnaise, and side dishes—not to mention the expense of the meal.

For this week, consider making a commitment to prepare your lunch at home in advance. Brown bagging enables you to plan a meal you will enjoy and control your nutritional intake. Take the money that you *would* have spent, and put it in an envelope for this purpose.

What kind of lunch works for you? Consider, for example, a low-fat tuna sandwich or salad and maybe some soup.

How can you prepare these favorite lunches in a healthy way and take them to work? Here are some ideas:

- For tuna salad, grill tuna the night before; then use the leftover tuna for salad.
- For soup, make a big batch on days off, and freeze it in small containers.
- For salad, prepare the night before and refrigerate in a plastic container. Bring dressing, if any, in a separate small container. Zippered bags work well for this.

Week 12, Day 2

If you work outside your home, then prior to the busy week, you need to make sure you have a menu in mind so that you can plan for what you will need. Here are some suggestions:

- Make a list and shop ahead for the food. Keep in mind that at this point in your lifestyle change program, we are trying to expand your choices—so this is an ideal time to experiment with new foods.
- Containers and wrappings are an often-overlooked practical necessity; if you are bringing salads, for instance, you will need to find a bowl with a lid—and something to put the salad dressing in (zipper snack bags are a good choice). Or you can keep a bottle of salad dressing at work (most dressings are safely left unrefrigerated for one week).
- Soups or other hot foods should be stored in a thermal container that closes tightly. And if you don't have access to refrigeration, you might need a frozen cold pack.

While our goal is to nutritionally balance your full day's menu, you may yet choose to keep your lunch option limited to something that has proved successful, such as a salad with protein.

In your journal or on your usual shopping list, write down everything you'll need to bring a healthy lunch.

Week 12, Day 3

Here are some suggestions to expand your list of lunch options that you may not have considered previously.

Soup is a great way to start a meal, even if it is just a broth. Hot liquids have been proven to decrease the amount of food eaten at a meal. A heavier soup may serve as most of your meal in and of itself—but do pay attention to portion size and ingredients, since many soups are loaded with calories and fats.

A sandwich prepared with lean fillings, such as turkey, ham, or roast beef, is a good choice. Put at least 4 ounces of meat and plenty of lettuce and tomato in the sandwich, and consider eating a side salad as well. Pay attention to bread size; limit calorie count from bread to 200 per sandwich.

Frozen packaged meals, such as Lean Cuisine or Weight Watchers meals, can provide variety and convenience if you have access to a microwave at work. There is also an increasing variety of healthy, low-fat soups and stews available in the canned food aisle in the supermarket.

Fruit and cottage cheese can be a satisfying option, particularly in the hot summer months. Many people enjoy adding some dry whole grain cereal for crunch.

Week 12, Day 4

People vary enormously in terms of how they like to spread their calories throughout the day. Some eat three meals and snack rarely, while others prefer many small meals. Put some thought into what works best for you.

As the midday meal, lunchtime can be viewed with flexibility; it may seem like the best time to eat your largest meal, or you may prefer instead to divide your midday calories into two or three portions for eating late morning, noon, and midafternoon. Consider experimenting with these different concepts, taking note of how you feel throughout the day. Each time you eat, try to take in a combination of nutrients so you are not just snacking on carbohydrates and sweets.

Record your thoughts on these questions in your journal:

- Do I like to have a midmorning snack (for example, a medium apple with nuts; cut bell peppers, celery, tomatoes)?
- Do I like to have a midafternoon snack (for example, sugar-free yogurt with nuts, a protein bar; a small meal like a piece of turkey with cheese and whole grain crackers)?
- Do I prefer bigger lunches? (In that case, double the volume of low-calorie and low-carb components, such as lettuce and other veggies, or have a filling and healthy dish like a nice piece of salmon with veggies.)

Week 12, Day 5

If you find that you like to eat a light lunch and supplement it with snacks in the morning and afternoon, here are some healthy snacking choices:

- 1 ounce of nuts, such as almonds, peanuts, or cashews. Premeasurement is critical, since nuts are very high in calories. Note that 1 ounce of nuts is typically about $1/4$ cup. Peanuts come prepackaged in snack-sized portions, so these can be a particularly useful choice.
- Low-fat cheese, presliced and packed with four to six whole grain crackers or fruit
- Cut-up vegetables, with $1/2$ cup of seasoned cottage cheese or a low-fat dip
- Protein shake or bar

A good rule of thumb is that a snack should be between 100 and 200 calories and should contain some protein in order to be maximally satisfying and energy sustaining.

Collect a list of snacks and categorize them as "yes" or "no" after consulting your nutritionist. Keep adding to the list. You are making a personal and customized snack database!

Week 12, Day 6

The one predictable thing about life is that it is unpredictable. Planning ahead for unforeseen situations will increase the likelihood that you will not falter from your long-term goal of healthy eating and lifestyle change. Here are some common situations and effective strategies:

- *Social events, such as birthday parties and group lunches.* If you have input into restaurant choice, select a place where you know you can get healthy food that you like. Don't be shy about ordering according to your needs. If everyone is eating dessert, share a portion with two or three people and order fruit if possible.
- *Travel, for business or pleasure.* Eating on the road presents its own challenges. If you have control over where you eat, choose delis or restaurants with fresh food. If you are limited to fast food, try to find a Subway and order from their low-fat menu.
- *Airplane travel.* Once again, bringing food with you is the best option. A protein bar or shake is a terrific strategy. Bring bottled water and fresh fruit and vegetables so you aren't tempted to eat the airline food. You also might order a special meal, such as vegetarian or kosher food, which often offers healthier alternatives.
- *Lunchtime meetings, where food is brought in.* Stick with the simplest sandwiches, avoid the mayonnaise-laden side salads, and try to steer clear of dessert. A protein shake before the meeting may take the edge off your hunger, so you are more likely to limit your intake.

Check the supplies you need to have available:

- Food scale
- Measuring cup
- Small snack bags
- Plastic wrap
- Small plastic containers with lids

- Aluminum foil
- Cold packs
- Cooler (if on the road a lot)
- Lunch bag
- Low-cal condiments (for work or to travel with)

Week 12, Day 7

Remember that envelope you started at the beginning of the week?

This week's reward is to take that money and buy yourself something fun and frivolous, something you don't really need and would not otherwise purchase. Packing your own lunch is financially and nutritionally smart, enabling you to be more in control.

If you have always packed your lunch, splurge a little on a food item that is out of the ordinary for you or may be exotic at first. Expanding your options and avoiding boredom are helpful for healthy eating. When possible, try fruits and veggies that are in season and preferably organic. Look for simple and tasty ways you can include them in your diet. For example, a frisée salad with walnuts and bacon or smoked salmon may be a new idea for lunch and may work well for you, since all the components can be kept refrigerated at work or prepared in the morning.

Write your ideas in your journal.

Week 13: Liberalizing Dinner

Week 13, Day 1

More than any other daily meal, the dinner hour presents logistical and emotional challenges. Depending on what your life is like, the dinner hour can be chaotic, stressful, exhausting, lonely—or the best part of your day. Part of our goal in this lifestyle change program is to help you to resolve the emotional aspects contributing to your unhealthy habits. So it is helpful to put some thought into the dinner hour at your home and how you might want it to be different. Here are some common situations and strategies for addressing them:

- *After work.* Whether you have a long commute home or often feel pressured to join your colleagues for "happy hour" or simply have a tendency of eating in the car, you should be aware that when you are tired, frustrated, stressed, and hungry, you are at extremely high risk of either overeating or eating foods that are not in line with your goals. You can avoid most of these situations by being proactive. Plan to eat a healthy snack late in the afternoon. Learn relaxation methods that are practical (such as going to a yoga class on your way home) and work for you. Do not compromise your goals to please others.

- *The first hour at home.* What happens when you walk in the door can set the stage for the entire evening. Think about your own pattern. Are you a mom, faced immediately with hungry kids—not to mention your own hunger and fatigue? Have something like cut-up veggies and a dip in the refrigerator that you can offer immediately while you take 10 minutes to relax.

- *Family meals.* The family dinner hour can be complex, depending on the ages and schedules of family members. Have a plan for specific situations: Will you make a separate meal for yourself if the family is eating foods you should stay away from? What will you do on evenings when everyone is going in different directions? Is it realistic to wait to eat until your spouse comes in if you are preparing an earlier meal for the children?

- *Special events.* Again, preplanning a strategy for holiday meals, parties, and family gatherings will help you get through these occasions without setbacks. Do not subvert your needs in making plans. Do whatever you need to do, including bringing your own food, to get through the occasion without regrets.

Describe in your journal the most difficult challenge you face around dinnertime.

Week 13, Day 2

There are many reasons why the dinner hour is considered a "danger zone" to individuals with weight issues. It can be hard to resist temptation all day long as the stress of the day accumulates, and you may be vulnerable to lapses when you get home in the evening. If the family comes together for dinner, this may be a time when it is hard to stick to your own meal plan. Dinner may be a social occasion; if liquor is involved, you may feel looser and less inclined to follow your rules. You may just feel tired of being hungry.

Think about your patterns of eating in the evening. It helps to identify ahead of time where you are likely to lapse. Then you can come up with a plan for distracting yourself, diverting your energy into a more positive direction.

Also, recognize that this period of lifestyle change is in some ways temporary, in other ways permanent. You may need certain strategies for getting through the period of change and other strategies for how you will arrange your activities when you have met your goal and moved into maintenance.

Articulate in your journal how you see this period of change affecting your eating habits at dinnertime. Describe how you see your future "maintenance" eating habits at dinnertime.

Week 13, Day 3

Many of us have a preconceived idea of what time we should sit down for our evening meal—but that is not always the time our body craves dinner. We may be hungry earlier and end up snacking too much before dinner, thereby eating two meals. Moms may be hungry when preparing dinner for the children while also planning to dine with their partner later in the evening, again taking in more food than intended. And if you eat too early, you may snack late into the evening.

Think about your own patterns at dinnertime, both in practical terms (when do you typically eat dinner, and why at that time?) and in physical terms (when are you really hungry?). Acknowledging the reality of what actually happens in your kitchen—as opposed to what you think *ought* to be happening—take a few minutes to consider your options. You might:

- Choose to eat your entire meal earlier in the evening—say, within a half hour of coming home—if you are always hungry at that time.
- Divide your entire dinner into two smaller meals, having some early on—when feeding the children or when you first arrive home—and saving the rest for later if you want to eat with your partner.
- Plan to consume part of your evening meal—say, soup and a salad—early, saving the entrée for later in the evening.

Many, if not most, of our patients have some snacks built into their eating plan for the day. If you like to snack at night, you may wish to experiment with how to divvy up your snacks so that you have some options in the evening.

What changes are working well for you? What changes are you having difficulty with?

Week 13, Day 4

While we have already discussed restaurant dining with respect to lunch, eating dinner out presents some of its own dilemmas. Here are some strategies to help keep you on track when you dine out in the evening:

- If it is within your power to choose the restaurant, select a place where you can get the kind of food that you are supposed to eat according to your meal plan. Bring in menus of restaurants that you frequent so that you and your nutritionist can discuss the best choices.
- Dining out is often about relaxing and enjoying the company of others, but by this point in the day fatigue is often a factor. This puts you in the position of being vulnerable to making poor choices—wolfing down rolls from the bread basket, for

instance—so that by the time the meal is served, you have already overeaten. Consider having a snack or low-calorie beverage in the car on the way home from work or on the way to the restaurant so that you don't arrive famished; ordering a seltzer or large glass of water immediately upon arrival; or ordering a salad right away and asking the waiter not to serve bread.

- While enjoying a drink may be a pleasant part of the dining-out experience, alcohol lowers your inhibitions and may therefore predispose you to abandon your meal plan. Know that, and plan accordingly.
- As discussed previously, warm beverages add to the feeling of fullness. Therefore, starting your meal with a cup of hot soup or ending it with a cup of coffee or tea can add to your sense of satisfaction.
- If you decide you really want to have dessert, options may include sharing with several people or ordering a fruit plate. Again, it is helpful to preplan.

Plan ahead what you will order at the restaurant (to the best of your knowledge of the menu). Think of alternatives. As an exercise, design in your journal a full meal for yourself. You are going to an Italian restaurant with your colleagues. Remember that when you order foods according to your plan, your self-confidence will earn you more respect in the eyes of your colleagues.

Week 13, Day 5

At the day's end, many people walk into the kitchen hungry and cranky and having put little or no thought into what to have for dinner. Some good options for evenings when you just want to grab something fast and easy include:

- Frozen entrées such as Lean Cuisine or Weight Watchers, coupled with premade salad (from bags or that you prepared in advance).
- Leftovers, which can be prepacked into meal-size portions and frozen, to be microwaved and eaten at a later date.

- Crock-Pots can be a great solution. Ask your nutritionist for recipes that fit your meal plan.
- Keep a list of nearby takeout restaurants that serve the sort of healthy fare that is on your meal plan. Again, it is a good idea to look at menus with your nutritionist so you can plan in advance for making good choices.
- Frozen vegetables are very nutritious and in fact are often more nutritious than fresh vegetables. Combined with deli turkey or an egg white omelet or one of the newer low-fat canned soups, this can make for a satisfying quick meal.

In your journal, write new foods to add to your shopping list.

Week 13, Day 6

It can be very easy to fall into the habit of treating mealtime as a low priority, something to be gotten through rather than a healthy and pleasurable part of taking good care of yourself—especially when you are eating alone. While it is admittedly less gratifying to spend time preparing a real meal for just yourself, it is good to make a point of treating yourself well and feeding yourself as a "loved one."

This can be accomplished without enormous time or effort, using the same principles we have already discussed. Try to be aware of your meal patterns, in addition to your eating patterns, so you can ascertain whether they accurately reflect the way you wish to live your life. Note your observations about your patterns in your journal and come up with ideas for changing any unhealthy patterns.

For example, if you are used to cooking large portions, note that and come up with ways to cook only what you (and whoever else is eating with you) should eat.

Week 13, Day 7

Our system of emphasizing weekly rewards is designed not only to give you something to work toward each week but also to help you learn to recognize other ways of feeling good.

Until now, we have made a point to keep all rewards unrelated to food. The reason for this is probably obvious: people who have become overweight usually have developed a pattern of using food to meet other needs beyond hunger and nutrition.

But in a healthy and balanced lifestyle, food can be a source of pleasure. It is important to learn to regulate yourself so you can enjoy the experience of dining out without sabotaging your health and lifestyle.

For this week's reward, we suggest that you go out to dinner—alone, if you are comfortable, or with someone to whom you feel close. Be strong, positive, energetic, and proactive about the evening. Choose a restaurant that serves a menu that works with your food plan. Select an appropriate entrée, one that you will enjoy and that will reinforce that this is a way you can live well and happily.

Concentrate on making this special meal a memorable, pleasurable event.

Describe your experience in your journal. What was enjoyable, what was frustrating, and how would you modify your choices in the future?

Week 14: Preventing Relapse (2)

Week 14, Day 1

One important aspect of preventing lapses is to learn ways and places to buy healthy and delicious treats so that you don't always look at food as something you are depriving yourself of.

Many of our patients have enjoyed the process of compiling a file that lists recipes, food products, takeout food, caterers, and restaurants that fit into their new lifestyle. It's a great idea to have a list of local resources to which you can turn when planning a special celebration, bringing a dish to a potluck, or when you just want to treat yourself especially well.

In compiling such a resource for yourself, you might consider:

- Clipping local restaurant reviews
- Asking friends for recommendations
- Saving recipes from books and magazines

- Cutting out advertisements for Internet or direct mail purvey-
ors of fine foods that are appealing and healthy

*How am I going to find restaurants or diners that have menus I am look-
ing for? Am I going to collect recipes? Do I find them in books, magazines, or
on the Web? I am interested in improving my cooking skills. How do I go about
it? Who are the people I can use as resources to help me?*

Week 14, Day 2

At various times during this period of lifestyle change, many (if not most)
people reach a point of weariness with the amount of effort involved.

Don't be hard on yourself when this happens. It is an inevitable part
of change that happens when you realize that there is no quick solution
to a process like this and that change is often an uncomfortable process
(which is why people are usually so resistant to change). Give yourself
credit for having come this far.

Take this opportunity to reconnect with your reasons for enrolling in
this lifestyle change program.

Ask yourself these questions, and write your answers in your journal:

- What feels great as I am changing my life? (*Possible answers:*
I have more energy. I feel proud of what I have accomplished.
I get compliments.)
- What would feel good if I stopped right now? (*Possible answers:*
I could eat a pint of ice cream. I wouldn't have to go to the gym
tomorrow morning. I could meet my friends at the bar without
feeling guilty about it.)
- What doesn't feel great about how my life is changing? (Possi-
ble answers: It is annoying to have to preplan every meal.
My family misses my baking. My husband is jealous now that
I have lost weight.)
- What might happen if I stopped right now? (Possible answers:
My diabetes would get worse. I'd gain weight again. My self-
esteem would suffer.)

What most people find, after doing this exercise, is that it is not the number of reasons in each category that matters to them, but the relative importance of those lists. Usually, the reasons for not changing—though they may be appealing in the short term—are far less compelling than the reasons to change.

You may just need a reminder of how vitally important this change is to the quality of your life.

What was the main reason you wanted to embark on changing your lifestyle?

Week 14, Day 3

Yesterday's list provides an excellent summary of the process of lifestyle change. A good idea would be to make your list into a "crib sheet" of sorts to carry with you as a reminder when you are tempted to make poor food choices.

Instead of pressuring yourself to be "perfect" at difficult times, try to choose one behavior on which to concentrate—such as eliminating late-night snacking or sticking to your exercise goal for just this week. Keep the rest of your eating under control to the extent that you can, but focus your energy on this one significant change—and the positive feeling you get from sticking to it.

Your goal for such a week might be:

- Exercising a certain number of total minutes (say, 300, which is 5 total hours)
- Eating only until you feel satisfied, but not "full"
- Eating meals at regular intervals
- Drinking 12 ounces of water with each meal

Describe your goal for the week. Be very specific. Define criteria of success. Revisit this goal throughout the week. Adjust your behavior accordingly. (*Example:* I will eat regular meals and check every day to see why I did not and determine what I can do to help myself stick with my goals.)

Here are some activities, hobbies, and interests that may help you expand your outlook and avoid boredom (check-mark the ones you are interested in):

- Listen to audiobooks and/or music
- Learn to do yoga or meditate at home
- Start an arts and crafts project
- Learn to play an instrument
- Learn a new language
- Learn to knit or quilt
- Read inspirational books
- Learn to paint or sculpt
- Make model cars or trains
- Learn to do woodworking
- Make use of healing home decorations
- Discover and enjoy new music
- Design an indoor or outdoor flower arrangement
- Experiment with Zen gardens or other indoor environments
- Consider an exotic fish tank
- Plan an exotic trip for the future

Write in your journal useful information about suppliers, instructors, fees, registration, and so on.

Week 14, Day 4

Studies have shown that being overweight is directly correlated to sedentary activities, such as TV watching or Internet surfing. (A fun fact to know is that your metabolism is actually lower while watching television than while reading a book!)

If you find that you are getting bored or irritated by the ceaseless requirements of following our intense lifestyle change program, it may be that you need to shift your focus somewhat. Take a look at the behaviors that may be contributing indirectly to your health problems and think about how you might make creative changes in your life and schedule.

Rather than looking at this as deprivation and another thing you have to do without, try instead to see the opportunity to expand your horizons. You can explore interests and divert your attention from eating to something exciting and interesting, to follow up on something you have found intriguing but never took the time to pursue.

Week 14, Day 5

"Plateauing" is a common and frustrating experience in the process of weight loss. When your weight gets stuck at a particular number and doesn't move despite your best efforts, there are several possible causes.

Your metabolic rate slows as you lose weight. It takes less energy to sustain a smaller body. Sometimes you need to reassess your calorie needs and make changes accordingly, whether it be eating less or exercising more.

The scale measures one number, but your body weight is composed of several different components. Changes in body fat occur slowly over weeks, but changes in water weight can occur even hourly. It is impossible to determine whether you are seeing an accurate reflection of body fat at a given moment in time. A better measure is how your clothes fit and how your body feels to you. Another option might be remeasurement of your body composition if you feel you have truly been stuck in the same place for a while.

Periodically, it is good to redouble your efforts to measure and weigh your portions to ensure accuracy. There is a phenomenon called "portion creep," whereby mere eyeballing of portions underestimates their actual size. An error of only 100 calories a day can make a 10-pound difference over the course of a year.

Week 14, Day 6

One common reason for lapses is frustration at aspects of life over which we have no control. Many people with a history of being overweight have turned to food as a source of solace and comfort, a dependable way to soothe themselves when other parts of life aren't going so well.

So part of our program focuses on helping to identify and deal with sources of frustration. There are things in our life over which we have no control. In fact, the only thing we truly can control is our own response.

Make two lists in your journal—things that frustrate you that you can change (not getting enough sleep, for instance) and things that frustrate you that you cannot change (your spouse's work problems). For each item you list, provide a possible solution (for example, going to bed earlier), or write next to it these words: "I will let it go."

The other thing you can do to reduce frustration is commit to saying no to people and things in your life that are not good for you. This list includes situations that stress you out, tempt you to make poor food or behavioral choices, exhaust you, or make you feel guilty or ashamed of yourself, as well as situations that you simply find unpleasant.

Things I Can Easily Change	Things I Cannot Easily Change
The color of my hair	My height or my body build
My work schedule	My career

Week 14, Day 7

For this week's reward, buy yourself a selection of magazines about healthy living, natural environments, or outdoor adventures. We like *Health Magazine,* which provides excellent coverage of a broad range of health and wellness topics, *Outside,* which is a youthful and inspirational outdoors magazine, and *O* (for Oprah!) for its interesting content, among others. The monthly arrival of an attractive, inspirational, lively, and readable magazine devoted to the cause of healthy living will be a periodic reminder of why you have committed to lifestyle change—and it will provide a regular source of new and useful ideas to keep you thinking about what it means to live well.

If you like inspirational images, you may wish to buy a poster or a calendar to place in a favorite spot at home or at work. Every time you see it, remind yourself of what it means to you and why you bought it.

As a visualization exercise focused on healthy living, you might try the following:

Choose an image of a place (like a beautiful, exotic, and peaceful beach) or an image that simply appeals to you and calms you down (like a dazzling sunset). Visualize that image, look around, imagine you are there. Feel relaxed, rested, and at peace. Now imagine a successful, healthy, happy you. Transfer the warm and rich feelings you just had when you were "seeing" that picture (the beach or the sunset) to feelings within you. Imagine and visualize again a fit, calm, and healthy you.

That is your reward. Feeling that positive emotion is your reward. The picture you choose to put on the wall or the magazine you choose to read as a reward should awaken these kinds of inspirational emotions within you.

Write in your journal a list of several different images and/or magazines you are interested in.

Week 15: Beginning to Exercise

Week 15, Day 1

Now that you have already experienced some success on our program (you have lost weight and feel lighter and better overall), you are ready to begin your commitment to regular exercise. If you have reached a plateau—a common frustration—beginning to exercise will help move weight loss along. Here are some points to recognize about exercise (if you are already exercising, you may want to review your program to fit current goals better):

- Always be safe. In the beginning, it is important to work with a fitness trainer to learn about how to exercise properly and safely.
- Plan on a three- to four-week period of introduction to exercise, during which you'll learn appropriate forms of exercise, technique, safety, and your personal limits.
- Hydration is key. Ask your clinician about what you should drink and when, especially if you have health conditions such as diabetes or heart disease.

- Pay attention to pain. Your fitness trainer will instruct you to avoid exercise that causes pain (as opposed to discomfort, which is often associated with being deconditioned) and to always speak out when something is painful.

- Faster is not necessarily better: When exercising, there is often more benefit from performing careful, controlled movements than going quickly. For example, in working with free weights, form is always more important than speed.

- Once you learn different kinds of exercises, it is optimal to vary your routines or programs from day to day to get better results and avoid injury.

- Pace your workouts by striving for regular sessions of moderate intensity as opposed to overtraining one day and taking several days off to recover.

- Even short sessions spread throughout the day (if you have trouble committing to a 1-hour workout) can be effective and can achieve effective results.

Week 15, Day 2

Here are different types of exercise you have probably heard about:

- *Aerobic exercise:* long-duration (30 minutes plus) activity, such as jogging or using a Stairmaster, that causes the body to utilize fat reserves for energy, as opposed to sugar.

- *Anaerobic exercise*: intense, short-duration exercise, such as sprinting, which does not burn many calories and is less useful for weight loss, but increases strength.

- *Fat-burning exercise:* long-duration, moderate-intensity aerobic exercise at approximately 60 percent the maximum heart rate and typically using all the muscles in the body. Examples: swimming, using an elliptical trainer.

- *Cardiovascular exercise:* long-duration, moderate to intense aerobic activity that is more intense than fat-burning exercise, defined as greater than 60 percent maximum heart rate. Examples: running, spinning.

- *Interval training:* combination of fat-burning programs with resistance training, the latter focused on various muscle groups, with very short rest intervals between the two types of exercise. Example: alternating aerobics and weight training with short rest intervals in between.

- *Resistance training:* strength training either utilizing the body's own weight, as with push-ups, or using free weights, tubings, and machines. Resistance training typically focuses on individual muscle groups and over time increases the weight and/or repetitions.

- *Core balance training:* exercises that take advantage of deep and big muscles that control posture and balance (deep abdominals, gluts, lower back muscles). Activating these muscles is an effective way to burn calories and tone the body while improving the sense of balance. Physioball training, Pilates, and yoga are considered core balance exercises.

- *Conditioning:* combination exercise routines at the gym typically prescribed by a personal trainer, with the goal of maintaining a desired level of fitness.

- *Circuit training:* similar to interval training but usually designed for group classes.

Here are some things you should know about exercise programs. Programs that raise the heart rate tend to improve the cardiorespiratory fitness and burn more calories during the exercise period. Exercises that help build muscle mass (such as resistance training) may burn fewer calories during the exercise period, but will increase the burn rate and thus the metabolism throughout the day, thereby speeding up the weight loss process.

Some exercises, such as core balance (yoga and Physioball), activate the big, core muscles (which are often not used enough) and improve flexibility and balance.

These recommendations should take into account any medical conditions or limitations you may have, such as bad knees or diabetes.

Week 15, Day 3

Do not exercise if you are under the influence of medications or alcohol or if you are very tired or feel ill. That's just common sense.

Always do a risk assessment before you decide to take on a new routine. For example, if you are at risk for knee injury—which may result in a major setback if you get injured—ask what exercises you should avoid and how far you can safely push yourself with the exercises that you do choose.

Pay particular attention to environmental conditions, such as temperature, humidity, weather conditions, and visibility. If you prefer outdoor activities, it is safer to exercise with a companion than alone.

Men cool off by sweating, women by increasing the circulation in their skin. No matter how your body cools off, there are limitations. If the temperature is above 100°F *or* if you exercise too long in hot weather, you are at risk for heat stroke. Ask your physician about preventive measures.

Always start with a 5- to 10-minute warm-up session, which is typically moderate aerobic exercise, such as using a treadmill or Stairmaster, followed by gentle stretching of all muscle groups.

Always cool down for 5 to 10 minutes by gently reducing the intensity of the exercise, followed by stretches again.

Drink plenty of water after exercising and up to 2 hours before you exercise. Eating or drinking a lot immediately before exercise may cause discomfort. The body requires gradual hydration; fluids taken in immediately before exercise are ineffective. Fluid taken in during exercise may not keep up with fluid loss.

If you have diabetes, you should know that while exercise is good for you, it may cause hypoglycemia. Ask your doctor about when, how, and what type of exercise may affect your diabetes control. If you have complications of diabetes, certain exercises may be dangerous. Ask your doctor.

If you have heart disease, hypertension, or circulatory problems, you should not be discouraged, because there are plenty of exercises you can safely do. Your doctor will provide you with this information.

If you have a chronic lung condition, such as asthma or emphysema, you may require an in-depth evaluation before embarking on an exercise program.

Never exercise when you are having an asthma attack or if your breathing is distressed.

No exercise is enjoyable if not done safely.

Week 15, Day 4

Many people feel frustrated that they don't have time for exercise, but others who've successfully incorporated fitness into their schedule have learned that exercise is something you make time for. In our experience, most people have, on average, 3 hours of disposable time every day, some of which can certainly be used for exercise and other healthy rituals.

The best time to exercise depends on a number of factors: your time and schedule, seasonal constraints, your individual stress level, and your fitness-related goals.

Medical conditions may shape your exercise schedule. For example, a person with type 2 diabetes who is overweight should try to engage in a gentle exercise program after meals. This will help regulate blood sugars and clear fat from the blood faster.

Stress is another factor to consider. Vigorous exercise in the morning, such as resistance training, can prepare you for a stressful day, while aerobic exercise and yoga can help you decompress in the evening.

Some people find it energizing to exercise in the morning, while others find that late-afternoon exercise provides a welcome energy boost. Exercise can raise stress hormones such as cortisol and catecholamines, which may be responsible for increasing energy level, especially in the afternoon, when these hormones are typically low.

Late-afternoon exercise of 30 minutes or more may help some individuals control their evening appetite. But in general, aerobic exercise tends to stimulate appetite—something to be aware of if your goal is weight loss.

In general, most experts recommend invigorating exercise in the morning and relaxing and calming exercise in the late afternoon or evening.

However, it is best to individualize your exercise program based on your personal preferences, body condition, schedule, and family obligations.

Week 15, Day 5

If your goal is weight loss, it is important to pay attention to what you eat before and after exercise:

- *Before exercise.* It is best to have a low-volume, high-protein meal or (preferably) drink 45 minutes before exercising. Obviously, eating a full meal before exercise results in discomfort and/or conditions such as acid reflux. Excessive carbohydrate intake before an exercise session will result in more cravings and hunger afterward. Patients with diabetes who are on insulin should ask for specific instructions regarding food and exercise and required adjustments to their insulin program.
- *After exercise.* Keep in mind that after exercise you will be hungry, and you may find yourself eating more than you have just worked off. Be mindful of your exercise session to get an idea of how many calories you have burned. If you drink plentiful fluids after exercising, you will find hunger to be less of an issue. If your goal is to build more muscle, you may have to eat a balanced meal or even a high-protein meal after exercise sessions. Ask your fitness trainer for information on this.

Week 15, Day 6

Your health care practitioner has, by now, analyzed your hormonal and metabolic profile, your body composition, your burn rate, and any possible medical conditions. An exercise program should reflect this comprehensive personal profile.

If you are overweight and have good muscle development in your legs, your exercise program should include upper body resistance training to increase your lean mass, as well as lower body aerobics to burn calories efficiently.

If you are overweight and have poor muscle development overall, you will see immediate benefits when you begin whole-body resistance training.

If you are overweight and have well-developed muscles (like a former football player would have), the focus should be on debulking and fat-burning exercise routines. Weight lifting alone will not meet your goals, so your exercise program should emphasize aerobics and stretching.

If you have medical conditions such as low back pain and/or cadiorespiratory limitations, you will need modifications in order to exercise safely, but the basic principles remain the same.

Our goal is to teach you exercise routines that you can practice on your own, at a gym or outdoors or elsewhere. Communicate any questions or concerns with your fitness trainer.

Week 15, Day 7

Looking good is a benefit of losing weight and taking care of yourself. Even while you work out, it is important that you feel comfortable about your appearance.

For your reward this week, invest in some clothing for exercise. Look for clothing that is comfortable and allows you to move easily and that fits well now but (if possible) will also accommodate your changing body shape. Choose the right fitness clothing for the kind of exercise you like best—and which will be most effective in helping you meet your personal goals.

While some people believe they prefer no-frills, no-fuss exercise clothing (the old-fashioned cotton tee and sweats, for instance), you should recognize that technology has come far in the world of fitness fashion. Many of the new fabrics help keep the body warm in cold weather and cool in hot weather, wicking away sweat to prevent chafing and rashes. Clothing designed for yoga moves comfortably but does not weigh much and holds on to your body when you do inverted poses. Layering is always a good idea for yoga, as your body temperature changes during the session.

Feet are precious. Yoga is done barefoot. But all other sport activities require particular attention to shoes.

Depending on whether you run or walk on the treadmill, trails, or pavement, you need different shoes. Depending on your weight, the size and shape of your feet, as well as other considerations, such as circulation and the nerves, your shoes have to be especially chosen for you. We recommend that you visit a shoe shop that provides you with individualized and expert service. Socks are important as well. Double-layer socks prevent blisters while walking or running, while the right sneakers prevent serious injury.

Week 16: Yoga

Week 16, Day 1
Why do we emphasize yoga?

To many, yoga seems exotic and perhaps even strange. Some men even consider it "feminine." However, yoga is a sophisticated form of exercise that can go from pure relaxation to power training. Yoga teaches proper breathing, improves range of motion, enhances flexibility, and, depending on the kind of yoga, provides either a nonimpact cardiovascular routine or resistance training.

In our experience, most overweight individuals are deconditioned and reluctant to exercise—often with good reason, because there is a very real risk of injury. At our center, patients are often eased into fitness training with private yoga classes. We have also discovered that yoga can be a powerful tool for stress management and, as such, facilitates lifestyle change. The breathing techniques, stretching, and some of the specific yoga postures are designed to relax the mind while strengthening the body—a truly powerful combination that benefits everyone. Even if you can only perform yoga at a very basic level, such as only doing upper body postures (neck and shoulder and back), you will still tap into the internal sense of strength and relaxation that this form of exercise confers. With time, you will be surprised by your own progress and new abilities.

To start, we recommend gentle yoga, which is designed for beginners, or restorative yoga for those who have musculoskeletal limitations. For stress management and aerobic exercise, we recommend Kundalini yoga (inquire for more information on this type of yoga). For a more advanced and powerful experience, a Vinyasa or Ashtanga class may be more rewarding. As a rule, our morning classes are more vigorous and our evening classes aim at stress relaxation.

Week 16, Day 2

The term *yoga practice* means turning your yoga routines into a fixture or anchor in your life. We often recommend that our patients begin with private (or "one-on-one") yoga classes, which provide a warm and trusting environment in which to learn the basics of yoga: the terminology, the postures, the breathing, and education on how to work with your individual strengths and limitations.

Even though you could continue private classes or do yoga at home or by video, we recommend that you eventually join a group class. The reason for this is that classes help you structure your week around yoga and ultimately provide the discipline that you need to practice yoga on your own. When you get to the point where you enjoy yoga as a special treat for yourself, you can use yoga sessions as rewards—something positive for your mind and body.

In the beginning of each yoga session, set a goal that you would like to achieve that day: relax, or regain a sense of internal focus and concentration, or stretch-stretch-stretch. Yoga will not let you down and will reinforce your new commitment to healthy living in a subtle and natural way.

Week 16, Day 3

How should you prepare for yoga?

Do not eat immediately before yoga. However, we recommend a small lean meal or a protein shake 45 minutes to an hour before class. Drink adequately before and after yoga class, but not during the sessions. This helps to avoid acid reflux and unnecessary distraction.

Come 10 or 15 minutes early for class and get your body and mind ready. You can't rush yoga.

Wear layered clothing so that you can adjust to your rising body temperature by removing the outer layers and then, at the end, put them back on during the relaxation phase. Clothing should be loose, stretchy, and comfortable—but not so loose that it drops over your face when you are bending down. Ask the instructor where to purchase suitable yoga clothing, a mat, and other accessories.

You should have your own mat. Most yoga classes require a non-stretching and sticky mat so you don't slide or slip. However, for restorative yoga, a thicker (cotton or foam) mat may be better. For Kundalini yoga, which has a lot of repetitive movements, a thicker mat (or two mats) is more comfortable.

In some yoga classes, you may be asked to bring props with you. Props include cushions, straps, blankets, and bricks. These are usually used in restorative classes, which emphasize deep relaxation, flexibility, and stretching. However, they may be used in other types of yoga, such as Ashtanga yoga. Your instructor will advise you as to what you may need.

Week 16, Day 4

In the United States, the practice of yoga is often reduced to the physical routines of flexibility and strength. However, a true yoga practice follows the progressive development of eight fundamental elements, a "path" to right living. Even though we don't expect strict adherence to this path, it is important to understand why yoga has been practiced for so many centuries as not only a powerful body and mind modality, but also a way of life and a vision of the world in which we live.

The fundamental aspects of a yoga practice include:

- *Self-control.* This refers to a group of virtues to be mindful of, such as honesty, forgiveness, cleanliness, sexual control, and harmlessness.
- *Observance.* This involves cultivating a contemplative state of mind and committing to spiritual mindfulness. It contains the following practices: faith, contentment, moral discipline, charity, modesty, and reflection.
- *Asana.* This term means "posture," relating to the culture of body and mind, using certain postures or positions in the yoga

ritual. This aspect of yoga brings purification and vitalization to the body and eliminates disease, fatigue, and aches and pains. It is often the starting point of Western yoga teaching.

- *Breath control, or pranayama.* The process of controlling prana (the core energy) is achieved through regulation of the length and depth of inhalation and exhalation, control of the upper airway (larynx, tongue, lips), and retention of the breath at different moments in the respiratory cycle. Control of the breath and the movement of the air in the lungs produces rhythmic effects on the mind, resulting in control, focus, stress management, relaxation, and mindfulness.

- *Sensory control.* This involves focusing on the big toe, ankle, calf, and other body parts, including the pelvic organs as well as head and neck structures, such as the tongue, eyes, and forehead. The sensory acknowledgment requires mental concentration and breathing aimed at those body parts to focus the wandering mind on sensory signals from within the body.

- *Concentration.* It is said that a well-controlled student should control the bioenergy by breath suspension. Thus controlled, the naturally restless mind becomes fit and able to undergo the process of concentration. Holding concentration has been defined as controlling the desiring mind; this is dharana, or holding concentration. Holding in the consciousness using breath and concentration is a fundamental aspect of yoga as a tool to prepare the mind for meditation and mindfulness.

- *Meditation.* Levels of concentration called "deep" (dhyana) and "super" (samadhi) refer to higher levels of mindfulness, often referred to as "divine." This level of concentration involves the use of visualizations to achieve a higher spiritual awareness.

- *Ashtanga yoga.* Ashtanga yoga is often referred to in the West as a type of yoga practice (as opposed to Kundalini or Hatha yoga), but the term itself means the eightfold yoga, or ecstasy, the sum total of all the above elements of practice.

Week 16, Day 5

Why all the emphasis on breathing?

For more than 5,000 years, yoga has focused on the art of breathing, which is often taken for granted. Through the practice of yoga, you will learn about specific types of breathing to raise body temperature, to cool the body down, to energize yourself and clear your mind, and to reach deep relaxation, as well as stress and fear and anger management techniques.

These ideas may seem strange at first, but by practicing, you will discover that these are truly different kinds of breathing, each with its own benefits. For example, in one form of breathing, emphasis is put on inhalation, resulting in an uplifting and energizing mood. In another form of breathing, it is the exhalation that is slowed and deepened, resulting in relaxation.

The "breath of fire" is a form of breathing that allows the body to warm up and increase the exercise capacity without hyperventilation. Yoga also uses breathing as a tool for relaxing muscle groups by combining breathing with body movements. You will learn techniques that you can use in day-to-day living to reduce muscle tension.

Week 16, Day 6

Why do people chant in yoga class?

You may feel uncomfortable doing the chanting in some of the yoga classes. These chants, also called mantras, often translate into very insightful concepts, but it is the actual sound and the rhythmic pattern of the chant that has a direct effect on the body. That is why they are done in Sanskrit rather than in English—because the sounds have been worked on for centuries in their original form.

Chanting can also activate the upper airway, torso, and abdominal muscles. This subtle and easy form of "exercise" is useful for obstructive sleep disorder and lung disease, among other things. Chanting is also used in meditation as a means to clear and relax the mind. Chanting also sets the pace and the duration of some of the yoga movements, as if counting repetitions.

Understanding the meaning of the chants also helps to elevate the practice to a more spiritual level, one that is far more satisfying to the soul.

Among the most common chants and their meanings:

- *Om* is one of the most common chants, often used to mark the beginning and the end of the yoga session. A representation of the mind, associated with a spot known as the third eye, located between the eyebrows. It is actually composed of three sounds—*a, u,* and *m*—thought to represent three states of consciousness. This mantra is repeated before each meditation and at the end to refocus the mind.
- *Ong . . . namo. . . guru dev . . . namo . . . is* an example of a more complex mantra that means "I call on the divine teacher or the universal wisdom."
- *Sat nam,* which means true identity, is an example of a mantra or chant used repetitively through the session for refocusing, while others, such as *Sa Ta Na Ma,* referring to existence, life, death, rebirth, is often used for breathing practices. Other mantras may be used for more complex energy work and healing.

Week 16, Day 7

As long as you remain hydrated, a full-body massage after yoga is a wonderful body and mind experience that can be used effectively as a special reward whenever you feel you need one.

This week, schedule yourself a massage immediately after a yoga class—or, if that isn't possible, have one the next day. Yoga stretches and relaxes your muscles, but it also develops muscles that you never knew you had. Massage would feel particularly good working on these new muscles.

A massage is a deeply personal and physical experience. When you are fully relaxed and you let the therapist work on your muscles and lymphatics, you are also soothing your mind and resting your body. Therapists have different styles or touches. In addition, the oils used can have subtle influences. The most commonly used massage is a deep-tissue or

Swedish full-body massage. However, athletic massages focus on particular muscle groups, while aromatherapy and Reiki massage aim at deep relaxation. Thai massage works the range of motion, and Shiatsu uses pressure points. It is important that you like and feel comfortable with your therapist and that you feel you "deserve" or "really want" a massage. No one should talk you into getting a massage if you don't feel like it. If you are uncomfortable about the idea of a massage, you may instead try a facial, which many find as delightful as a massage.

In our experience, massage is a great reward—especially if you are "due for one." Use massages—given by a therapist or by your loved one—as a way of sinking deep into a physical form of relaxation that soothes your mind and heals your stressed muscles and joints.

Full-body massages are also useful for your skin health, circulation, lymphatic drainage, and nerves.

No matter what, drink lots of water after a massage (in particular after deep-tissue work and if you have combined a massage session with yoga or fitness training). Communicate with your therapist and let her or him know how you feel. Enjoy!

Week 17: General Exercise Information

Week 17, Day 1

Many people are under the misconception that when you engage in regular physical activity, it is important to use dietary supplements for additional energy or improved recovery from exercise. Not so. For the kind of exercises that you will most likely do, the only supplementation you need in addition to a balanced diet is hydration—preferably water rather than sports drinks that add extra calories.

Here are some common terms relating to nutritional supplementation:

- *anabolic:* Increasing muscle tissue.
- *ergogenic:* Increasing energy for athletic performance.
- *anticatabolic:* Inhibiting the breakdown of tissue and helping to build muscle mass.

- *coenzyme:* A compound that binds to an enzyme and activates it. For example, B vitamins are coenzymes.
- *cofactor:* An organic or inorganic substance that is required for the proper functioning of enzymes. Vitamins and minerals, like zinc, often serve as cofactors.
- *free radicals:* Damaging substances produced during metabolism that cause cellular injury.
- *antioxidants:* Free-radical scavengers that promote health and recovery.
- *functional foods:* Nutritional products that are assumed to provide enriched health benefits beyond their substantive food quality.
- *phytochemicals:* Substances that are extracted from plants for their health benefits and which may or may not be part of the natural diet.
- *nutraceuticals:* Commercial food-related products that are often synthetic or that may be concentrated extracts of plants, vegetables, or animal proteins.

Week 17, Day 2

Here are some anabolic and exercise-enhancing supplements with *presumed* anabolic benefits. Write down the supplements you may be taking and ask your doctor or your dietitian about them. You could also research them at a library or on the Internet.

Androstenedione

Argenine

Chromium

CLA, or conjugated linolenic acid

Creatine

Whey protein

Glutamine

Bee pollen

Ginseng

Lecithin

Vanadium

Vitamins B_1, B_2, B_{12}

DHEA

Antioxidants or substances with *presumed* free-radical-scavenging capability:

Green tea

Grape-seed extract

Omega-3 fatty acids

Tumeric

CoQ10

Flaxseed

GLA (gamma-linolenic acid)

Prescription hormones that may affect metabolism:

Testosterone

Growth hormone

Week 17, Day 3

The term *metabolic equivalent,* or *MET,* is used to describe the intensity of any physical activity, ranging from mowing the lawn to weight lifting. It is useful to know both the technical definition of MET and a measure of the intensity of various physical activities in order to have a better understanding of how to evaluate day-to-day energy expenditure.

A single MET is equivalent to the amount of energy expended during 1 minute of rest. Therefore, exercise at a metabolic rate that is five times oxygen consumption (VO2 rate) is considered 5 METs. Energy expenditure depends on body size, gender, age, and other factors. However, for simplicity's sake, 1 MET represents an energy expenditure of 1.2 kilocalories (what we generally call calories) per minute for a 70-kilogram (154-pound) person.

Here are some common physical activities and their corresponding
MET score:

Bicycling leisurely at less than 10 mph	4.0 METs
Stationary cycling, light effort	5.5 METs
Stationary cycling, vigorous effort	10.5 METs
Gentle calisthenics (push-ups, pull-ups, sit-ups)	4.5 METs
Vigorous calisthenics	8.0 METs
Circuit training	8.0 METs
Weight lifting (bodybuilding)	6.0 METs
Weight lifting (light workout)	3.0 METs
Health club exercise	5.5 METs
Low-impact dancing (ballet, ballroom)	3–5.0 METs
Aerobic high-impact dancing (jazzercise)	7.0 METs
Daily activity (housecleaning, shopping, vacuuming)	2–5.0 METs
Lawn and garden work	3–6.0 METs
Sexual activity (active, vigorous)	5.0 METs
Vigorous sports (running, swimming laps, hockey)	8–12.0 METs
Jogging	7.0 METs
Slow sports (golf, gymnastics, badminton)	3–5.0 METs
Winter sports (skiing, skating)	6–7.0 METs

To calculate caloric expenditure, multiply the number of METs by the
number of minutes engaged in the activity by 1.2. For instance, half an
hour of jogging for an average-sized man would result in 30 minutes ×
7 METs × 1.2 = 252 calories.

Week 17, Day 4

It is important to learn about dehydration and exercise. When you exercise,
you may lose as much as 5 percent of your body weight in water. This represents a loss of approximately 3 to 4 liters, or 7 percent of the total body
water. A reduction in total body water by as little as 2 percent (approximately
half a liter) may lead to a significant detriment in exercise performance and
endurance. Even when you replenish fluids throughout exercise, the rate of

loss remains high, at roughly 1 liter per hour. This is often referred to as voluntary fluid loss and corresponds to approximately one-third of the total fluid loss. The remainder of the fluid loss is typically replenished during the 24 hours after exercise. Therefore, it is extremely important to prepare for exercise by drinking water prior to working out and to continue replacement during and after exercise (for up to 24 hours).

While you are working out, fluids are redistributing in your body, resulting in different amounts of fluid loss in different parts of the body. For example, the loss in blood volume is compensated by an increase in cardiac output and redistribution of blood flow to ensure that the organ systems are properly nourished. Gender is a factor: Women typically sweat less and cool off by redistributing their blood circulation toward the skin, while men tend to cool off by perspiration, resulting in more fluid loss. By itself, sweating in a hot climate can lead to fluid loss as high as $1^1/_2$ liters per hour. With sweating comes loss of electrolytes, such as sodium, potassium, and chlorate.

Fluid and electrolyte replacement play a critical role during long-duration exercise and exercise in a hot climate.

Because of fluid distribution and the excessive loss of fluid during exercise, it is important that rehydration be started as much as 12 to 24 hours before strenuous exercise. For moderate exercise, free access to water during exercise and responding to thirst signals for several hours afterward is generally sufficient. Individuals with particular medical conditions, such as diabetes or respiratory or cardiac disorders, should discuss hydration with their doctor. Ask about the amounts of fluid, the kind of fluid, and the risks of dehydration prior to any aggressive exercise program.

Week 17, Day 5

We do not recommend that you buy sophisticated home equipment until you have had proper training and a better understanding of what your exercise requirements and preferences will be.

However, certain exercise equipment is relatively inexpensive and easy to purchase. Ask your fitness trainer for help in deciding what would be useful to have in your home. These could include simple equipment like free weights, tubing, and a Physioball or pricier pieces like a stationary bike, elliptical trainer, or stair-climber. You may even decide to give away or sell old equipment that is accumulating dust and taking up space as a reminder that you are making a lifestyle change.

Do not forget that safe and efficient clothing and footwear is an important part of "equipment." If you have diabetes or other medical conditions, such as swelling of the legs or excessive abdominal girth, you may require customized fitness clothing to make exercise safe and appealing to you. A superlarge and long T-shirt and baggy sweatpants may be a good temporary solution for overweight women. Later you can buy the new high-tech outfits that you will enjoy wearing.

When You Travel

Your basic exercise equipment while traveling is your body. If you are always on the move, you need to learn strength yoga and calisthenics (for example, push-ups and sit-ups) and combine these with transportable equipment, such as tubing and jump ropes. If you have more than one home, you may wish to equip each with minimal exercise equipment. When choosing your hotel, make a point to ask about gym and other fitness facilities. Your trainer may offer further helpful tips.

Week 17, Day 6

Two thoughts to motivate and inspire you:

> There is only one corner of the universe you can be certain of improving, and that is your own self.
>
> ALDOUS HUXLEY

> Success is dependent on effort.
>
> SOCRATES

Week 17, Day 7

There is nothing better than a nice, relaxing bath after an exercise session. This could be combined with a steam shower or sauna. Certain oils, such as arnica, are used for muscle aches. Bath salts are used for joint aches. Make it a routine to take a bath, massage and stretch your muscles, and look for blisters and bruises if your circulation is poor.

Depending on the kind of exercise you engage in and the climate in which you live, as well as the season, you may treat your skin by adding oils to the bath or by applying an antioxidant skin mask while in the bath. This is a true finale to your worthy efforts.

Try this recipe for a comforting, healing bath using oils that help improve body tissue tone: Run a hot bath to the temperature you like. While the water is running, add the following oils (available at most natural food stores):

5 drops grapefruit oil
5 drops lemon oil
5 drops sage oil
5 drops basil oil

Week 18: Finding Inspiration

Week 18, Day 1

People draw inspiration from a variety of sources, but many are able to find meaningful motivation in the pages of a book. We've compiled this partial list of titles that our patients have found helpful in navigating the sometimes turbulent waters of lifestyle change:

The Gift of a Year: How to Achieve the Most Meaningful, Satisfying and Pleasurable Year of Your Life, by Mira Kirshenbaum (Dutton, 2000). A one-year plan for instituting major or minor life change, with a special focus on women's issues.

How to Find More Time for Yourself Every Day: A 7-Step Plan That Will Change Your Life, by Stephanie Culp (Better Way Books, 1994). Organization and time management tips and strategies.

The Simpler Life: An Inspirational Guide to Living Better with Less, by Deborah Deford (Readers Digest Books, 1998). Realistic advice on how to make your life more satisfying with a soulful voice.

Take Time for Your Life: A 7-Step Program for Creating the Life You Want, by Cheryl Richardson (Broadway Books, 1999). A "coach" for lifestyle change.

Life Makeovers: 52 Practical and Inspiring Ways to Improve Your Life One Week at a Time, by Cheryl Richardson (Broadway Books, 2000). An idea a week for life improvement.

The Emotional Energy Factor: The Secrets High-Energy People Use to Beat Emotional Fatigue, by Mira Kirshenbaum (Delacourt Press, 2003). How to figure out what's draining your energy.

Time Management from the Inside Out: The Foolproof System for Taking Control of Your Schedule—and Your Life, by Julie Morgenstern (Holt, 2000). An intuitive view of time management.

Choosing Happiness: Keys to a Joyful Life, by Alexandra Stoddard (HarperCollins, 2002). Fresh ideas on connecting to the joy of life.

Week 18, Day 2

It is wise to cultivate the habit of regularly reevaluating how your life is feeling and working for you. Here is a list of questions to help you figure out whether you are doing a good job of balancing your needs and responsibilities to others with your commitment to living the life you want:

- What was the last "big thing" I did just for myself?
- I can name a long list of people I take care of, but where is my own name on that list? Do I feel guilty when I put my needs before those of others?
- What do I dream about doing? Am I taking any steps toward accomplishing that goal?
- What do I consider "essential" in my life? Do the choices I make honor that?
- What drains my energy? Is there a way to reduce negative flow?
- What sustains me? Is there a way to add more of that to my life?

Week 18, Day 3

It is easier for many people to give help to others than to ask for it for themselves. Yet to be successful in changing your life—and making that change permanent—you will need support from the people who are close to you. Our lives are connected to the lives of others. The changes you make in your life will affect the lives of those close to you, so it is important that you make clear the reasons you want and need to change, that you describe clearly what payoff you seek.

Here are some ideas on how to receive useful, valuable support from the people in your life in a way that feels good to you and to them:

- Consider the impact your actions will have on others. If you are responsible for them—say, because you prepare your family's meals and will now only be eating the foods on your plan—come up with an alternative that will consider how their needs will be met (for example, buying takeout food).
- Cultivate a positive attitude so that your enthusiasm is apparent and the people who love you will understand the importance of this change to you. Believe that others will want you to succeed and will be happy to help you.
- Don't allow neediness on the part of others to get in your way.
- If you encounter resistance, pay close attention to what is being said. If obstacles are put in your path, work together to solve them. If a person is fearful that change means that he or she will be left behind, provide reassurance of your feelings and evidence that you, happier, will be a better partner, parent, or friend, for example.

Week 18, Day 4

In the same way that you need to see results for your efforts—looking better, feeling better, movement on the scale—the people you are asking for support will appreciate evidence that they are valued and that their efforts are appreciated.

- To whatever extent is comfortable for you, communicate with generosity about what is going on in your life, and with this program in particular. Talk about how you feel. Note your progress. Celebrate your victories.

- Regularly thank people for their support. Be specific about how much it means to you. Be clear about what a difference it makes to know they are in your corner. A small gift of appreciation or a handwritten thank-you note is a good idea.
- Communicate your needs clearly, cleanly, specifically. Use "I" statements, asking for what you want without being accusatory or defensive.
- Do not apologize. Remember that you have a right to ask for what you want.
- Ask how you can trade favors. It might be that your progress in changing your life motivates someone close to you to tackle a problem of his or her own. You can provide support for each other and both be richer for the experience.

Week 18, Day 5

It is inevitable that changing your health will lead you to evaluate how other parts of your life are working. This is a time to get in touch with who you *really* are and what you *really* want in life. That doesn't mean that you have to change everything. Rather, it is a call to be authentic, to laugh—hard—when you want to laugh, to cry when you need to cry.

Take time to focus on your feelings, and identify what it is you are feeling at a particular point in time. Knowing this is the first step to communicating it (or deciding when *not* to communicate, because not every feeling needs to be shared).

Pay attention to what makes you happy. This is what you need more of in your life.

Pay attention to what ties your stomach in knots. This is what you need to get rid of in your life.

It may be a radical thought, but remember, you have a right to a life that you enjoy! Do what you need to do to make that a reality, not a distant goal.

Week 18, Day 6

An important key to succeeding at life change is learning to recognize when you are getting in your own way—for instance, playing a "tape" of negative thoughts in your head—and changing it. One effective way to do this is quite simply to change the negative tape to a positive one.

This is called using *affirmations*. An affirmation is a simple statement that you repeat to yourself—as a reminder, a reinforcement, a motivator, an inspirational tool. It is a way to reprogram yourself to think positive thoughts that will help you build the life you want, as opposed to negative thought, which only discourage you. Thoughts can become self-fulfilling prophecies, so it makes sense to make those thoughts productive ones.

An affirmation is a statement that helps create the state of mind you want to have for yourself. It reinforces your beliefs. It is useful when you learn to stop yourself when you begin to feel stressed, anxious, or about to lose control.

Breathe deeply, and replace what you are thinking with what you *should* be thinking.

Here are some ideas on how to create an affirmation, or set of affirmations, that will prove powerfully motivating to you:

- Use the present tense, so your affirmation describes you in the here and now. ("I am strong and healthy.")
- Describe yourself as you want to be. ("I am calm and relaxed.")
- Be personal, using "I" statements and words that are meaningful to you. ("I value myself.")
- Be positive. ("I am accomplishing my goal" rather than "I am working to lose 100 pounds.")
- Visualize yourself achieving what it is you are working toward.
- Repeat as necessary throughout your day!

Week 18, Day 7

Is there a quote that you have found inspirational—either in your recent efforts at changing your life and getting healthy or perhaps that has always been meaningful?

Consider whether you have encountered words of wisdom that have made a difference in your life—that perhaps provided the inspiration to change at a time when you struggled with a difficult question or transition. Or perhaps it was a comment—spoken by a friend or mentor, read in a book, or just picked up from the general wisdom of the culture—that is particularly apt at summarizing what you believe life to be about.

Take this quote and make something of it. Write it in your own penmanship, and decorate it. Use your computer to create a small poster. Needlepoint or embroider it. Have it inscribed on a favorite photo.

Place this quote in a place where you will see it and be able to draw inspiration from it. While we each need to figure out for ourselves what is important in life, it can be enormously comforting—and motivating—to think of the others who've faced similar challenges successfully.

Week 19: Time Management

Week 19, Day 1

Many of our patients find that the process of taking control over their physical self, losing weight and committing to getting healthy, propels them to take control over other parts of their life as well. The sense of empowerment can be contagious!

You now have some experience in what it means to take care of yourself by eating right and exercising. When you first began the program, it is likely that your day felt upended; all the time you needed to spend planning your meals and shopping for and preparing different foods might have been overwhelming. By now, though, you have worked this new routine into your life, and it feels normal.

What does your daily schedule look like? How has it been altered by your commitment to healthy living?

What other changes would you like to make in your life?

Take some time to consider those questions. Think about your job and whether you want to work more or fewer hours. Think about your family and whether you feel you are devoting an appropriate amount of time to the people you love. Think about your hobbies and passions and whether you have made room for their pursuit in your life. And think about your finances and whether you are handling money in a responsible, timely manner.

The answers to these questions will help determine how to allocate your time during the day and during the week.

Week 19, Day 2

Understanding and being clear about what you want in life, in the big picture, is the essential first step in putting time to work for you. And—perhaps surprisingly—that is the goal, to have a life that is organized around what you want, rather than organizing yourself completely around what life is asking of you.

Think about the different categories in your life, and make a list that reflects what your life is about. A typical list might include:

Self
Family
Friends
Work
Money
Home
Spirituality
Interests/Hobbies

The next question to ask yourself is, What do I want from each of these categories? Just one or two goals for each is sufficient. For *self*, for instance, you might identify "health" and "happy relationships." For *home* you might say "inviting" and "neat"; for *spirituality*, "sense of purpose," "connection with a higher being" or "giving to the community."

Now that you have laid out on paper what you want from life, the next step is to devise a concrete plan that will get you there. Think about immediate and long-term plans: To make your home more inviting, you might schedule one day to eliminate clutter immediately, while a long-term plan might be to add on a family room.

When you begin to make a practice of identifying priorities and strate-gizing how to make them happen, you are committing yourself to change and providing the tools to succeed. This is how you take control over your schedule—one step at a time.

Week 19, Day 3

If you are frustrated with how your life feels, it is probably because you have allowed others to set your priorities for you. While it is true that few of us have *total* control over what we do with our time, it is also true that we have more control than we may believe. For instance, there are many chores and responsibilities that constitute good parenting; you need to love, care for, feed, play with, listen to, read to, and spend time with your child. But running the PTO is not an essential task of motherhood. For some men and women, involvement in school affairs is personally rewarding—and it certainly is a valuable and important way to spend your time. But your involvement is strictly optional: Your first commitment should be to your family and yourself, and if you don't have time to run bake sales this year because you are trying to take better care of yourself, *that is okay.*

The first step in learning to say no is figuring out what you want to do and what you don't want to do. The exercises of the last two days should have helped you to identify your goals and priorities.

The second step in learning to say no is recognizing that you cannot do everything. Taking on a new responsibility means letting something else go (unless boredom and lack of purpose has been a problem for you). When someone asks something of you, ask yourself what impact it will have on your schedule.

The third step is giving yourself permission to say no to those activities and commitments that are optional and that don't fit well into your plan for what you want from life.

The fourth, and final, step is *just saying it. Just say no!* Many people make up excuses or offer long lists of reasons why. If you feel compelled to explain yourself, then do so. But as you gain practice in saying no for the right reason—because the request doesn't fit into your view of what you should be doing with your time—you may find that the simplest response is accepted unquestioningly.

Week 19, Day 4

Professional organizers have many tricks and strategies for streamlining record keeping and organizing, for controlling clutter, and for saving time. It's a good idea to routinely pick up books or articles on organization and time management and scan them for ideas that might be useful in your life.

Here are a few we like:

- Designate a place near your entry to keep bags, keys, calendars, backpacks, umbrellas, cell phones, and other things you often need on the way out the door.
- To simplify food shopping, plan several weeks' meals in advance. Make a master shopping list. Try out Internet shopping with delivery service if it is available in your area.
- Set up "task centers" around your home for laundry, financial management, homework, TV/video viewing, and so forth. Plan for storage of all related items so you don't have to waste time searching for the remote control, a video, a warm blanket, and so on.
- Schedule tasks—such as grocery shopping, laundry, and bill paying—so they rotate predictably through your weeks and months.
- Organize systems for filing everything you keep—not only financial records but also photos, journals, greeting cards, and recipes.
- Figure out which tasks you dislike, and evaluate whether there is a way to delegate by trading with someone else or hiring outside help.
- Write in your personal calendar time commitments for exercise, seeing friends, even reading—all activities that are vital to your sense of self and satisfaction.
- Multitask when it makes sense. Bring reading material to appointments or car pools where you will have empty time on your hands; chat on the phone with a friend while cooking dinner.

Week 19, Day 5

Being organized about your eating habits reduces the likelihood that you will lapse from the healthy diet you are working to establish as a routine. Here are some strategies that will help keep you on track in the dietary realm:

- Organize the food storage systems in your home in a way that makes sense to your own needs and those of your family. Keep your healthy snacks in one place, snacks for your children in another. Store breakfast foods together. Keep cut-up fresh vegetables in a crisper so they are always available.
- Sort foods in your cabinet so you can easily find what you are looking for.
- If some family members want foods that are problematic to you, designate an out-of-the-way place to keep them where you won't encounter temptation all the time.
- Schedule food shopping into your week for a time when you can do the job with mindfulness—and when you aren't hungry.
- Shop with a plan, not only for meals but also for snacks and even an occasional healthy indulgence, so you are prepared in advance for your hunger.
- Evaluate your calendar with an eye toward situations that are likely to present challenges to you, and build in an advance strategy for healthy coping. For instance, if you have a dinner party on a weekend evening, make sure you have time to exercise earlier in the day, and eat a light snack beforehand so you aren't tempted to overeat out of intense hunger.

Week 19, Day 6

It is not just the physical aspects of your life that need to be consciously organized but also your "internal" space—your mind and how you approach your daily and weekly schedule.

Here are some suggestions to help you feel—and *be*—more in control of your life.

- Cluster activities in your schedule in a way that makes sense: nature of activity (shopping), location (southeastern part of town), energy required (if you are a slow starter, avoid scheduling activities in the early morning), even attire (things you need to be "dressed up" for).
- In earlier sections, we have discussed how different it is to take time to care for yourself—for exercise, healthy food preparation, your rewards. Schedule this time into your day, writing down these commitments as "appointments" that you must fit into your day.
- Consider the rhythm of your day and week and how you like it to feel. Do you like a very structured routine? Do you like variety? Do you prefer a similar pace to all your days, or do you like to have some that are busy and others that are relaxed? To the extent that you can control your schedule, consider your preferences in making appointments and engagements. (You don't have to share your reasoning when you say "I can't make it" because you want a relaxed pace to a particular day.)

Week 19, Day 7

For this week's reward, we suggest that you upgrade your organizational tools. Think about your personal style and about the various types of scheduling devices—electronic, paper, portable, desk based—that are currently available. What intrigues you? What feels most natural? What do you find appealing in an aesthetic and sensory way?

Budget considerations are always valid, but remember that your organizational tool is an essential, vital aspect of your life and one with which you will interact numerous times every day!

So, whether you are buying a lovely red leather calendar to carry in your bag, the latest PDA in a slick black case, or new software for your home computer, choose the tool that will give you pleasure *and* purpose in your life!

Week 20: Mindfulness

Week 20, Day 1

Most of us spend most of our lives somewhere else, somewhere other than where we are. As we go about our days, doing our jobs, being with our families and friends, running the machinery of our lives, our minds are elsewhere. We are not paying much—if any—attention to ourselves and the world around us, which is why life can be so unsatisfying.

Mindfulness is the concept of being fully alert, fully conscious—alive and aware and involved—in the present moment as opposed to having your mind wander aimlessly around, wondering what other people are thinking about you, as opposed to processing your preconceived ideas about people, places, activities, as opposed to assuming that you have access to the thoughts, attitudes, and motivations of others around you, as opposed to planning the next thing you will say or do, as opposed to preparing your response to what someone is saying to you, as opposed to wishing you were somewhere else, as opposed to planning and living in the future, as opposed to remembering and living in the past.

You get the picture: Mindfulness is the ability to stay in the here and now, to experience fully what is happening in your mind, body, and environment. While it means allowing yourself to feel and experience things you may wish to avoid (boredom, unhappiness in a relationship), the practice of mindfulness also enables you to fully experience satisfaction and joy.

Week 20, Day 2

Mindfulness is very much a matter of practice. It involves a commitment to being mindful and a decision to keep returning to awareness of the moment—the one you are in *right now*! Mindfulness does not happen naturally. The tendency of the mind to wander is not a *bad* thing for which the owner should be judged; it is a natural tendency of the lazy, untrained mind. We can teach ourselves ways to gently bring the mind back into the moment, to where we are now, in order that we may have the experience of living our actual lives.

Here is a common exercise to introduce the concept of mindfulness:

Take one raisin—only one. Sit quietly for a moment, and concentrate on how your body feels. Do nothing else. Now look at the raisin, slowly, noticing its size, its shape, its contours, and the interplay of light and shadows. Touch the raisin, and feel its size, texture, consistency. Place the raisin in your mouth—don't chew. For a moment, just feel the raisin on your tongue; notice how your mouth responds to its presence. Begin to chew, slowly, again noticing the different sensations and tastes. Swallow the raisin as slowly as you can, with awareness of what you are experiencing. Sit quietly for another few minutes and think about what you are feeling.

This exercise helps to illuminate how incredibly rich and complex even the simplest experiences in our lives can be if we are mindful. Our body—not our mind—is our most valuable tool for living; yet all too often we allow our mind to dictate our reality.

Several times a day, make a practice of focusing on your body and how it feels. Use your experience with the raisin as a template. Sit quietly. Notice how your feet, legs, knees, thighs, seat, stomach, chest, arms, shoulders, neck, jaw, cheeks, forehead, and scalp feel. Scan your body, head to toe, taking in awareness of your physiological response to the things that are going on in your life. Don't judge, just notice—and relax each body part. This is mindfulness.

Week 20, Day 3

We consider breathing to be an involuntary action, one that occurs naturally, without intent. Yet the breath can be a powerful tool for connecting mind and body and for taking control over your unpleasant or destructive emotions and feelings. With training and attention, the breath can be used to energize or relax, to heat up the body or cool it down. Conscious, intentional breathing through the nose or mouth can also be used for other, more specific purposes, such as stress management, fear control, anger control, and meditation.

Throughout the day, take a few minutes to stop what you are doing, sit quietly, and focus on your breathing. As you become more attuned to your breathing, it is likely that you will also begin to notice how your breathing fluctuates with regard to your activity level, your mood, and your state of mind. When you are tense, breathing becomes rapid and shallow. Breathing in a relaxed state is slow, deep.

There is a physiological connection between how you breathe and how you feel, which means that you can actually use your breath to help you achieve a different emotional state. When you feel agitated, stop for a moment, and concentrate on taking long, slow breaths. Notice how your body responds: your heart rate slows down, your mind clears.

Here are a few exercises you can try to help you give attention to your breathing and achieve a different emotional state:

- Sit comfortably in an upright position, placing your right index finger on your left nostril. Breathe in through your right nostril, then put your thumb on your right nostril and breathe out through your left nostril. Do this for 2 minutes, and see how your body feels. Reverse, for another 2 minutes, and notice the difference in how your body feels.
- Inhale four times, counting 1—2—3—4. Once you have reached full lung capacity, breathe out the same way, in four short sniffs, 1—2—3—4. Repeat several times as a way to clear and relax the mind.
- To clear your mind during physical activity, such as walking, running, or using a stair-climber, focus on counting your breaths—breathing consciously, two breaths in, two breaths out. Each time you feel your mind begin to wander, gently return to your counting.

Week 20, Day 4

As we have discussed previously, many people who have ended up overweight have a history of interpreting many different sorts of feelings as "hunger" in the physical sense and substituting food for other sources of satisfaction. Fear, boredom, unhappiness, anger—these are all feelings that are unpleasant to face and that we may have assuaged with cookies, chips, or other unhealthy foods that are eaten as a distraction rather than for nourishment.

We need to be mindful—aware—emotionally, as well as physically.

An important aspect of being mindful is slowing down enough that you can take the time to notice and process what you are feeling. If your life and schedule are so full that you never sit down, never have time to think, the odds are that you have a difficult time knowing and understanding what you are feeling.

Developing the habit of checking in with yourself and labeling your feelings is another aspect to mindfulness. Several times during the day, make a point to stop and focus on how you feel—and why. If you are feeling agitated (and are taking it out on a customer, your significant other, or your child), stop and ask yourself whether your anger or annoyance should be directed at this person—or if there is perhaps another cause, maybe even one you are trying not to pay attention to (fear that you might lose your job, anxiety over mounting debt, or perhaps a marital issue, for instance).

Understanding what you feel is the most important aspect of emotional health. Not all problems can be solved, especially in relationships, but identifying your emotions helps to put them in context. Once you understand what is bothering you, you can figure out whether this is a problem that can be solved or one you need to learn to live with, without allowing it to control your life—and without looking for a solution in the refrigerator!

Week 20, Day 5

The exterior world can be a rich source of pleasure, inspiration, and connectedness—or it can drag you down, making you tense, uneasy, even angry. There is no question that our physical surroundings have a profound impact on our state of mind—whether or not we are aware of it.

Think about how you feel on a gorgeous, sunny day. The first warmth of spring, the crisp cool of autumn—these are environmental cues that fuel our sense of well-being. Conversely, a cold and rainy day; a crowded shopping mall, your aunt Matilda's small, dark, smoky living room may be environments that stress you to your limits.

Awareness of your surroundings and their impact is important in understanding your own emotional state. There are things you cannot change: rain, crowds, the discomfort of Aunt Matilda's home may be out of your realm of control. But understanding their effect on your mood (and the likelihood that you may overeat or lash out in frustration) will help you control your response.

Week 20, Day 6

We may believe that our feelings of overload, insignificance, or unworthiness are unique to us and to the stressful times in which we live. Not so. These are normal and timeless human feelings that people have struggled with forever. (Consider the universal themes of the writings of William Shakespeare, for instance). This beautiful, calming, inspirational piece was written in the sixteenth century. Read it and recognize that your emotions are part of the human condition:

> *Go placidly amid the noise and haste, and remember what peace there may be in silence. As far as possible, without surrender, be on good terms with all persons. Speak your truth quietly and clearly, and listen to others, even the dull and ignorant; they too have their story. Avoid loud and aggressive persons, they are vexations to the spirit. If you compare yourself with others, you may become vain and bitter, for always there will be greater and lesser persons than yourself. Enjoy your achievements as well as your plans. Keep interested in your career, however humble; it is a real possession in the changing fortunes of time. Exercise caution in your business affairs; the world is full of trickery. But let this not blind you to what virtue there is; many persons strive for high ideals, and everywhere life is full of heroism. Be yourself. Especially do not feign affection. Neither be cynical about love, for in the face of all aridity and disenchantment it is perennial as the grass. Take kindly to the counsel of the years, gracefully surrendering the things of youth.*

Nurture strength of spirit to shield you in sudden misfortune. But do not distress yourself with imaginings. Many fears are born of fatigue and loneliness. Beyond a wholesome discipline, be gentle with yourself. You are a child of the universe, no less than the trees and the stars; you have a right to be here. And whether or not it is clear to you, no doubt the universe is unfolding as it should. Therefore, be at peace with God, whatever you conceive him to be, and whatever your labors and aspirations, in the noisy confusion of life, keep peace with your soul. With all its sham, drudgery and broken dreams, it is still a beautiful world. Be careful. Strive to be happy.

Week 20, Day 7

This week has been about reflecting on the world and the rightness of everything within it. Our preconceived notions about how things are, how people are, often limit the experience we have.

This week's reward is the following poem, which describes the quality of mindfulness in relationships:

You and I

We meet as strangers, each carrying a mystery within us.

I cannot say who you are. I may never know you completely.

But I trust that you are a person in your own right, possessed

Of a beauty and a value that are the earth's richest treasures.

I will impose no identities upon you, but will invite you to

Become yourself without shame or fear. I will hold open a

Space for you in the world and allow your right to fill it with

An authentic vocation and purpose. For as long as your

Search takes, you have my loyalty.

AUTHOR UNKNOWN

Weeks 21 and 22: Try Something Different

Week 21: Breathing and Relaxation

Time of Day	M	T	W	T	F	S	S
Morning	Breathing Meditation	Breathing Meditation	Breathing Meditation	Breathing Meditation	Breathing Meditation	Walk in the woods	Garden or walk or hike
Noon							
Afternoon	Yoga class or video	Massage	Aerobics		Yoga class or video	Massage	
Evening	Aromatherapy Bath						

Week 22: Exercising to Rewire Your Body

Time of Day	M	T	W	T	F	S	S
Morning	Pilates video	Core strength	Pilates video	Core strength	Resistance training	Pilates video	
Noon							Tai chi workshop
Afternoon	Yoga class or video		Massage		Yoga class or video	Massage	
Evening		Hot salt bath					

Weeks 21 and 22 require you to set up different schedules. It's time for you to take a break from your established routines and try something different. You may need to purchase videos, go to new yoga and meditation classes, and make a point of getting pampered. You will also need to ask your trainer to teach you new routines or sign up for Pilates and other fitness styles you have not tried yet. See page 305 for some examples. Feel free to modify as you wish.

Week 23: Secondary Benefits of Your Weight Loss

Week 23, Day 1
Weight Gain and Chronic Disease
Since the early 1970s, more than thirty large studies, involving more than 750,000 individuals, with long-term follow-up, have shown clear-cut correlation between incremental rise in BMI and risk of the following diseases:

- Type 2, or adult-onset, diabetes
- Hypertension
- Coronary heart disease
- Stroke
- Gallbladder disease
- Osteoarthritis
- Cancer

In addition, many studies have shown that weight loss can reduce the risk of these diseases in an incremental manner. It is currently estimated that over 64 percent of American adults are overweight and obese. As a society, it is important that we direct our efforts toward improving our lifestyle, with the goal of weight loss as one of our top national priorities.

Make a list of your loved ones (for example, your spouse) and close friends who you think suffer from one of the above conditions. Do a Web search on obesity and their specific condition. Read it and inform yourself. Then discuss it with them. If you are sensitive and gentle, you may help them take the first step toward lifestyle change.

Week 23, Day 2

Therapeutic Lifestyle Change Targeting Weight Loss for Diabetes Prevention
Several well-designed studies have now confirmed that as little as 5 to 7 percent body weight loss can have a profound impact in diabetes risk reduction. In a well-publicized study published in the prestigious *New England Journal of Medicine* in the fall of 2001, a group of European investigators showed that this degree of weight loss reduces risk of diabetes by approximately 58 percent. That means that one out of two people who would otherwise get diabetes were able to avoid it for as long as they maintained their "healthy" lifestyle.

A more recent (2002) and larger study conducted by the National Institutes of Health confirmed the earlier findings of the European study, showing that regardless of age, gender, and ethnicity, weight loss results in approximately 58 percent risk reduction for type 2 diabetes. In this study, a combination of diet and moderate exercise gave better—in fact, twice as good—results than metformin, the medication currently used for diabetes prevention.

One out of three American females and one out of four American males will have diabetes during their life. Discuss diabetes prevention with your coworkers at lunch. By now you know more than most of them. If you are sensitive and gentle, without suggesting that you have anyone specific in mind, you may help them take the first step toward lifestyle change.

Week 23, Day 3

Fat Loss and Cardiovascular Disease (review discussion in the book)
Even a modest weight loss of 5 percent body weight has beneficial effects in reducing cardiovascular disease risk. Numerous studies have shown that fat loss, in particular abdominal fat loss, results in a rise in the "good" (HDL) cholesterol and a drop in the "bad" fats (such as triglycerides and LDL). With even a minimal improvement in the cholesterol profile, there is a significant benefit for heart disease prevention. Therefore, even minor dietary and lifestyle changes in the long run have significant impact on mortality from heart disease. In addition to its beneficial results in cholesterol profile, physical activity results in improved cardiac oxygenation,

better vascular tone, lower blood pressure, and a reduced chance of arrhythmia and clotting risks. Finally, regular exercise plays a significant role in stress reduction and recovery from depression.

To reach cardio protective levels, you have to exercise the equivalent of 1,500 calories per week. This would correspond roughly to moderate-intensity aerobic exercise 30 minutes five days per week. It could, however, be divided into shorter but more intense routines, such as spinning, or longer and less frequent workouts, such as long-distance walking or jogging.

Week 23, Day 4
Weight Loss and Cancer

Weight loss reduces the risk of all cancers. But cancers that are hormone dependent, such as breast, ovarian, and prostate cancer, are particularly impacted by excess body fat. In addition, risk of death from these cancers, once they are diagnosed, also increases dramatically with obesity. Risk of breast cancer death *doubles*, for example, in women who are obese.

Reach out to cancer survivors you know. Call them up and ask them if they want to engage in an exercise program with you. Let them know about your weight loss efforts, your diet, your experience with yoga, and so on. Get them interested in weight loss without sounding intrusive or "pushy." You are a role model now. Use your power and help others, but be gentle and sensitive.

Week 23, Day 5
Weight Loss and Other Medical Conditions

One out of four American adults has metabolic syndrome. People with metabolic syndrome have a 200 to 400 percent increase in their risk of mortality from cardiovascular disease. Cardiovascular disease in metabolic syndrome is often silent for years.

You may be able to save the lives of your loved ones. If you are sensitive and gentle, you may encourage someone you care for who has metabolic syndrome to have a cardiac evaluation. If you are not sure they have metabolic syndrome, you may copy the screening survey for metabolic syndrome in this book and give it to them. They will contact their doctor, and they will thank you.

There is not a single medical condition not negatively impacted by weight gain. In fact, after tobacco, obesity is now considered the number two preventable killer.

Consider donating money, time, or resources to fight against obesity.

Week 23, Day 6
Childhood Obesity
You probably have some children in your extended family who are obese. Contact them, give them your love, stay in touch with them. Do not pressure them into any forced change. Give them unconditional love in ways that are not food related.

Week 23, Day 7
Weight Loss and Body Image: A Nonmedical Reward
You may have relatives who have low self-esteem because of their body image. You may have been one of them. Reach out to them. Ask them to come and visit. Let them talk to you about their fears, their disappointments. Just listen; they need someone to talk to. Leave the counseling to others, but you can share your new feelings about an improved sense of inner self and body image with them.

Week 24: Maintenance

Week 24, Day 1
Congratulations! You are very near the end of our six-month weight loss program. It is important to realize, however, that this doesn't mean that you can return to your old life—at least not if you like the changes you have made.

The process of losing weight may have taken six months, but the process of keeping it off will take the rest of your life. As we say at our center, the postobese state is a state of remission, not cure. This means that you will need to commit to living a healthy lifestyle forever—but that's good news, not bad news.

Taking care of yourself—in every way, in all the ways we have discussed these past six months, not just in terms of food choices—is key to living a satisfying life. *Living, that is—not merely existing.*

In the twenty-first century, we have reason to expect a longer, healthier life than humans have ever experienced. It is not a birthright, however; it is our personal obligation to invest now in our health so that we can maintain our vitality into our later years.

Week 24, Day 2

Key to succeeding not only at weight loss but also at weight maintenance is understanding that there is a fundamental change in the philosophy of how you are living your life.

While you may have motivated yourself these past six months with a vision of what it would mean to *lose* weight and get healthy, you are now shifting to a new paradigm: health maximization.

This means that you are eating, exercising, and living your life with a vision of who you now are, a healthy and active person.

Think of ways you can affirm that in your life.

Week 24, Day 3

Assuming you have reached your goal, you can now expand your repertoire of foods to include many that have formerly been off limits. Now there is room for some discretionary use of "fun" or "recreational" foods. However, the key is learning what the limitations are—how these foods fit into a healthy lifestyle and how you can make trade-offs from one food to another on occasion.

There will likely be up to several hundred more calories per day that you can add to your food plan. If you overdo it, you will regain weight, so expect a learning curve to include a few ups and downs on the scale.

Eventually, you will learn the fine art of self-regulation—which is tomorrow's topic.

Week 24, Day 4

Most people who maintain a healthy weight actually fluctuate within a range of up to 5 pounds. Most of this fluctuation is due to water weight. At this point in your life, when weight loss is new and maintenance is newer yet, it is a good idea to be in the habit of weighing yourself several times a week, if not daily.

It is important, however, to recognize that the scale will move up and down. You might want to graph your weight over time to see how these fluctuations play out. Most of our patients find that over the course of a month, you can draw a line through the ups and downs that will average out as a straightish line.

Do not allow the number on the scale on any single day to change how you eat or how you feel about yourself. Consistency with the process will bear out over time.

If you are doing the right things most of the time, your weight will be stable and healthy.

In time, many people reach a point where they become confident in their ability to maintain a healthy weight. They no longer need daily or even weekly weigh-ins, because they are attuned to how their body looks and feels. This process of self-regulation will become a normal and natural aspect to taking excellent care of yourself.

Week 24, Day 5

Our population as a whole is heavier than ever before, despite apparent awareness of what it takes to lose weight. Children are heavier at an earlier age and are now coming down with diseases formerly associated with middle age, such as adult-onset diabetes and hypertension. Clearly, knowledge is not enough.

What is discouraging is that a high percentage of people who have managed to be successful at weight loss end up regaining their weight, and sometimes even more, within a few years. So it is important to recognize that maintenance is difficult, but doable.

Research has shown that certain behaviors typically accompany successful long-term weight loss:

- *Consistent, frequent exercise.* This is the single most important predictor of an individual's ability to sustain weight loss. While there is not yet a consensus as to the optimal amount or type of exercise, generally speaking, it's more than you think. Aim to include significant physical activity in your life, most days of the week. Optimally, this should include a combination of cardiovascular, strengthening, and flexibility components.

- *Periodic checking in on portion size and total caloric intake.* Over time, many people add a little bit here and a little bit there, but don't consider that extra spoonful of sugar to be significant in their daily intake. As noted before, just 100 additional calories a day will add 10 pounds in body weight over the course of one year. If you are eating ten items a day and you make an error of just 10 calories per item, barely perceptible in quantity, there is the extra 100 calories!

- *Belief in your ability to sustain the changes.* Called "internal locus of control," this has been found to be an important factor in making any changes permanent. This means that you have taken responsibility and accountability for your own actions and choices, despite the obstacles life throws in your direction.

Week 24, Day 6

As you are losing weight, the changes that you see and feel are apparent, not only to you but to others around you. Every week you look different. You get compliments, you buy clothing in smaller sizes, you decrease medications, you have more energy, you feel and look better. These, in and of themselves, provide compelling motivation and reinforcement for your efforts.

However, a year later, people will no longer be paying as much attention to how well you are doing, and your reinforcements and motivators must come from within.

It is important, therefore, to maintain a real connection with yourself. Part of taking care of yourself, as we have discussed in previous weeks, is knowing what you feel and when you are feeling it. Now that you have lost weight, make sure you *notice* how good you look and feel—and conversely, take note of what happens when you are less focused on eating well and exercising (as inevitably happens at times). How you feel can and should be a powerful motivating tool.

It's worth noting, also, that a common misconception among people who have worked hard to lose a lot of weight is that once the weight is off, life will be perfect. Not so!

You will have many of the same problems—you will just be thinner and healthier. What is good, however, is that you can use the same problem-solving skills to address other issues in your life, hopefully with as much success as your weight loss efforts.

If you had previously been using food to cope with the discomforts and disappointments of life—for instance, the unfairness of having diabetes, losing a job, caring for sick parents, being single or in an unhappy marriage—you will now need to find nonfood solutions or ways to make yourself feel better. During the weight loss phase, adherence to a structured eating plan provides comfort and a sense of control that feels really good. During maintenance, when there is less structure, it may feel scary to have to rely on yourself.

This is where getting in touch with your feelings and needs becomes imperative. Seeking the appropriate response to your needs, rather than translating every sensation to one of hunger, is challenging and requires significant dedication. Fortunately, you have already seen how effective and rewarding the process of changing your life can be.

Week 24, Day 7

The weekly reward has been a significant aspect of our program—and it is one that our patients tell us they really begin to look forward to. We have experimented with lots of different ways of providing rewards—some are external, others come from within.

This week, take some time to think about the many different sorts of rewards you have experienced over the course of the program. Which ones did you find most meaningful? Which ones didn't make much difference to you?

Choose your favorite reward, and try it again this week. If it was going out for a healthful meal, call a friend and schedule dinner out, and go with the confidence that you can savor your meal without sabotaging your health. If you enjoyed your first massage, have another.

You deserve to feel good—and you don't need to indulge in unhealthy eating. Think about what it is you like most about this type of reward, and consider how you can incorporate it into your life on a regular basis. If it is massage, for instance, you might set aside money you would normally use to buy lunch and bring lunch from home instead. Chances are, the money will accrue quickly enough that you can afford a biweekly or monthly massage. If you love the way you look in your new smaller and more fashionable clothing, decide to treat yourself regularly. Some rewards, of course, cost nothing at all. Spending time with friends, taking long walks at the beach, writing in your journal—these are all ways to reward yourself, connect with the parts of yourself you like the best, and feel good without overindulging!

Go for it!

Selected Bibliography

Metabolic Syndrome and Related Conditions

Bjorntorp, P. "Etiology of Metabolic Syndrome." In *Handbook of Obesity*, 2nd ed., edited by G. A. Bray and C. Bouchard, Chapter 32. New York: Marcel Dekker, 2004.

Bjorntorp, P., and R. Eosmond. "Hypothalamic Origin of the Metabolic Syndrome X." *Annals of the New York Academy of Sciences* 892 (1999): 297–307.

Bouchard, C., et al. "The Response to Long-Term Overfeeding in Identical Twins." *New England Journal of Medicine* 322 (1990): 1477–82.

Bouchard, C., and L. Perusse. "Genetics of Obesity." *Annual Review of Nutrition* 13 (1993): 337–54.

Carr, M.C. "The Emergence of the Metabolic Syndrome with Menopause." *Journal of Clinical Endocrinology and Metabolism* 88, 6 (2003): 2404–11.

Damcott, C.M., P. Sack, and A.R. Shuldiner. "The Genetics of Obesity." *Endocrinology and Metabolism Clinics of North America* 32, 4 (2003): 761–86.

Eckel, R.H., and R.M. Krauss. "American Heart Association Call to Action: Obesity as a Major Risk Factor for Coronary Heart Disease." *Circulation* 97 (1998): 2099–100.

Ferrai, P., et al. "Altered Insulin Sensitivity, Hyperinsulinemia and Dyslipidemia in Individuals with a Hypertensive Parent." *American Journal of Medicine* 91 (1991): 589–96.

Ferrannini, E., et al. "Insulin Resistance and Blood Pressure." In *Insulin Resistance*, edited by G.M. Reaven and A. Laws, 281–308. Totowa, NJ: Humana Press, 1999.

Ford, E.S., W.H. Giles, and W.H. Dietz. "Prevalence of the Metabolic Syndrome Among US Adults." *Journal of the American Medical Association* 287, 3 (2002): 356–59.

Flegal, K.M., et al. "Prevalence and Trends in Obesity Among US Adults, 1999-2000." *Journal of the American Medical Association* 288, 14 (2002): 1723–27.

Gohlke-Barwolf, C. "Coronary Artery Disease: Is Menopause a Risk Factor?" *Basic Research in Cardiology* 95, S1 (2000): 177–83.

Grundy, S.M. "Obesity, Metabolic Syndrome and Cardiovascular Disease." *Journal of Clinical Endocrinology and Metabolism* 89 (2004): 2595–600.

Grundy, S.M., et al. "Clinical Management of Metabolic Syndrome: Report of the American Heart Association/National Heart, Lung and Blood Institute/American Diabetes Association Conference on Scientific Issues Related to Management." *Circulation* 109 (2004): 551–56.

Haffner, S.J., and H. Cassells. "Hyperglycemia as a Cardiovascular Risk Factor." *American Journal of Medicine* 115, 8A (2003): 6S–11S.

Hansen, B.C. "The Metabolic Syndrome X." *Annals of the New York Academy of Sciences* 891 (1999): 1–24.

Kuusisto J., et al. "NIDDM and Its Metabolic Control Predict Coronary Heart Disease in Elderly Patients." *Diabetes* 43 (1994): 960–67.

Montague, C.T., and S. O'Rahilly. "The Perils of Portliness: Causes and Consequences of Visceral Adiposity." *Diabetes* 49 (2000): 883–88.

Ogden, C.L., et al. "Prevalence and Trends in Overweight Among US Children and Adolescents, 1999–2000." *Journal of the American Medical Association* 288, 14 (2002): 1728–32.

Reaven, G.M. "Banting Lecture 1988: Role of Insulin Resistance in Human Disease." *Diabetes* 37, 12 (1988): 1595–607.

Reaven, G.M. "Insulin Resistance: A Chicken That Has Come to Roost." *Annals of the New York Academy of Sciences* 892 (1999): 45–47.

Reaven G.M., H. Lithell, and L. Landsberg. "Hypertension and Associated Metabolic Abnormalities—The Role of Insulin Resistance and the Sympathoadrenal System." *New England Journal of Medicine* 334, 6 (1996): 374–82.

Rocchini, A.P. "Childhood Obesity and a Diabetes Epidemic." *New England Journal of Medicine* 346 (2002): 854–55.

Sowers, J.R. "Obesity as a Cardiovascular Risk Factor." *American Journal of Medicine* 115, 8A (2003): 37S–41S.

Stratton, I.M., et al. "Association of Glycaemia with Macrovascular and Microvascular Complications of Type 2 Diabetes (UKPDS 35)." *British Medical Journal* 321 (2000): 405–12.

Venkat Narayan, K.M., et al. "Lifetime Risk of Diabetes Mellitus in the United States." *Journal of the American Medical Association* 290, 14 (2003): 1884–90.

Biology of Metabolic Syndrome: Hormones, Body Composition, and Excess Fat

Albu, J.B., et al. "Fat Distribution in Health and Obesity." *Annals of the New York Academy of Sciences* 904 (2000): 491–501.

Asakawa, A., et al. "A Role of Ghrelin in Neuroendocrine and Behavioral Responses to Stress in Mice." *Neuroendocrinology* 74 (2001): 143–47.

Baldi, J.C., and N. Snowling. "Resistance Training Improves Glycaemic Control in Obese Type 2 Diabetic Men." *International Journal of Sports Medicine* 24 (2003): 419–23.

Batterham, R.L., S.R. Bloom. "The Gut Hormone Peptide YY Regulates Appetite." *Annals of the New York Academy of Sciences* 994 (2003): 162–68.

Batterham, R.L., et al. "Inhibition of Food Intake in Obese Subjects by Peptide YY3–36." *New England Journal of Medicine* 349 (2003): 941–48.

Bergman, R.N. "Lipid Effects on Carbohydrates." *Endocrine Reviews* S21–1 (2004).

Bergman, R.N., et al. "Burst-like Control of Lipolysis by the Sympathetic Nervous System in Vivo." *Journal of Clinical Investigation* 111 (2003): 257–64.

D'Agostino. F.A., et al. "Elevated Levels of Acute-Phase Proteins and Plasminogen Activator Inhibitor-1 Predict the Development of Type 2 Diabetes: The Insulin Resistance Atherosclerotic Study." *Diabetes* 51 (2002): 1131–37.

Despers, J.P., et al. "The Insulin Resistance-Dyslipidemic Syndrome: Contribution of Visceral Adiposity and Therapeutic Implications." International *Journal of Obesity and Related Metabolic Disorders* 44 (1995): 141–46.

Farooqi, I.S., et al. "Effects of Recombinant Leptin Therapy in a Child with Congenital Leptin Deficiency." *New England Journal of Medicine* 341 (1999): 879–84.

Fernandez-Real, J.M., et al. "Novel Interactions of Adiponectin with the Endocrine System and Inflammatory Parameters." *Journal of Clinical Endocrinology and Metabolism* 88 (2003): 2714–18.

Funlhouser, A.B., et al. "Measurement of Body Fat During Weight Loss in Obese Women: Comparison of Four Methods." *Annals of the New York Academy of Sciences* 904 (2000): 539–41.

Garg, A. "The Role of Body Fat Distribution in *Insulin Resistance*." In Insulin Resistance, edited by G.M. Reaven and A. Laws, 83–96. Totowa, NJ: Humana Press, 1999.

Gavrila, A., et al. "Diurnal and Ultradian Dynamics of Serum Adiponectin in Healthy Men: Comparison with Leptin, Circulating Soluble Leptin Receptor and Cortisol Pattern." *Journal of Clinical Endocrinology and Metabolism* 88 (2003): 2838–43.

Heymfield, S.M., et al. "Recombinant Leptin for Weight Loss in Obese and Lean Adults: A Randomized, Controlled, Dose Escalation Trial." *Journal of the American Medical Association* 282 (1999): 1568–75.

Hotta, K., et al. "Plasma Concentrations of a Novel Adipose-Specific Protein, Adiponectin, in Type 2 Diabetic Patients." *Arteriosclerosis, Thrombosis, and Vascular Biology* 20 (2000): 1595–99.

Janand-Delenne, B., et al. "Visceral Fat as a Main Determinant of Plasminogen Activator Inhibitor 1 Level in Women." *International Journal of Obesity and Metabolic Disorders* 22, 4 (1998): 312–17.

Karelis, A.D., et al. "Metabolic and Body Composition Factors in Subgroups of Obesity: What Do We Know? *Journal of Clinical Endocrinology and Metabolism* 89 (2004): 2563–75.

Kershaw, E.F., and J.S. Flier. "Adipose Tissue as an Endocrine Organ." *Journal of Clinical Endocrinology and Metabolism* 89, 6 (2004): 2548–56.

Kissebah, A.H., and A.N. Peiris. "Biology of Regional Body Fat Distribution: Relationship to Non-Insulin Dependent Diabetes Mellitus." *Diabetes/Metabolism Reviews* 5 (1989): 83–109.

Kockx, M., et al. "Relationship Between Visceral Fat and PAI-1 in Overweight Men and Women Before and After Weight Loss." *Thrombosis and Haemostasis* 82 (1999): 1490–96.

Landsberg, L. "Role of the Sympathetic Adrenal System in the Pathogenesis of the Insulin Resistance Syndrome." *Annals of the New York Academy of Sciences* 892 (1999): 84–90.

Lemieux, P.A., et al. "Age-Related Increase in Visceral Adipose Tissue and Body Fat and the Metabolic Risk Profile of Premenopausal Women." *Diabetes Care* 22 (1999): 1471–78.

Lohman, T.G. "Assessing Body Composition and Changes in Body Composition: Another Look at Dual Energy X-Ray Absorptiometry." *Annals of the New York Academy of Sciences* 904 (2000): 45–54.

Lovejoy, J.C., et al. "Exogenous Androgens Influence Body Composition and Regional Body Fat Distribution in Obese Postmenopausal Women—A Clinical Research Center Study." *Journal of Clinical Endocrinology and Metabolism* 81 (1996): 2198–203.

Lustig, R.H. "The Neuroendocrinology of Obesity." *Endocrinology and Metabolism Clinics of North America* 30, 3 (2001): 765–85.

Lyon, C.J., and W.A. Hsuch. "Effect of Plasminogen Activator Inhibitor-1 in Diabetes Mellitus and Cardiovascular Disease." *American Journal of Medicine* 115, 8A (2003): 62S–68S.

Masuzaki, H., et al. "A Transgenic Model of Visceral Obesity and Metabolic Syndrome." *Science* 294 (2001): 2166–70.

Montague, C.T., et al. "Congenital Leptin Deficiency Is Associated with Severe Early-Onset Obesity in Humans." *Nature* 387 (1997): 903–8.

Morton, N.M., et al. "Novel Adipose Tissue-Mediated Resistance to Diet-Induced Visceral Obesity in 11ß-hydroxysteroid Dehydrogenase Type 1-Deficient Mice." *Diabetes* 53 (2004): 931–38.

Okamoto, Y., et al. "An Adipocyte-Derived Plasma Protein, Adiponectin, Adheres to Injured Vascular Walls." *Hormone and Metabolic Research* 32 (2002): 47–50.

Ouchi, N., et al. "Novel Modulator for Endothelial Adhesion Molecules: Adipocyte-Derived Plasma Protein Adiponectin." *Circulation* 100 (1999): 2473–76.

Petersen, K., and G. Schulman. "Pathogenesis of Skeletal Muscle Insulin Resistance in Type 2 Diabetes Mellitus." *American Journal of Medicine* 90, 5A (2001).

Reaven, G.M. "The Pathophysiological Consequences of Adipose Tissue Insulin Resistance." In *Insulin Resistance*, edited by G.M. Reaven and A. Laws, 233–46. Totowa, NJ: Humana Press, 1999.

Rohner-Jeanrenaud, F. "Hormonal Regulation of Energy Partitioning." *International Journal of Obesity and Related Metabolic Disorders* 24, S2 (2000): S4–S7.

Rosmon R., et al. "Stress-Related Cortisol Secretion in Men: Relationship with Abdominal Obesity and Endocrine, Metabolic and Hemodynamic Abnormalities." *Journal of Clinical Endocrinology and Metabolism* 83 (1998): 1853–59.

Stegnar, M.A., et al. "Impact of Adipose Tissue on Plasma Plasminogen Activator Inhibitor-1 in Dieting Obese Women." *Arteriosclerosis, Thrombosis, and Vascular Biology* 19 (1999): 1582–87.

Toth, M.J., et al. "Menopause-Related Changes in Body Fat Distribution." *Annals of the New York Academy of Sciences* 904 (2001): 502–6.

Van der Lely, A.J., et al. "Biological, Physiological and Pharmacological Aspects of Ghrelin." *Endocrine Reviews* 25, 3 (2004): 426–57.

Vicennati, V., and R. Pasquali. "Abnormalities of the Hypothalamic-Pituitary-Adrenal Axis in Nondepressed Women with Abdominal Obesity and Relations with Insulin Resistance: Evidence for a Central and Peripheral Alteration." *LCEM* 85 (2000): 4093–98.

Weyer, C., et al. "Hypoadiponectinemia in Obesity and Type 2 Diabetes: Close Association with Insulin Resistance and Hyperinsulinemia." *Journal of Clinical Endocrinology and Metabolism* 86 (2001): 1930–35.

Wynne, A., et al. "The Gut Regulation of Body Weight." *Journal of Clinical Endocrinology and Metabolism* 89, 6 (2004): 2576–82.

Xydakis, A.M., et al. Adiponectin, Inflammation, and the Expression of the Metabolic Syndrome in Obese Individuals: The Impact of Rapid Weight Loss Through Caloric Restriction." *Journal of Clinical Endocrinology and Metabolism* 89 (2004): 2697–703.

Yang, W.S., et al. "Weight Reduction Increases Plasma Levels of an Adipose-Derived Anti-Inflammatory Protein, Adiponectin." *Journal of Clinical Endocrinology and Metabolism* 86 (2001): 3815–19.

Yannakoulia, M., et al. "Body Fat Mass and Macronutrient Intake in Relation to Circulating Soluble Leptin Receptor, Free Leptin Index, Adiponectin, and Resistin Concentrations in Healthy Humans." *Journal of Clinical Endocrinology and Metabolism* 88 (2003): 1731–36.

Preventing Metabolic Syndrome and Its Complications: Lifestyle Interventions

Azziz, R., et al. "Troglitazone Improves Ovulation and Hirsutism in the Polycystic Ovary Syndrome: A Multicenter, Double Blind, Placebo-Controlled Trial." *Journal of Clinical Endocrinology and Metabolism* 86 (2001): 1626–32.

Azziz, R., et al. "The Prevalence and Features of the Polycystic Ovary Syndrome in an Unselected Population." *Journal of Clinical Endocrinology and Metabolism* 89 (2004): 2745–49.

Demaree, S., et al. "Fundamentals of Exercise Metabolism. In *ASCM's Resource Manual for Guidelines for Exercise Testing and Prescription*, 4th ed., edited by J. Roitman, Chapter 14, 133–40. Baltimore: Lippincott Williams & Wilkins, 2001.

Diabetes Prevention Program Research Group. "Reduction Incidence of Type 2 Diabetes with Lifestyle Intervention or Metformin." *New England Journal of Medicine* 346 (2002): 393–403.

Eriksson, J., and F. Lingarde. "Prevention of Type 2 (Non-Insulin-Dependent) Diabetes Mellitus by Diet and Physical Exercise: The 5-Year Malmo Feasibility Study." *Diabetologia* 34 (1991): 891–98.

Esposito, K., et al. "Effect of Weight Loss and Lifestyle Changes on Vascular Inflammatory Markers in Obese Women." *Journal of the American Medical Association* 289 (2003): 1799–804.

Gibson, S.A. "Are Diets High in Non-Mil Extrinsic Sugars Conducive to Obesity." *Journal of Human Nutrition and Dietetics* 9 (1996): 283–92.

Foster, G.D., et al. "A Randomized Trial of a Low-Carbohydrate Diet for Obesity." *New England Journal of Medicine* 348, 21 (2003): 2082–92.

Hamdy, O., et al. "Lifestyle Modification Improves Endothelial Function in Obese Subjects with Insulin Resistance Syndrome." *Diabetes Care* 26 (2003): 2119–25.

Hu, F., et al. "Elevated Risk of Cardiovascular Disease Prior to Clinical Diagnosis of Type 2 Diabetes." *Diabetes Care* 25 (2002): 1129–34.

Huber-Bucholz, M.M., et al. "Restoration of Reproductive Potential by Lifestyle Modification in Obese Polycystic Ovary Syndrome: Role of Insulin Sensitivity and Luteinizing Hormone." *Journal of Clinical Endocrinology and Metabolism* 84 (1999): 1470–74.

Ludwig, D.S., K.E. Peterson, and S.L. Gortmaker. "Relation Between Consumption of Sugar-Sweetened Drinks and Childhood Obesity: A Prospective, Observational Analysis." *The Lancet* 357 (2001): 505–478.

Manson, J.E., et al. "Physical Activity and the Incidence of Noninsulin Dependent Diabetes in Women." *The Lancet* 338 (1991): 774–78.

Manson, J.E., et al. "A Prospective Study of Exercise and Incidence of Diabetes Among U.S. Male Physicians." *Journal of the American Medical Association* 268 (1992): 63–67.

Meckling, K.A., et al. "Comparison of a Low-Fat Diet to a Low-Carbohydrate Diet of Weight Loss, Body Composition, and Risk Factors for Diabetes and Cardiovascular Disease in Free-Living, Overweight

Men and Women." *Journal of Clinical Endocrinology and Metabolism* 89, 6 (2004): 2717–23.

Nielson, S.J., and B.M. Popkin. "Patterns and Trends in Food Portion Sizes, 1977–1998." *Journal of the American Medical Association* 289 (2003): 450–53.

O'Connor, A. "Study Details 30-Year Increase in Calorie Consumption." *New York Times*, February 6, 2004, A20.

Pan, X., et al. "Effect of Diet and Exercise in Preventing NIDDM in People with Impaired Glucose Tolerance. The Da Qing IGT and Diabetes Study." *Diabetes Care* 20 (1997): 537–44.

Pasquali, R., et al. "Effect of Long-Term Treatment with Metformin Added to Hypocaloric Diet on Body Composition, Fat Distribution, and Androgen and Insulin Levels in Abdominally Obese Women with and without the Polycystic Ovary Syndrome." *Journal of Clinical Endocrinology and Metabolism* 86 (2000): 2757–74.

Saltin, B. "Genes, Skeletal Muscle Metabolic Capacity, and Health." *Cardiovascular Reviews and Reports* 23, 6 (2002): 326–32.

Samaha, F.F., et al. "A Low-Carbohydrate as Compared with a Low-Fat Diet in Severe Obesity." *New England Journal of Medicine* 348, 21 (2003): 2074–82.

Schulze, M.B., et al. "Sugar Sweetened Beverages, Weight Gain, and Incidence of Type 2 Diabetes in Young and Middle-Aged Women." *Journal of the American Medical Association* 292 (2004): 927–34.

Taylor, A.E. "Polycstic Ovary Syndrome." *Endocrinology and Metabolism Clinics* 27, 4 (1998): 877–902.

Troiano, R.P., et al. "Energy and Fat Intake of Children and Adolescents in the United States: Data from the National Health and Nutrition Examination Surveys." *American Journal of Clinical Nutrition* 72 (2000): 1343S–53S.

Tuomilehto, J., et al. "Prevention of Type 2 Diabetes Mellitus by Changes in Lifestyle Among Subjects with Impaired Glucose Tolerance." *New England Journal of Medicine* 344 (2001): 1343–50.

Index